Lyn Cockburn

THE DECADE OF WOMEN
A *Ms.* HISTORY OF THE SEVENTIES IN WORDS AND PICTURES

EDITED AND PRODUCED BY
SUZANNE LEVINE AND HARRIET LYONS
WITH JOANNE EDGAR,
ELLEN SWEET, MARY THOM

INTRODUCTION BY GLORIA STEINEM

DESIGNED BY STEVE PHILLIPS

A PARAGON BOOK

Paragon Books
are published by
G.P. Putnam's Sons
200 Madison Avenue
New York, New York 10016

Library of Congress Cataloging in Publication Data

The Decade of Women.

"A Paragon book."
Includes index.
1. Women—United States—History—20th Century—Addresses, essays, lectures.
2. United States—Social conditions—1960– I. Ms.
HQ1426.D38 1980 301.41'2'0973 79-3543
ISBN 0-399-12490-X
ISBN 0-399-50473-7 pbk.

Printed in the United States of America

With special thanks for help and ideas to Patricia Carbine, Judy Clarke, Susan Dworkin, Evelyn Elder, Jim Harrison, Barbara Hendra, Barbara Kraus, Robert Levine, Gillian Lyons, Marilyn Phillips, Kate Sisk, Cynthia Stoddard, Jill Storey, Ruth Sullivan, Marlo Thomas, Wendy Weil.

Cover Photo by Bettye Lane

A widely published photojournalist since 1959, Bettye Lane identified with the renewed struggle in the '70s for women's rights and began photographing the demonstrations, conferences, events, and leaders challenging and redefining the role of women in our society.

We are indebted to all the photographers in this book for the visual chronicle of feminist activism and change that shaped the decade.

CONTENTS

1970

☐ Women's Equity Action League (WEAL) officer Dr. Bernice Sandler files first formal charges of sex discrimination under Executive Order 11246 against the University of Maryland. Suits against more than 300 colleges follow in the next two years.

☐ The United Auto Workers becomes the first major national union to endorse the ERA.

☐ Hawaii, Alaska, and New York become the first states to liberalize their abortion laws.

☐ The first women's caucus in the federal government is formed by women in the Department of State, the Agency for International Development, and the U.S. Information Agency.

☐ The first national commercial newsletters to serve the Women's Movement are started: "Women Today," by Myra and Lester Barrer in Washington, D.C., and "Spokeswoman," by Susan Davis in Chicago.

☐ First annual National Conference of Women Law Students sponsored by New York University Law School Women's Rights Committee.

☐ *Notes from the Second Year*, the radical feminist journal, is published.

☐ The New York City Women's Center and other centers across the country open as meeting places and information centers for women.

☐ The Interstate Association of Commissions on the Status of Women is organized and elects Dr. Kathryn Clarenbach its first president.

☐ The Women's Bureau of the U.S. Department of Labor holds fiftieth anniversary conference and endorses the ERA.

☐ Senate holds the first ERA hearings since 1956.

☐ House subcommittee hearings on sex discrimination in education are the first in U.S. history.

☐ Department of Justice files first Title VII suit of sex discrimination in employment against Libbey-Owens, United Glass and Ceramic Workers of North America (Ohio); settled by consent decree.

☐ New York City is first major U.S. city to pass a bill banning sex discrimination in public accommodations. The change followed feminist demonstrations to "liberate" the Biltmore Hotel men's bar, and other similar protests.

☐ Activists disrupt Senate subcommittee hearings on the Pill, protesting that most witnesses are male doctors and that women are being used as "guinea pigs" in testing.

☐ First annual nationwide Women's Strike for Equality, celebrating the fiftieth anniversary of suffrage. On August 26, 50,000 people march down Fifth Avenue in New York City.

☐ Twelve stewardesses file multimillion-dollar sex-discrimination suit against TWA.

☐ First woman Lutheran pastor is ordained.

☐ First all-women's professional tennis tour is announced.

☐ National Press Club, Washington, D.C., votes to admit women members.

☐ Women from 43 tribes and 23 states organize the North American Indian Women's Association.

☐ First women generals are commissioned—Elizabeth Holsington, director of the Women's Army Corps, and Anna Mae Hays, chief of Army Nurse Corps.

☐ Forty-six editorial staff women win a settlement of their suit charging sex discrimination at *Newsweek* magazine.

☐ Dr. Edgar F. Berman resigns from Democratic Party Committee on National Priorities after arguing that women cannot hold decision-making roles because of their "raging hormonal imbalance."

☐ The League for Women's Rights forms to restructure marriage and divorce laws, calls for recognition of home-making as "recompensible employment."

☐ Women on the staff of *Rat* take over the New York radical underground newspaper.

☐ Sit-in at *Ladies' Home Journal* by 100 women leads to special supplement in August, 1970, issue.

☐ Congress To Unite Women meets in New York City. Lesbians stage Lavender Menace Action, one of the first asserting the right to be public lesbians.

☐ *Time* and *Newsweek* do cover stories on the Women's Movement.

☐ Chicana feminists in California found the *Comision Feminil Mexicana Nacional*. They start a model service center for working women and two child-care centers. Founders include Gracia Molina Pick, Francisca Flores, Graciella Olivares, Yolanda Nava.

☐ Radical Lesbians is founded. Write landmark "Woman-Identified Woman" piece.

☐ *off our backs* (Washington, D.C.), *Ain't I a Woman?* (Iowa City, Iowa), and *It Ain't Me, Babe* (Berkeley, California), feminist newspapers, begin publishing.

☐ Gray Panthers founded by Maggie Kuhn to gain national attention for the rights of the elderly.

☐ Diana Oughton, member of the Weathermen, is killed in a revolutionary bomb factory (West 11th Street, New York City).

☐ Singer Janis Joplin dies of a heroin overdose.

THE WAY WE WERE—AND WILL BE

Think for a minute. Who were you before the '70s began?

Trying to remember our way back into past realities, past rooms, past beliefs is a first step toward measuring the depth of change in ourselves and the world. It's also a reminder that the progress we may now take for granted is the result of many major accomplishments of the past and just the beginning of more changes to come.

Sharing these past measures of change—in the same way we have learned to personally share current problems and solutions in consciousness-raising groups—is probably the most accurate, bias-proof, and feminist way of identifying and recording our own history. After all, if women of diverse experience and age and background and even nationality can begin to see patterns of similarity emerge from the telling of past learning-moments and milestones, then we are probably on the track of an accurate historical pattern. And if we can accomplish this sharing, then history may cease to be limited mainly to the documented acts of national leaders, or to the interpretations of scholars proving a particular theory. We can begin to create a women's history—and finally a people's history—that is accurate, nourishing, and accessible.

Of course, massive change proceeds more as a spiral than a straight line. We repeat similar patterns over and over again, each time in a slightly different circumstance, so experiences that appear to be circular and discouraging in the short run may turn out to be moving in a clear direction in the long run. Those of us who were taught the cheerful American notion that progress is linear and hierarchical, for instance, may have had to learn with pain in the '70s that no worthwhile battle can be fought and won only once. Whether the struggle is as clear-cut as an individual woman's right to equal pay—and to decide for herself when and whether she will have a child—or as complex as the cross-cultural principles of economic equity and reproductive freedom, the issues still repeat

1971

☐ New York Radical Feminists hold "Speak-out on Rape."

☐ Berkeley, California, initiates women's studies in primary schools.

☐ U.S. Supreme Court rules that companies cannot refuse to hire mothers with small children unless same policy applies to fathers with small children.

☐ New York Board of Education votes to allow high school girls and boys to compete in noncontact sports.

☐ The University of Michigan becomes first university to incorporate an affirmative action plan for hiring and promotion of women, including goals and timetables, as the result of a class action suit filed by Michigan FOCUS.

☐ The Professional Women's Caucus files a class action sex-discrimination suit against every law school in the country receiving federal funds.

☐ Boy Scouts of America admits girls into its Explorer Scout Division (ages 15 to 20).

☐ Girls are appointed as Senate pages for first time in U.S. history.

☐ The National Women's Political Caucus is organized to put more women who speak for women's issues and all less powerful groups into positions of elected and appointed political decision-making.

☐ Stoughton High School, Stoughton, Wisconsin, offers one of first-known high school courses in the history of women in America.

☐ Repeal of antiabortion laws is the impetus for formation of the Women's National Abortion Coalition.

☐ Billie Jean King, at 27, becomes the first woman athlete to earn more than $100,000 in a year (more than any American male tennis player that year).

☐ Nixon vetoes Comprehensive Child Development Bill, which would have provided $2 billion for comprehensive child care.

☐ Erin Pizzey starts the first battered women's shelter in England. It was the beginning of a movement that spread throughout Europe and the United States in the '70s.

☐ *Harper's* magazine devotes an entire issue to Norman Mailer's *Prisoner of Sex*.

☐ Jill Johnston breaks up symposium on women at New York's Theater for Ideas by embracing a lover on stage. Other panelists are Norman Mailer (who was offended), Germaine Greer, Diana Trilling, and Jackie Ceballos.

☐ Patricia Buckley Bozell takes a swing at Ti-Grace Atkinson at Catholic University in Washington, D.C., after Atkinson announces that the Virgin Mary has been "used."

☐ The "Fourth World Manifesto," by Detroit feminists, challenges politics of New Left women and men after feminists call for a boycott of a meeting with a delegation of Vietnamese women in Canada because those organizing the meeting are too revisionary. The meeting, the Indo-Chinese Women's Conference, took place with American feminists and women from North Vietnam, Laos, and Cambodia.

☐ First feminist fund is formed, Sisterhood Is Powerful, Inc., with royalties from the best-selling anthology.

☐ FBI reports that the increase in women's crime rate is up sharply over men's.

☐ Three hundred forty Frenchwomen sign a petition, the "Manifesto of 340 Bitches," declaring they have had abortions. In the U.S., *Ms.* Magazine publishes a similar petition in 1972, initially signed by 53 prominent women and later by thousands of *Ms.* readers.

☐ The Women's Action Alliance, first national center on women's issues and programs, is founded in New York City by Gloria Steinem and Brenda Feigen Fasteau.

themselves in different ways and in constantly shifting arenas. The process goes on and on—until the spiral has passed through the superficiality of official phrases or newspaper reports and moved into the deeper regions of everyday acceptance and culture. In fact, truly successful politics are probably definable simply as "culture."

Our own personal spirals of growth blend in with the larger one wherever it touches most directly on our experience.

My memory tells me, for instance, that I was certainly old enough to understand these well-educated, white, upper-middle-class housewives who began to rebel in the '60s against a feminine mystique that had kept them and their sisters locked out of professions and into the suburbs. Nonetheless, I not only felt little personal connection between their words and my own life, but was often put off by their emphasis on getting a piece of the existing professional pie: on bringing women, as the National Organization for Women put it in 1966, "into full participation in the mainstream of American society" and on becoming "a civil rights movement to speak for women, as there has been for Negroes"—this last seeming to imply either that all women were white, or that Negro women didn't suffer from sex discrimination.

As a journalist, I was already near the mainstream of my profession and very far from the suburbs; yet I was still suffering from a world in which I was assumed to be far less "serious" (and to need far less money) than my male colleagues, and where the highest praise I could earn was, "You write like a man." I felt mysteriously alienated among the powerful men of that "mainstream," and mysteriously attracted to the farm-worker meetings or black-run community child-care centers about which I chose to write; yet those early reformers of NOW couldn't help me to understand why. On the contrary, they seemed to want to become the "token woman" I already was.

Only in the late '60s when many women who had grown up in the peace or civil rights movements began to propose feminism—that is, an analysis that included all women as a caste and called for a transformation of patriarchy, not just integration into it by a few women—did my own feelings of recognition, empathy, and hope begin to explode. Many of these feminists had rejected their own hard-won but subordinate places inside male-run professions or political groups. Some had the courage to expose the real sexual caste systems inside movements that were supposed to be about social justice, but whose revolutionary sons treated women the same or with less equality than their conservative fathers had done. A few took on both political and literary heroes by occupying a prestigious publishing house that was actually supporting itself with sadomasochistic pornography, or by writing well-documented attacks on the sexual politics of male cultural heroes.

In each case, there was some odd echo of an experience that I had thought was idiosyncratic and mine alone. One woman told of the years she had spent doing much of the research and background work for radical male colleagues, for instance, but her major reward was to be called "a real brother." I had been doing free-lance editing jobs for the male editor of a national women's magazine who always handed me manuscripts with the instruction (intended as praise, since he had such contempt for his readers), "Pretend you're a woman and read this." Furthermore, I had always felt resentful or depressed when reading much-admired literary works in which women were humiliated, yet I assumed I had no right to criticize.

Instead of demonstrating outside posh "men only" lunch havens, as some of the reformers were then doing, these feminists were declaring their common bonds with women as a group, and holding public speak-outs on such populist and still illegal issues as abortion. For the first time, I understood that the abortion I had kept so shamefully quiet about for years was an experience I had probably shared with at least one out of four American women of every race and group.

And for the first time, I realized that our bodies, much less the rest of our lives, could never be entirely our own as long as we were viewed and controlled by society as the most basic means of production: the means of reproduction. Women were supposed to be a subordinate caste, with authority taking the various forms of the church or family or patriarchal state—and if we rebelled, each of us was often made to feel falsely aberrant and alone.

In addition to taking on such visceral subjects as the politics of reproduction, sexuality, and housework, the feminist analysis of women as a subordinate caste uncovered the age-old parallels and interdependencies with caste systems based on race. Sometimes, this realization came from figuring out that the men of the racially powerful group had to restrict the freedom of "their" women in order to preserve racial purity, but could produce more workers by making sure that all men had easy access to the bodies of women in the powerless group. Often, the message came from black women who had lived through the parallel myths of "natural" inferiority based on race and sex, or from black men in particular and women in general who simply found themselves dealing with some common pattern of discrimination or common adversary. In our various ways, we were mutually uncovering the secret of this land of opportunity. If you aren't born white and male in America, you are statistically likely to end up as some sort of support system for those who are.

We shouldn't have had to learn this the hard way. Our 19th-century counterparts of the first wave of feminism in America and the abolitionist movement had shared much of their struggle to challenge a system that defined black men and all women as chattel: the legal possessions of masters, husbands, or fathers. In coalitions that were both consciously built on issues and unconsciously created around shared sympathies, the movements against the intertwined caste systems of race and sex worked together—until the patriarchy divided the movements by allowing only "Manhood Suffrage"; that is, a few black men were allowed to vote, but no women. Seventy years later when women of all races finally won the vote, the obvious differences in cruelty or intimacy of race/sex caste systems had been successfully used to divide the two and to forestall the danger of another 19th-century

1972

A staff meeting at *Ms.*

□ Congress passes the Equal Rights Amendment, first introduced in 1923; Hawaii is the first state to ratify.

□ The Equal Employment Opportunity Act of 1972 empowers the EEOC to go to court with discrimination cases.

□ Title IX of the Education Amendments of 1972 is passed, prohibiting sex discrimination in most federally assisted educational programs. Opens up a debate in the area of sports that remains unresolved throughout the decade.

□ The National Conference of Puerto Rican Women is organized in Washington, D.C., by Carmen Maymi, Paquita Vivo, and others.

□ Dr. Donna Allen's Women's Institute for Freedom of the Press begins publishing *Media Report to Women*.

□ The Equal Pay Act of 1963 is extended to cover administrative, professional, and executive employees.

□ The Feminist Press starts "Women's Studies Newsletter" (in 1977, the National Women's Studies' Association is formed; by 1978, the number of women's studies courses exceeds 15,000).

□ *Ms.* magazine publishes its Preview Issue.

□ The University of Minnesota lets women into the marching band.

□ The Maritime College of the State University of New York admits women.

□ Women's Lobby, Inc., is formed by Carol Burris to lobby Congress on women's issues.

□ The Civil Rights Commission is given jurisdiction over sex discrimination. Loses jurisdiction over abortion in 1978.

□ Women's issues, including the right to abortion, are included in the platform of *La Raza Unida*, a Mexican-American political movement, as the result of pressure from its Chicana caucus.

□ Sally Priesand is first woman ordained a rabbi.

□ Marlo Thomas and friends produce the record "Free To Be . . . You and Me," the first record of nonsexist, multiracial songs, poems, and stories for children.

□ The Washington *Post* eliminates sex-segregated classified ads.

□ New York City is the scene of the First International Festival of Women's Films.

□ Shirley Chisholm runs for President.

□ Women are 40 percent of the delegates to the Democratic National Convention (13 percent in 1968); 35 percent of the Republican.

□ Frances ("Sissy") Farenthold comes in second in Democratic Convention Vice-Presidential nomination.

□ Jean Westwood is unanimously selected chair of Democratic National Committee (first woman in either party).

□ Margo St. James and other prostitutes start COYOTE (Cut Out Your Old Tired Ethics).

□ Judy Chicago, Miriam Schapiro, and members of the Feminist Art Program at the California Institute of the Arts open 17-room *Womanhouse* exhibit seen by 4,000.

□ New Ways to Work (California) initiates part-time and job-sharing model programs.

□ American Heritage publishes first dictionary (a wordbook for children) to define "sexism," include the phrase "liberated women," and recognize "Ms."

□ Ms. Foundation is formed, only nation-wide funding source specifically for women.

□ League of Women Voters endorses the ERA.

□ Gail and Thomas Parker are appointed president and vice-president respectively of Bennington College (Vermont)—first wife-husband team.

□ Revised Order 4 requires companies doing business with the federal government to form written affirmative action programs for hiring and promoting minorities and women.

□ First conference of Older Women's Liberation held in New York City.

□ Poet Marianne Moore, winner of the Pulitzer Prize and National Book Award, dies.

□ Women elected to Congress are Elizabeth Holtzman (D.-N.Y.), Yvonne Brathwaite Burke (D.-Calif.), Barbara Jordan (D.-Tex.), Patricia Schroeder (D.-Col.) and Marjorie Holt (R.-Md.).

□ On the tenth anniversary of her suicide, Marilyn Monroe becomes the subject of articles, poems, and books analyzing her victimization as a sex symbol.

majority coalition. Black women and men—but especially white women—had been encouraged to believe that all progress was to be achieved by identifying upward, by attaching oneself to serving the most powerful men available, and not by banding together ourselves or with other less powerful groups to enforce political change. No wonder that I and many other women had been so educated to believe that salvation lay in either marrying into the right group or becoming an accepted "token" within it. And no wonder we were so surprised if we accidentally discovered that we felt more in common or at ease in all the wrong groups. It took feminism, and not the earlier upwardly mobile reformism, to reveal the politics of everyday life and the shared interests of women as a caste; to make sense of emotions and political sympathies by explaining that women were some degree of "out" group, too.

On the other hand, thousands of women had been strengthened and started on paths of lifelong change by hearing their experience as wives, mothers, and frustrated professionals accurately described by those reformers of the '60s. They then went on to discover that success in the mainstream simply wasn't possible through the efforts of one group of women alone, or through changing only our work lives. By the '70s, almost all the early reformers had become feminists through realizing that they were strengthened by alliances with women of different races and classes, women who were welfare mothers or employed in traditional "women's work," women who were lesbians or who had chosen unconventional lifestyles. After all, a woman might start out identifying "upward" with her male boss and not "downward" with another secretary, but both often realized that they shared problems as women, and they needed to support each other to have any power at all. As for rights of sexual expression and reproductive freedom, women finally discovered that all of us were endangered when one group was denied.

At the same time, most of the early feminists were learning the importance of being inside as well as outside those structures that need change; of legislative lobbying and electoral politics; in short, of the skills that their reformist sisters often possessed. We have even admitted the degree to which stylistic differences kept us from seeing that shared issues had been there all along. In retrospect, for instance, I realize that NOW had made a dignified and courageous demand for "repealing penal laws governing abortion" in 1967, almost two years before so many of us experienced the more dramatic revelation of hearing women demand the same repeal by speaking out publicly about their experiences of illegal abortions. If I had been willing to look beyond the superficial style differences of women who picketed against employers in their mink coats (in order to prove, as one of them now ruefully recalls, "that we were demonstrating out of principle, not need"), I might have started to work on the vital issue of abortion two years earlier. And if more of the early reformers had been willing to look beyond the boots-and-jeans uniform and impersonal rhetoric with which some of us emerged from the male-dominated Left, they might have realized that we were neither so far from them on issues nor such a political liability as we seemed.

1973

The Los Angeles Woman's Building; Jeanette Rankin at a 1972 rally.

□ Supreme Court legalizes abortion following successful arguments by lawyers Sarah Weddington and Marjorie Pitts Hames (*Doe v. Bolton* and *Roe v. Wade*).

□ National Black Feminist Organization is formed to deal with dual problems of racism and sexism.

□ Billie Jean King beats Bobby Riggs in "Battle of the Sexes" tennis match in Houston's Astrodome.

□ Supreme Court outlaws sex-segregated classified ads.

□ Kalamazoo, Michigan, group files first Title IX textbook complaint with Health, Education, and Welfare Department.

□ AFL-CIO National Convention endorses the ERA.

□ Women admitted to U.S. Coast Guard officer-candidate program.

□ American Stock Exchange adopts affirmative action hiring plan.

□ Los Angeles Woman's Building opens—housing art galleries, studios, workshops, and stores.

□ University of Chicago establishes athletic scholarships for women.

□ Government Printing Office stylebook accepts "Ms." as a prefix.

□ Men and women get equal money at the U.S. Open tennis tournament (Forest Hills, New York).

□ New Jersey opens Little League to girls.

□ Child-care deduction in federal income tax is allowed for volunteer workers.

□ Labor is first federal department or agency to grant paternity leave.

□ Dr. Benjamin Spock renounces his earlier sexist views on child care and revises his classic book.

□ AT & T signs a $35-million settlement with the EEOC and Labor Department agreeing to back pay, goals and timetables for increasing the role of women and minorities.

□ Supreme Court outlaws discrimination against women officers and their husbands in military benefits (Frontiero).

□ Federal Home Loan Bank Board bars sex bias by savings and loan institutions.

□ Civil Service Commission ends discriminatory height-and-weight requirements for park police and jobs in fire prevention and narcotics control.

□ Stewardesses for Women's Rights formed to support job rights, a dignified public image, and health issues of women flight attendants.

□ Daughters Inc., and Diana Press are among the earliest book publishers run by and for feminists.

□ Artemisia and A.I.R., nonprofit art cooperatives for women, are founded in Chicago and New York City, respectively.

□ Catholics for a Free Choice is organized to work for abortion rights.

□ Midwest Academy (Chicago) is founded by Heather Booth to train women to organize.

□ Women Employed (Chicago), Women Office Workers (New York), and 9 to 5 (Boston) are among earliest citywide groups of office workers.

□ The first Feminist Federal Credit Union is formed in Detroit.

□ First National Lesbian Feminist Conference is held in Los Angeles.

□ Robyn Smith is first woman jockey to win Aqueduct Stakes.

□ U.S. homemakers organize national week-long meat boycott to protest rising beef prices.

□ Jeanette Rankin, the first Congresswoman (R.-Mont.)—from 1917-19 and from 1941-43—and a staunch supporter of women's rights, dies.

□ National Association for Repeal of Abortion Laws (NARAL), founded in 1969, changes its name to the National Abortion Rights Action League (same acronym) and makes its goal to preserve the 1973 Supreme Court decision.

□ First exposé of the Dalkon Shield is published in the *National Observer* by reporter Barbara Katz, leading to eventual withdrawal of this IUD from the market.

Mary McNally

Bettye Lane

This personal note on two different paths to feminism is only a hint at the diversity of experience that each of us would count as vital in summing up the '70s: the first full decade of the Second Wave of feminism in America. Each of us would probably choose a different way of measuring how far the revolution has come.

If we are sociologists or statisticians, we might explain that every major issue raised by the Women's Movement now has majority support in national public opinion polls: from the supposedly "easy" ones like equal pay, women in political office and equal access to education to the supposedly "controversial" ones like the Equal Rights Amendment, a woman's right to choose abortion and "would-you-work-for-a woman?" That represents a major change from the beginning of the decade when most such issues were supported by only a minority; and an even bigger change from the '60s, when they weren't taken seriously enough to be included in public opinion polls at all.

If we are history buffs or students of revolution, we might see the '70s as a time of massive consciousness-raising: of breaking the conspiracy of silence on the depth of sex-based inequities, both nationally and internationally, and of achieving token victories that disproved "biology is destiny" and that raised women's hopes. Having successfully forged a majority change in consciousness, we are now ready for more institutional, systematic change in the '80s. A redistribution of power in families, a revolution in the way children are raised and by whom, flexible work schedules outside the home, recognition of work done by women (and men) in the home, a lessening of the violence that is rooted in the cult of masculinity, the redistribution of salary and services that would begin if we actually got equal pay for comparable work: all these structural changes are possible in the '80s because hopes were raised in the '70s.

If, on the other hand, we are simply among the millions of women struggling to survive the double burden of working outside the home, yet carrying the major responsibility for homemaking and raising children, we might describe the '70s as the decade in which we advanced *half* the battle. We've learned that women can and should do "men's jobs," for instance, and we've won the principle (if not the fact) of getting equal pay. But we haven't yet established the principle (much less the fact) that men can and should do "women's jobs": that homemaking and childrearing are as much a man's responsibility as a woman's, and that those poorly paid jobs in which women are concentrated outside the home would probably be better rewarded if more men became secretaries and file clerks, nurses and schoolteachers, too.

Obviously, society in general and women in particular will have to make more demands on men as equal parents in the '80s. Job patterns must allow both fathers and mothers of young children to arrange shorter workdays or shorter workweeks. (We'll also have to return to the battle for quality child care that we lost at the beginning of the '70s; this time with a clear statement that free child-care centers are not for the benefit of "working mothers," any more than free schools are. They are simply the right of every child.) Existing antidiscrimination laws and affirmative action

1974

☐ Coalition of Labor Union Women is organized in Chicago with more than 3,000 women from 58 unions attending; Olga Madar of UAW first president.

☐ More than 1.5 million domestic workers are covered by minimum wage requirements.

☐ "Marriage, Divorce, and the Family" newsletter begins publishing (Betty Berry, editor).

☐ Mexican American Women's Association (MAWA) is founded.

☐ Supreme Court outlaws mandatory maternity leave for teachers.

☐ Merchant Marine Academy admits women; Ruth Johnson first woman to join the 175-year-old U.S. Marine Corps Band.

☐ National Little League Baseball, Inc., agrees to admit women.

☐ Federal Office of Workman's Compensation Programs becomes Office of Workers' Compensation Programs.

☐ Housing and Community Development Act outlaws sex bias in housing.

☐ Washington state court grants lesbian mother living with lover custody of her children.

☐ Pennsylvania outlaws sex bias in insurance.

☐ Passport Office allows use of "maiden" name.

☐ "Woman Alive!" special documentary series, produced for and about women, is telecast over Public Broadcasting stations.

☐ Connecticut judge says women can register to vote under "maiden" name.

☐ Ella Grasso is elected Governor of Connecticut, first woman governor elected in her own right.

☐ Mary Ann Krupsak elected lieutenant governor of New York State.

☐ Elaine Noble, elected to Massachusetts state legislature, is first self-declared lesbian elected to state office.

☐ Abortion is legalized in France.

☐ Eleven women are ordained as Episcopal priests (not recognized by church hierarchy).

☐ National Association of Women Business Owners is formed.

☐ McGraw-Hill, Inc., publishes nonsexist guidelines for its nonfiction authors.

☐ Equal Credit Opportunity Act prohibits discrimination in credit on basis of sex or marital status.

☐ Mary Louise Smith becomes chair of Republican National Committee.

☐ Françoise Giroud is appointed French Secretary of State for the Condition of Women.

☐ Betty Ford and Happy Rockefeller are frank about their mastectomies in order to help other women.

☐ National Association of Broadcasters rejects *some* of National Airlines' proposed "I'm going to fly you like you've never been flown before" commercials as sexist.

☐ Electrical, Radio, and Machine Workers adopt a 10-point antisexism resolution.

☐ Laura Cross, 11, wins National Soap Box Derby.

☐ National Congress of Neighborhood Women forms to upgrade status of working-class women.

☐ National Women's Music Festival is held at the University of Illinois.

☐ National Women's Football League is formed.

☐ All-America Girls' Basketball Conference.

☐ Patricia Hearst is kidnapped.

☐ Bennington, Vermont, school board votes to ban *Ms.* magazine.

☐ Kathryn Kirschbaum is denied a BankAmericard unless she gets her husband's signature, even though she earns $15,000 a year as mayor of Davenport, Iowa.

☐ Congress passes the Women's Educational Equity Act, providing for funding nonsexist training.

☐ Anne Sexton, winner of the Pulitzer Prize for poetry in 1967, commits suicide.

☐ *WomenSports* magazine is founded, published by Billie Jean King.

☐ *Quest*, a feminist theoretical quarterly, is started.

☐ Olivia Records is formed. First record is by Meg Christian and Chris Williamson.

☐ Kathy Kozachenko wins election to city council as an openly gay woman, from a predominantly student ward in Ann Arbor, Michigan.

☐ First president of a major university is Lorene Rogers, appointed president of the University of Texas (Austin).

☐ Pop singer Cass Elliott, of The Mamas and the Papas, dies.

☐ Mrs. Martin Luther King, Sr., is killed in her husband's church by a black gunman who believes that black ministers exploit their congregations.

☐ Elizabeth Gould Davis, author of *The First Sex*, commits suicide because of cancer.

☐ Acquittal of Portuguese feminist writers, the Three Marias, by the new revolutionary government in Portugal. The acquittal followed the first internationally coordinated feminist demonstrations protesting the government charges.

☐ *Ms.* sponsors Metric Mile at Madison Square Garden, the first race of that length held in the U.S. Olympic Invitational Track Meet. Francie Larrieu wins in both 1974 and 1975.

measures will have to be used to integrate men into "women's jobs," and not just the other way around; especially where large employers can be forced to pay decent salaries to *all* workers in order to attract men. Yet this integration *must* retain its first stage. If men become flight attendants but women don't become pilots and airline executives, for instance, women will still be on the losing end.

Politicians and organizers would surely measure the success of the '70s—and the danger of the '80s—by the force of the right-wing backlash against all of these majority changes in hopes and values. Representatives of a social order that depends solely on sex, race, and class privilege for its power, and is often justified by the mythic and economic force of patriarchal religions, are clearly feeling endangered. They have paid this first full decade of the Second Wave of feminism the honor of beginning to oppose it very seriously indeed.

As a writer, however, I find myself focusing on change as reflected in language and words: not just such vital but obvious shifts as *girls* to *women*, or *Congressmen* to *Congresspeople*, but the newly coined words and phrases that capture transformations of perception, and sometimes of reality itself.

At the beginning of the '70s, for instance, we were still discussing *population control* and worrying about the *population explosion*. Those were negative phrases that implied outside, authoritarian decisions on the one hand, and endless impersonal breeding as the alternative. Though feminists were expected to come down on the side of *population control*, one of its underlying assumptions was that women themselves could not possibly be given the power to achieve it. Liberal men who were the majority of the population experts assumed that women gained security or were fulfilled only through motherhood, and so would choose to bear too many babies. (Unless, of course, they could achieve a higher degree of literacy and education, thus becoming more rational, more like men.) Many conservative or very religious males, a group that often seemed intent on increasing the numbers of the faithful, treated women as potentially sex-obsessed creatures who would use contraception to behave sinfully, perhaps with men not their husbands, thus weakening the patriarchal family and civilization itself.

By the end of the '70s, however, feminism had transformed the terms of discussion by introducing *reproductive freedom* as a phrase and as a basic human right. This umbrella term included safe contraception and abortion, freedom from forced sterilization, and health care during pregnancy and birth. In other words, *reproductive freedom* states the right of the individual to decide to have or not to have a child. Though obviously more important to women, this right also protects men; especially those from less powerful groups who have sometimes been subjected to coerced sterilization. It also allowed new trust and coalitions between white and "minority" or Third World women in this country and elsewhere, who had rightly suspected that the authoritarian power implied by *population control* would be directed at some races and economic groups more than others.

To the surprise of the liberal population experts, the choice of *reproductive freedom* has been exercised carefully and eagerly by women wherever it has been even marginally allowed. By the late '70s, population journals were full of mystified articles about the declining rate of population growth in many areas of the world, even where the tragic rate of illiteracy among women was still increasing. A 1979 United Nations' women's conference of East and West Europe concluded that women were not only limiting their pregnancies for obvious health reasons, but were, statistically speaking at least, on something of a "baby strike" because of double-role problems; that is, the burden of working both outside and inside the home. Some countries recommended the logical remedy of encouraging men to share child-rearing equally, but other more authoritarian governments simply tried to ensure compulsory childbearing by suppressing contraception and abortion. Since U.S. government population experts were speaking of our "unsatisfactorily low birth rate" quite openly by 1979, the question of whether childbearing and child-rearing are to be supported and aided by both men and women (as feminists advocate) or simply forced on women (as the ultra-right wing advocates) will be a crucial question of the '80s.

Needless to say, conservative religious authorities were greatly alarmed by these evidences of women's increasing efforts to control our own lives and bodies. Seizing control of the means of reproduction could eventually undermine the sexual caste system itself. Wherever religious patriarchs asserted themselves, from the United States Bishops' Conference to the newly theocratic government in Iran, the sinfulness of contraception, abortion, and all sex outside marriage—in fact, of any ways in which women could autonomously decide our own reproductive and sexual lives—was fervently condemned and punished.

Obviously, the phrase *reproductive freedom* is simply a more universal way of stating the basic need that waves of feminism had been advancing long before the '70s. Witches and gypsies were literally freedom fighters for women, and their knowledge of contraception and abortion had made them anathema to patriarchs of the past. In the worldwide wave of feminism of the 19th and early 20th century, advocating "birth control" or "fertility control," even for married women was enough to jail many feminist crusaders.

But the '70s contribution was the stating of *reproductive freedom* as a fundamental human right; at least as important as other protected freedoms. Regardless of marital status, racist desires to limit or increase certain populations or nationalistic goals of having more or fewer workers, individual women have the right to make this decision for themselves. Men who want children must at least find women who share that wish, and governments that want increased rates of population growth must resort to such humane measures as lowering infant mortality rates, improving health care during pregnancy, sharing the work of child-rearing through child care and parenthood, and protecting the health of older people.

Obviously, this ultimate bargaining power on the part of women is exactly what male-supremacists fear most. Because their authoritarian impulse was so clearly against any sexuality not directed toward family-style procreation (that is, forbidding extramarital sex, homosexuality, and lesbianism, as well as

1975

Junko Tabei (*left*, with guide) conquers Everest; Mary Ann Krupsak opens account at The First Women's Bank.

☐ Supreme Court outlaws automatic exclusion of women from jury duty.

☐ Womanschool opens in New York City.

☐ United Nations declares International Year of the Woman, holds world conference in Mexico City.

☐ New Jersey and New York voters reject state ERAs.

☐ Supreme Court outlaws different majority ages for women (18) and men (21).

☐ U.S. District Court says Arkansas cannot require "Miss" or "Mrs." for voter registration.

☐ Laurie Shields and Tish Sommers start Alliance for Displaced Homemakers in California.

☐ Supreme Court ruling gives widower with minor children in his care the same right to Social Security benefits for the child's care as a widow is allowed.

☐ *Ms.* publishes petition for freedom of sexual expression signed by 100 prominent women. More than 11,000 readers respond in support.

☐ First American Indian Women's Leadership Conference meets in New York City.

☐ Harris Poll shows jump in just four years of those who favor improved status of women from 42 to 59 percent; those who favor legalized abortion from 46 to 54 percent; those who favor more child-care centers from 56 to 67 percent.

☐ Pentagon outlaws automatic discharge of pregnant women from armed services.

☐ New York State outlaws sex discrimination in insurance coverage.

☐ Japanese homemaker is first woman to climb Mount Everest.

☐ U.S. District Court Judge W.D. Murray (Butte, Montana) rules the military draft unconstitutional as sex discrimination.

☐ *Signs*, a feminist scholarly journal edited by Catharine Stimpson, starts publication.

☐ Federal court decisions give federal employees right to sue for sex discrimination.

☐ Supreme Court allows publication of ads for abortion services.

☐ First Women's Bank opens in New York City.

☐ Women's Action Alliance coordinates U.S. National Women's Agenda, a bill of rights outlining 11 areas of concern to more than 100 women's organizations.

☐ Carla Hills is appointed Secretary of Housing and Urban Development—third woman ever to serve in U.S. Cabinet.

☐ Working Women United Institute formed to fight sexual harassment on the job.

☐ Joellen Drag is Navy's first woman helicopter pilot. Later files successful class action suit against the Navy for not allowing women pilots to land at sea.

☐ Women's Ordination Conference forms to encourage Roman Catholic priesthood for women.

☐ National Council of Negro Women publishes landmark report on discrimination against women in housing.

☐ California Elected Women's Association for Education and Research (CEWAER) forms model network for state women in political office.

☐ National Organization for Women sponsors "Alice Doesn't! Strike Day"; but most women continue to work.

☐ NOW lobbyist and board member Ann Scott dies of cancer.

☐ *Ms.* and New York Philharmonic present a "Celebration of Women Composers" conducted by Sarah Caldwell.

☐ National Socialist-Feminist Conference at Yellow Springs, Ohio.

☐ Congress passes a bill requiring the service academies to admit women.

☐ National Advertising Review Board issues position paper on "Advertising and Women," which points out that it is "a counterproductive business practice to try to sell a product to someone who feels insulted by the product's advertising."

☐ Ten California Chicanas file a suit, sponsored by the *Comision Feminil Mexicana Nacional*, claiming they were involuntarily sterilized at a county medical center.

☐ Of prescriptions written in 1975, 80 percent of amphetamines, 67 percent of tranquilizers, and 60 percent of barbiturates are prescribed for women.

☐ Valentina Nikolaeva Tereshkova, first woman astronaut, heads the Soviet delegation to International Women's Year meeting in Mexico City.

☐ The NOW Subcommittee on Toys denounces the Mattel toy company for "Growing Up Skipper," a doll that grows breasts when you twist her arm.

☐ Hannah Arendt, German-born U.S. political philosopher and author of *The Human Condition*, dies.

☐ First national women's health conference, sponsored by Our Bodies, Ourselves Collective and 20 other women's health groups, held at Harvard Medical School; 4,000 women attend.

☐ Jacqueline Kennedy Onassis takes a $10,000-a-year consulting editor job at Viking, later moves to Doubleday as associate editor.

☐ Time magazine breaks tradition in naming the Man of the Year by designating ten women for cover honors.

UPI

Bettye Lane

contraception and abortion), feminists of the '70s were strong enough to stand clearly and publicly on the side of any consenting, freely chosen sexuality as a rightful form of human expression. Words like *lovers, sex partners, sexual preference* or *gay rights* began to be used positively in this decade. *Homophobic* was invented to describe irrational fear of any sexual expression between people of the same gender; a fear that had been so often accepted as normal in the past that it rarely needed a name. Because some women's ability to love other women and to be sexually independent of men was even more threatening to patriarchal values than male homosexuality, there was special emphasis on stating *lesbianism, lesbian separatism, lesbian mother*, and *lesbian child-custody rights* as positive choices.

When we entered the '70s, any sex outside marriage was often called the *Sexual Revolution*, a nonfeminist phrase of the '60s that simply meant women's increased availability on men's terms. By the end of the '70s, feminism had brought more understanding that real liberation meant choice; that sexuality was to be neither forbidden nor enforced. With that in mind, words like *virgin, celibacy, autonomy, faithfulness* and *commitment* took on positive meaning. And such condemning, propagandistic words as *frigid* and *nymphomaniac* were being replaced in medical literature by nonjudgmental ones like *preorgasmic* and *sexually active*, thanks mostly to women's new honesty and willingness to challenge male authorities.

It still took some legal procedure and explaining, but many more women kept their *birth names* in the '70s (not *maiden names*, with all the sexual double standard that implies). *Ms.* entered common public usage as a choice added to *Mrs.* or *Miss* and removed the necessity of identifying all females by the presence or absence of a man. A few women tried role reversal by exchanging their *patriarchal names* for invented, *matriarchal* ones ("Mary *Ruthchild*"), or followed the Black Movement tradition of replacing former owners' names with place-names or letters (for instance, "Mary *Indiana*" or "Mary *X*"). Many tried to solve the dilemma of husbands' names with the reformist step of taking both ("Mary *Smith Jones*"), thus ending up with two last names while men still needed only one. Hardly anyone succeeded in interrupting the patriarchal flow of naming children, whether they were still given father's names only, or their mother's names as the dispensable ones in the middle. It remains for the '80s to legalize the egalitarian choice of giving children both parents' names (thus eliminating not only inequality but explanations like, "This is my daughter by my first marriage, and my son by my second"); and then allowing them to choose their own names for adulthood, whether it is either parent's or one entirely different, when they are old enough to work or to register to vote.

In any case, these 10 years made us realize and experiment with the power of naming, and with the invention of words that allow more choice.

Parent or *parenting* began to take some of the solitary burden from *mother* and *mothering* for instance, as well as to make men feel welcome and

1976

□ International Tribunal on Crimes Against Women held in Brussels. Women's International Information and Communications Service (ISIS) begins publishing.

□ ERAmerica forms as coalition to mobilize support for ratification of the ERA.

□ National Women's Health Network brings together health centers, self-help groups, consumers, and health professionals in the only consumer organization devoted to women and health.

□ Supreme Court requires federal agencies to end discrimination in the industries they regulate.

□ FDA requires uniform standards for the safety and effectiveness of intrauterine devices.

□ General Convention of the Episcopal Church votes to ordain women, and recognize those already "illegally" ordained. Jacqueline Means is first woman officially ordained an Episcopal priest in 1977.

□ Amendments to the Education Act aimed at eliminating sex-stereotyping in vocational programs.

□ 1976-1985 declared UN Decade for Women, Equality, Development, and Peace.

□ Air Force agrees to train women pilots but not for combat.

□ Supreme Court rules that pregnant women cannot be denied unemployment benefits automatically in the weeks before and after childbirth.

□ Roberta A. Kankus, 23 (Secane, Pennsylvania), is licensed as first woman commercial nuclear power plant operator.

□ National Aeronautics and Space Administration (NASA) announces it will accept women for astronaut training; it had rejected qualified women in the past. The first women astronauts are selected in 1978.

□ Wisconsin women are first to be listed with their own names, not solely their husbands' names, in phone book.

□ Janet Guthrie is the first woman driver to race at Indianapolis 500.

□ Sarah Caldwell is first woman to conduct at the Metropolitan Opera after Beverly Sills refuses to sing unless Caldwell conducts.

□ Carter appoints Juanita Kreps (Commerce) and Patricia Harris (HUD) to Cabinet.

□ Women's basketball included as an event at the Summer Olympics (Montreal).

□ Article in American Psychiatric Association journal declares male chauvinism a certifiable psychiatric illness.

□ Britain's Rhodes Scholarship program admits women applicants. The following year, 13 women (and 19 men) are named Rhodes Scholars.

□ Simone de Beauvoir heads French Ligue du Droit des Femmes to defend legal rights of women.

□ ". . . Remember the Ladies . . . : Women in America 1750-1815" makes national Bicentennial museum tour.

□ Barbara Walters signs million-dollar contract with ABC.

□ U.S. Department of Labor reports that, despite gains by women in employment (more entering the labor force, and more in better-paying jobs), the wage gap between men and women has actually *increased* in the past 19 years. Women earn 57 cents for every dollar earned by men. Of all full-time, year-round workers earning $15,000 or more, only 5 percent are women.

□ New research gives hitherto unacknowledged credit to geneticist Rosalind Franklin for her work in solving the riddle of the DNA molecule.

□ National Alliance of Black Feminists forms in Chicago.

□ Los Angeles Women Against Violence Against Women begin nationwide protest over the release of pornographic film, "Snuff," which depicts the dismemberment and murder of a woman as sexual entertainment. Three years later, four Rochester, New York, WAVAW members are convicted for demonstrating outside a local theatre showing the film.

□ Radcliffe College starts oral history project on the lives of black women.

□ French prostitutes stage nationwide strike.

□ Women in Iceland hold day-long strike to show their importance to the economy, virtually shutting down the country.

□ National Association of Black Professional Women forms in San Diego, California.

□ Chiang Ch'ing, Madame Mao Tse-tung, is denounced in China as one of the Gang of Four.

□ Dixy Lee Ray, former head of the Atomic Energy Commission, is elected governor of Washington State.

□ Martha Mitchell, outspoken wife of Watergate-indicted Attorney General John Mitchell, dies of cancer.

to underline the revolutionary discovery that children have (or could have) two equally responsible parents. A few workers and unions began to press for *parental leave* as an expansion of *maternity leave,* in recognition of fathers' importance during childbirth and the care of new babies. *Homemaker* replaced *housewife* as a way of making clear that women were definitely not married to houses; that men could be homemakers, too. *Household worker* was chosen by women who had been called *maids* or *domestics,* and their efforts to put a decent monetary value on work done in the home was complementary to the efforts of *homemakers,* to the whole re-definition of *work.*

Pro-choice began to replace the adjective *pro-abortion,* a media-created term that implied women were advocating abortion as something more than a last resort. And a decade that had begun with the shocking necessity of proving the Freudian-dictated *vaginal orgasm* to be neurologically impossible—plus explaining the *clitoral orgasm* to be literally true—finally ended up more equally with just *orgasm* (no adjectives necessary) being both talked about openly and experienced by women and men.

It was also a time of reclaiming words, in a spirit of defiance, humor, and pride. *Witch, bitch, dyke* and other formerly pejorative epithets turned up in the brave names of small feminist groups. Some women artists dubbed their new female imagery *cunt art,* and a few activists actually put *cunt power!* on political buttons. Women pinpointed the problem of being *male-identified,* of feeling like half-people without men, by calling ourselves *man-junkies,* a first step toward kicking the addictive habit. More seriously the term *woman-identified woman* began to be used with significance and pride.

Click! turned up as a way of describing that instant of recognizing the sexual politics of a situation: any moment of feminist truth. (As in "May you have sons to take care of you in old age." *Click!*) Humor encouraged many such clicks, from the invention of *jockocracy* to describe the social power of a certain male obsession with athletics and victory, to *loserism* as a rueful recognition of women's cultural discomfort with anything as "unfeminine" as competence or success. *Supermom* and *Superwoman* were words that relieved us all by identifying the Perfect-Wife-and-Mother—plus or minus the Perfect-Career-Woman—as humanly impossible goals. *D & C* was lifted from gynecology to satirize the *divide-and-conquer* tactics used against women. *Horizontal hostility* explained the temptation of directing anger at each other instead of upward at those in positions of power. *Ejaculatory politics* made fun of the impatience of a certain masculine political style of the '60s and '70s. (As in "If the revolution doesn't happen this month, I'm going home to my father's business.") The *machismo factor* and the *hairy-chested syndrome,* particularly as applied to American foreign policy and the history of the war in Vietnam, identified a dangerous attraction to aggression and violence on the part of policymakers who seemed to feel the need of proving "masculinity".

Women's Libber was a trivializing term that feminists tried to argue against. (Would we say "Algerian Lib"? "Black Libber"?) By the end of the '70s, its use had diminished—but not disappeared.

The nature of *work* was a major area of new understanding—beginning with the word itself. When the '70s began, work was largely defined as what men did, and a *working woman* was someone who labored outside the home and got paid for it, masculine style. By the end of the '70s, the term *working woman* was identified as inaccurate and a put-down: a way of excluding (and thus not rewarding with either money or respect) all the homemaking and human-support services that women have traditionally done at home. We began to speak carefully of work *inside the home,* work *outside the home.* Obviously, people who did the former also needed money of their own, Social Security, pensions, disability benefits, and the protection of a partnership principle that the Equal Rights Amendment would bring. At the death or desertion of a spousal partner, homemakers might need as much help with job retraining as any other worker. *Displaced homemakers,* a term invented in the '70s by women who found themselves in that position, spread throughout the country as women organized into self-help groups, and finally pressured the federal government for special funding and legislation.

This breaking of boundaries between and among women by defining all socially worthwhile work as valuable and dignified was an important feminist step. It also underlined the *double-role problem* that had been identified in the '60s—that is, the double burden of millions of women who worked both inside and outside the home—and gave birth to such slogans as *Wages for Housework* and *Every Mother Is a Working Mother.*

Equal pay for equal work, the concept with which we entered the decade, turned out to fall short of helping women in the mostly female *pink collar ghettos* of service, clerical, and other largely nonunionized jobs where women needed help the most. What did "equal pay" do for the waitress or secretary, for instance, who was getting the same low salary as the woman working next to her? By the end of the '70s, *equal pay for comparable work* was the new goal, and comparability studies were going forward on the many *blue-collar jobs* (done by men) that required less education, fewer skills but got more pay than *pink collar jobs* (done by women). In the '80s, the research results on comparability are likely to be introduced in discrimination suits and tested in the courts.

This decade transformed many ideas by adding one crucial adjective: *women's credit union, women's bank, women's rock group, women's studies, women's poetry collective, women's self-help clinic, women's caucus.* Most such groups also added a lot of new content: child care, different hours, new definitions of creditworthiness, new symbolism, new lyrics, sharing and learning from the textbooks of each other's lives. They also experimented with new structures. Whether out of a conscious belief that hierarchy was rooted in patriarchy or an unconscious discomfort with authority and giving orders, women's groups usually replaced vertical forms of organization with more lateral ones. *Collective, communal, cooperative, supportive, constituency* and *skill-sharing* were all more likely to be heard than *chain of authority, organizational chart,*

1977

Anita Bryant gets pie from irate homosexual; Anaïs Nin's last book, *Delta of Venus*, is published.

☐ Two Austin, Texas, Girl Scout leaders burn their uniforms to protest their organization's endorsement of the ERA, but survey shows that sale of Girl Scout cookies is up due to ERA supporters.

☐ Harris Poll finds that 55 percent of Americans find homosexuals most discriminated against group in the country.

☐ Dade County, Florida, voters reject a resolution to protect lesbians and gay men from discrimination in employment, housing, and public accommodations, after singer Anita Bryant leads an emotionally charged Save Our Children campaign.

☐ NOW sponsors national ERA Walkathon.

☐ Supreme Court allows a widower who is dependent on his wife's income to collect survivor's benefits automatically, just as widows do.

☐ Ohio women form LUNA (Loose Umbrella Network Association) as statewide political resource and talent bank for women office seekers.

☐ Coalition of Labor Union Women leads consumer boycott of J.P. Stevens textile products as protest against the company's 14-year resistance to unionization of its plants.

☐ Fifty-six states and territories hold International Women's Year (IWY) meetings, elect delegates to National Women's Conference in Houston.

☐ Women assigned as permanent shipboard crew members by Navy.

☐ National Communication Network for Elimination of Violence Against Women is formed.

☐ Seven Philadelphia women's groups form fund-raising coalition, Women's Way, to parallel the United Way, which funds few women's programs.

☐ Women's Caucus of National Gay Task Force formalized.

☐ Coalition of Women's Art Organizations vows to lobby for greater role for women in the arts.

☐ NBC signs $1.7 million agreement with the EEOC for back pay and programs for women.

☐ Dr. Ben Munson, the only doctor performing abortions in South Dakota, is acquitted of manslaughter charges in a death following an abortion he performed.

☐ Massachusetts Supreme Judicial Court overturns conviction of Dr. Kenneth C. Edelin for manslaughter in the death of a fetus after a legal abortion.

☐ Women on staffs of foundations and corporate philanthropies form organization to work for more funding for women's programs (Women and Foundations / Corporate Philanthropy).

☐ Virginia Dill McCarty nominated as first woman U.S. Attorney (Southern District of Indiana).

☐ AT&T announces it's ready to allow dual listings of married people in phone books.

☐ South Australia Parliament becomes first in the world to make rape within marriage a criminal offense.

☐ Infant Formula Action Coalition (INFACT) sponsors nationwide boycott of Nestlé products to stop the company's promotion of infant formula in Third World countries where improper use has led to infant malnutrition and even death.

☐ The Army restores Medal of Honor to Dr. Mary Edwards Walker, who was cited in 1866 for services as surgeon in the Union Army, but whose medal was revoked in 1917 for insufficient evidence of her "gallantry."

☐ Supreme Court rules that states and cities may bar use of public funds and public hospital facilities for elective, nontherapeutic abortions. Carter endorses the decisions, saying that "there are many things in life that are not fair. . . ."

☐ Women and minority employees of Crocker National Bank (San Francisco) win landmark settlement of a suit, with no upper limit on amount the bank may be required to pay those filing claims.

☐ Congresswomen's Caucus is formed by 15 women Representatives and one Senator.

☐ *Reader's Digest* agrees to pay more than $1.5 million in back pay and immediate salary increases to 2,600 women employees.

☐ Barbara Kopple's "Harlan County U.S.A." wins the Academy Award for best documentary.

☐ Rosalyn Yalow wins the Nobel Prize in medicine for development of the radioimmunoassay.

☐ Kitty Genovese Women's Project in Texas publishes names of 1,500 men indicted for rape or sex-related crimes from 1970-1976.

☐ Alice Paul, a leading suffragist who also drafted the ERA, dies.

☐ Author Anaïs Nin dies.

☐ Fannie Lou Hamer, a sharecropper who became a civil rights leader, dies.

☐ Indian Prime Minister Indira Gandhi is voted out of power; at the end of the decade, she is trying to regain power.

☐ FDA requires warning labels on menopausal estrogen prescriptions as a result of National Women's Health Network legal suit.

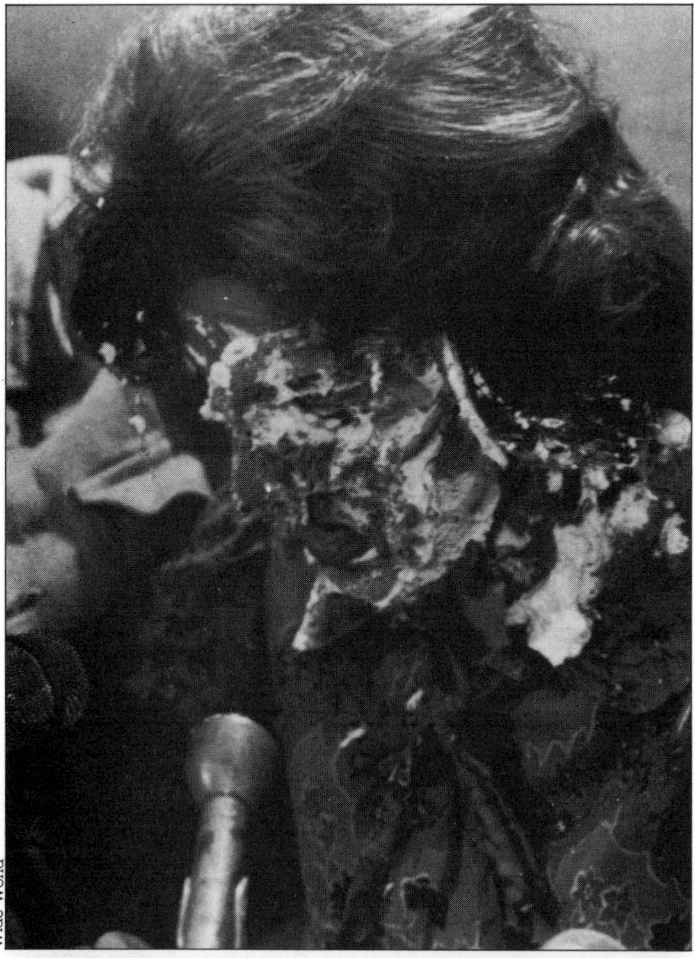

Wide World

Margo Moore

credentials, professional, employer or *employee.*

In short, all the truth-telling about women's lives and the creation of alternate institutions began to create a *women's culture;* a set of perspectives that differed from and could transform a masculinist value system.

The word *culture* was very important. Unlike the more biology-based philosphy of 19th-century feminism, this first decade of Second Wave feminists rarely suggested that females were intrinsically better or more moral. But they were also very clear about not wanting to simply imitate or integrate the masculine-patterned mainstream, even if that were possible to do. The point was that women's cultural experience had given us values, skills, and understanding that men's superior and dominant role had denied them—as well as vice versa. For each of us, progress lay in completing the circle; in facing the direction we had not been.

Challenging the basic power relationships between men and women—and thus the root of division between races and classes—brought a new definition of politics: no longer was it only the ballot box or even concentrations of corporate wealth; it was now seen as including every power relationship in our daily lives. Anytime one group or individual is systematically dominant over another—not because of ability, talent, or experience, but because of sex or race or class—that is *politics.*

Just as *politics* was enlarged by redefinition, *power* was redefined in the hope that it could be diminished and humanized. When feminists talked about powerlessness and the need to have more *power,* for instance, we often explained with care that we meant power to control one's own life but not to dominate others.

Language was also useful in shifting some of the burden back where it belonged. *Alimony* was sometimes referred to as *back salary.* After all, if even the Labor Department counted the replacement value of a homemaker at about $11,000 a year—and if many wives had worked outside the home to put their husbands through school besides—why might not a wife be entitled to back salary or to education money of her own? Similarly, many feminists in the '70s stopped pleading with corporations and professional groups for *contributions*—and started to ask for *reparations.* Womens' Studies, Black Studies, Hispanic Studies, and the like were often referred to by the "out" groups advocating such courses as *remedial studies.* A Constitutional Amendment against all abortions, an ultra-rightwing goal that surfaced in the late '70s, was dubbed the *Women's Death Amendment.* The self-description of the same antiwoman backlash as "pro-family" caused many feminists to take great care about using the plural, *families,* in order to show that the point was choice, and that the right-wing wished to enforce the patriarchal nuclear family (father as breadwinner, woman at home with children) that literally excluded and branded as abnormal almost 85 percent of all American households.

Of course, an importance of words is their power to exclude. *Man, Mankind,* and the *Family of Man* have made women feel left out, usually accurately. *People, humanity,* or *humankind* were suggested as partial remedies. So were rewrites like *The Human Family* or *Peace on Earth, Good Will to People.*

1978

□ California voters defeat Proposition Six (the Briggs Initiative), which would have allowed school boards to fire teachers who are openly homosexual outside their classrooms.

□ Oregon residents defeat referendum that would have denied state monies for abortion.

□ State of Missouri files suit against NOW for its economic boycott of states that have not ratified the ERA; in 1979, U.S. District Court upholds right to boycott.

□ Abortion clinics in several states are harassed and vandalized.

□ HEW strengthens regulations against sterilization abuse, following testimony by feminist groups on both sides of the issue.

□ Faye Wattleton is first woman (and first black) to be elected president of Planned Parenthood since the organization was founded by Margaret Sanger.

□ Labor Department issues regulations to increase number of women in blue-collar construction jobs.

□ Congress extends deadline for ratification of the ERA to June 30, 1982.

□ Congress passes bill prohibiting introduction of the victim's reputation in cases of rape or attempted rape.

□ The Federal Employees Part-Time Career Employment Act calls on all government agencies to create part-time career-level jobs.

□ Harris Poll reports that support for the ERA is up to 55 percent (38 percent opposed), after two-year period of erosion.

□ Kansas City, Missouri, is site of first Women's Jazz Festival.

□ Anthropologist Margaret Mead dies at age 76.

□ Golfer Nancy Lopez wins $161,235—setting a record for a rookie, man or woman.

□ Congress passes bill requiring pregnancy disability benefits for pregnant workers, but fails to require abortion coverage.

□ Comprehensive care for pregnant teens and support of programs to prevent teen pregnancy is approved by Congress.

□ Congress votes to cut coverage of most abortions to military employees and families, and to Peace Corps volunteers.

□ National Alliance of Businessmen changes name to National Alliance of Business.

□ French feminist magazine, *F*, begins.

□ Report by National Association of Secondary School Principals finds percentage of women high school principals has *declined* from 10 percent in 1965 to 7 percent in 1978.

□ The number of women applying to medical schools increased 87 percent between 1973 and 1978, according to the Women and Health Roundtable; women were 23.7 percent of those enrolled in 1977-78.

□ National Lesbian Feminist Organization is formed in Los Angeles.

□ Monsanto Textiles Company pays Barbara Taibi $10,000 in largest individual settlement to date of a sexual harassment suit.

□ Coal Employment Project is organized by Appalachian women's and citizens' groups to encourage hiring of women and minorities in coal mines.

□ Maria Elaine Pitchford, the first woman ever to be tried for performing an illegal abortion on herself, is acquitted.

□ New York is first state to pass a bill to locate the children of women who have taken the cancer-linked synthetic hormone diethylstilbestrol (DES).

□ U.S. District Court rules that women sportswriters cannot be barred from major league baseball locker rooms.

□ Congress allocates $5 million to Department of Labor to set up centers for displaced homemakers.

□ First national feminist conference on pornography is sponsored by Women Against Violence in Pornography and Media in San Francisco.

□ In New York City, after a coalition of women brought suit, and in New Haven, Connecticut, police agree to arrest husbands who beat their wives, even if the wife does not bring charges.

□ National Cancer Institute reports that lung cancer in women increased 30 percent between 1973 and 1976.

□ Five women at American Cyanamid Company's West Virginia plant are sterilized in order to keep their jobs, after the firm declares that women of reproductive capability would be barred from jobs with exposure to lead compounds.

□ Hanna Holborn Gray is appointed president of the University of Chicago.

□ First woman elected to head the governing body of the Presbyterian Church is Sara Berneice Mosely of Sherman,Texas.

□ More women than men enter college for the first time in American history.

□ Supreme Court rules 5-4 to affirm a lower court order requiring the University of California Medical School to admit Allan Bakke, a white male who claimed "reverse discrimination." (It also rules 5-4 that race can be considered as a factor in admissions.)

□ John Rideout, the first man charged by his wife with raping her while they were living together, is acquitted by an Oregon Circuit Court.

□ National Coalition Against Domestic Violence is formed.

Feminists also tried to educate by asking men how they would feel if *they* received a *Spinster of Arts* or *Mistress of Science* degree on graduation, and then had to apply for a *Sistership*.

Minorities, both women and men, have sometimes been defined in the negative as *nonwhite* (would we speak of white people as *nonblack*?), and in any case, those who are counted as *minorities* in the United States are actually the *majority* in the world. In order to be more accurate and cross-cultural, feminists often adopted the description of *Third World* or *women of color* for themselves or others. (*Fourth World* was also used in the early '70s as a way of describing the commonality of *all* women in the patriarchal world, regardless of race, but that term was taken over in the late '70s as a description of the poorest, nonindustrialized countries. To continue this reference in the '80s, women may have to become the Fifth World—or whatever number is left.)

In order to reach each other and men across the barrier of race, feminists also tried to be sensitive to other linguistically divisive habits; for instance, using images of darkness or blackness as negative ("the dark side of human nature," "a black heart," "blackmail") and whiteness as positive (a good well-meaning lie is "white", "white magic" is good, so is "fair of face").

Similarly, *qualified* was a word mainly for "out" groups, as if white men were intrinsically *qualified*. They remained the adult, the professional (*worker, doctor, poet*), while the rest of us still needed adjectives (*woman worker, black doctor, lady poet*) for our descriptions.

The difficult efforts to make language more gender-free and thus more accurate often included the invention of such new alternatives as *chairperson* or *spokesperson* to designate positions in mixed organizations where the individual in question could be a woman or a man. (Obviously, only single-sex organizations could use *chairman* or *chairwoman* with accuracy.) The balance of power being what it is, however, these gender-free words were used by nonfeminists to neuterize women, and to leave men in the *status quo*. Thus, a woman might might become a *spokesperson*, but a man remained a *spokesman*. Females might become people, but men remained unchanged.

This awkward middle stage of change was probably inevitable, but we sometimes collaborated with our own exclusion by skipping to unifying, gender-free words too soon. *Humanism* was a special temptation. (As in, "Don't be threatened by feminism, we're really just talking about humanism.") *Androgyny* also raised the idea that female and male culture could be perfectly blended in the ideal person; yet because the female side of the equation had yet to be recognized and honored, so-called *androgyny* usually tilted toward the male. As a misunderstood concept, it also raised people's anxiety levels by conjuring up some vision of a conformist unisex; the very opposite of the individual liberation and uniqueness that feminism is actually about.

The lesson of both life and language was clear. Without the equal power that must precede it, integration meant either complete assimilation or going right back to our usual slot in the hierarchy. By the decade's end, we were more likely to recognize our "feminine" fear of conflict, and to hear warning bells when it led us toward some dangerous pretension of a unity that didn't yet exist. That made clear both the necessity of an independent feminist movement, and of consciousness-raising through gender-specific language. For instance, "Judges will be elected on their merits" is a perfectly okay, inclusive sentence. But "A judge will be elected on her or his merits" is a sentence that forces us to remember that women judges do exist.

Another symbolic confusion of the '70s was the invention of *male chauvinist pig*, a hybrid produced by the early reformers' misuse of *chauvinist* combined with the Leftist women's use of *pig;* an imitative willingness to reduce adversaries to something less than human as a first step toward justifying violence against them. (Though years of being *chicks, dogs,* and *cows* may also have led to some understandable desire to turn the tables.) Police had been *pigs* in the masculinist '60s—as in *Off the pigs!*—so all prejudiced men became the same.

In fact, *male chauvinist* itself was a problem: since *chauvinist* referred to a superpatriot, all we were saying was that this was a man obsessed with loyalty to his country. Instead, many feminist writers began to use *male supremacist* as a more accurate description of the problem at hand, but some *male supremacists* delightedly took advantage of the earlier error by wearing ties and pins proclaiming, "I am a male chauvinist pig." (An indication, of course, of the lack of seriousness that was also a mark of sexism in the '70s. No matter how prejudiced, there were fewer people who would still so cheerfully proclaim, "I am an anti-Semite" or "I am a racist.")

The depth and acceptability of the differences in power between women and men were most evident in an area where the two groups met: sexuality. Masculine dominance and female submission were still defined as "natural"; so much so that even violence toward women was accepted as a normal part of sexual life. Sadomasochism, Saturday-night beatings,and the idea that women "wanted" to be forced were all accepted to some degree. One of the most courageous acts of feminists in the '70s was attempting the long, difficult task of untangling sex from violence.

Rape, for instance, was finally redefined in the '70s, and understood as an act of violence and woman-hatred, not "natural" sexual need. The victim was no longer routinely assumed to have "asked for it" (that is, to be masochistic), and the rapist was no longer assumed to be acting in an excessively sadistic, but somewhat excusable, masculine way. Since the legal definition of *rape* had also depended on the completion of the sex act—not the severe sexual beating or humiliation which was more often the point—that definition was often legislatively changed to *sexual assault*, a term that was more accurate, and protected males who were rape victims of other men.

Battered women was a phrase that uncovered a major kind of violence that had been long hidden. It helped us to reveal the fact that most violence in America takes place in our homes, not in the streets. *Sexual harassment on the job* also exposed a form of aggression and intimidation from which many women

1979

Rideouts on "Good Morning, America," after 1979 reconciliation; dethroned Miss North Carolina reacts.

☐ National Coalition Against Sexual Assault is formed by rape-crisis centers in 20 states.

☐ Carter dismisses Bella Abzug as cochair of National Advisory Committee for Women. Co-chair Carmen Delgado Votaw and more than half the committee resign in protest.

☐ Twelve citywide office worker groups form Working Women, National Association of Office Workers.

☐ Abortion Rights Action Week is held nationally, sponsored by more than 50 organizations.

☐ Supreme Court rules that welfare benefits must be paid to families left needy by the mother's loss of her job, just as to families with a father left unemployed.

☐ The Episcopal Church votes against ordaining anyone sexually active outside marriage, thus excluding homosexuals.

☐ Lawsuits in Alaska, Massachusetts, Minnesota, Washington, D.C., and Philadelphia, challenge 1978 Jaycee decision to ban women.

☐ Debbie Shook smashes her Miss North Carolina crown after state Jaycees retract her title for saying that being a beauty queen was not "a bed of roses."

☐ Harris Poll finds Americans favor "efforts to strengthen and change women's status," by 65 to 28 percent (up from 42 to 41 percent in 1970).

☐ U.S. Treasury issues Susan B. Anthony dollar coin.

☐ Supreme Court rules that Congressional employees can sue for sex discrimination.

☐ Commemorative Conference on Feminist Theory held in New York City on the thirtieth anniversary of the publication of *The Second Sex* by Simone de Beauvoir.

☐ Supreme Court rules that a Massachusetts law giving absolute preference to veterans in civil service employment is *not* discriminatory against women.

☐ WOMEN, USA, is formed by Bella Abzug, Yvonne Brathwaite Burke, Patsy Mink, and others to work for equality and economic justice.

☐ The Air Force and Navy introduce maternity uniforms for pregnant military women. Rear Admiral James Hogg says: "The people in the Navy look on motherhood as being compatible with being a woman."

☐ A U.S. Court of Appeals rules that employers may not require their female employees to wear uniforms if comparable male employees can wear customary business attire.

☐ More than 290 women hold seats on boards of major corporations, almost double the number in 1975, according to Catalyst, a career-service organization.

☐ U.S. Census announces end of "head of household" designation beginning in 1980.

☐ National Weather Service starts naming storms for men, alternating with women's names.

☐ Margaret Thatcher of Great Britain elected Europe's first woman prime minister.

☐ Supreme Court rules in the Weber case that employers and unions can establish affirmative action programs, including quotas.

☐ *Emma* brings suit against *Stern* magazine in West Germany to stop it from portraying nude women on its cover.

☐ National Archives for Black Women's History and the Mary McLeod Bethune Memorial Museum open in Washington, D.C.

☐ Phyllis Schlafly hosts a victory party in Washington, D.C., to celebrate "the End of an ERA" on March 22, the original deadline for ratification.

☐ Los Angeles Superior Court judge denies Michelle Triola Marvin's breach-of-contract claim for half of actor Lee Marvin's earnings. Instead, he awards Marvin's common-law wife $104,000 for rehabilitation.

☐ Rose Kushner, author of *Why Me?*, persuades National Institute of Health to endorse a two-stage breast biopsy procedure, enabling women to have a choice in their breast surgery for cancer.

☐ National Women's Health Network sets up nation's only Depo Provera registry to assist victims of this experimental contraceptive hormone shot.

☐ National march on Washington, D.C., for lesbian and gay rights is held.

☐ Supreme Court rules that a minor has a constitutional right to an abortion, but upholds a Massachusetts' state law requiring her to persuade the judge that she is mature enough to make the decision.

☐ Sister Theresa Kane, president of the Leadership Conference of Women Religious, calls on Pope John Paul II in Washington, D.C. to "regard the possibility of women being included in all ministries of the church." The Pope had earlier called on nuns to wear habits and ruled out ordination for women.

The many sources from which this chronology was drawn include: *Rebirth of Feminism*, by Judith Hole and Ellen Levine (Quadrangle); *The Spirit of Houston*, the National Commission on the Observance of International Women's Year (U.S. Government Printing Office); *Ms.* Magazine, 1972 to 1979.

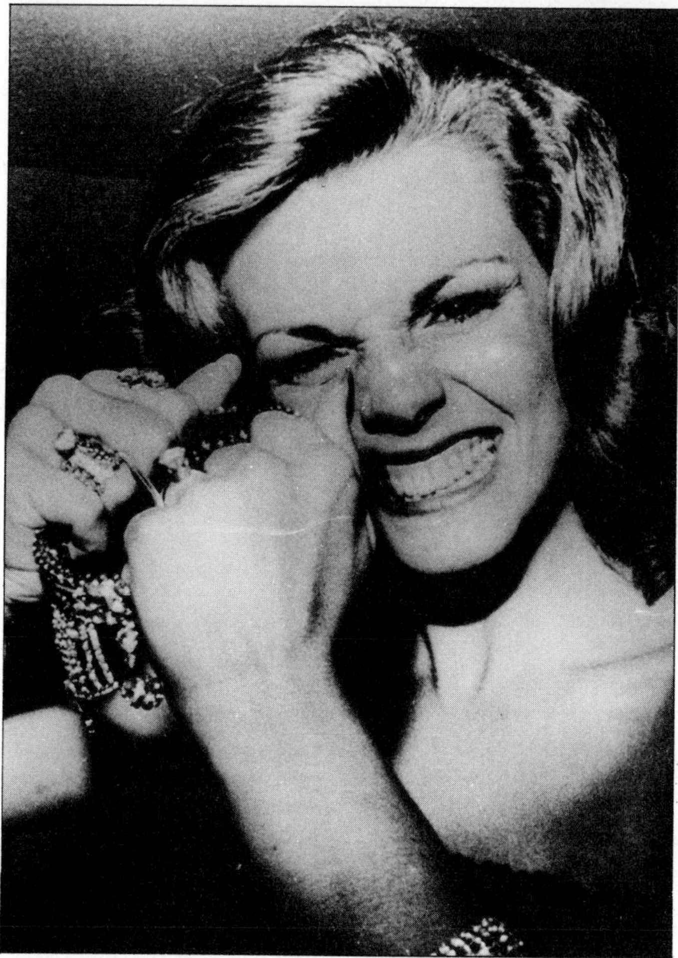

UPI

workers suffer. Talking about it openly inspired women to come forward, stop blaming themselves or other victims, and begin to penalize the aggressors. By identifying *pornography* (literally, "writing about female slaves") as the preaching of woman-hatred, and thus quite different from *erotica* with its connotation of love and mutuality, there was also the beginning of an understanding that such antiwoman propaganda is a major way in which violence and dominance are taught and legitimized.

We also uncovered the full horror of measures taken to turn women into passive possessions and child-bearers as we learned the meaning of such words as *cliterodectomy* (the total or partial excision of the clitoris), *infibulation* (cutting off the labia and forcing the raw edges to grow together so the vaginal entrance is blocked), plus other forms of brutal, routine sexual mutilation. Whether the outrage is the *psychic cliterodectomy* performed by Freud or the *physical cliterodectomy* still being performed on many little girls and women of Africa or the Middle East (and once an occasional medical treatment for non-conforming women and girls in America as well), the purpose of possessing the means of reproduction is clearly the same. Even *female sexual slavery* (once known by the 19th-century racist term *White Slavery*, since it was the only form to which whites were also subject) was rediscovered and exposed in the '70s as a flourishing business and a fact of international life.

In response, it's no wonder that *radicalism* lost its equation with excess, unreasonableness, smallness, or failure. By exposing the injustice of the sexual caste system and its role as a root of other "natural" injustices based on race and class, *radical feminism* laid the groundwork for a unity of women. And by challenging this masculine/feminine, dominant/passive structure as a cause of violence, it has also shown that *radicalism* can take nonviolent forms, and can act to challenge the roots of violence itself.

This understanding is obviously the basis of a cooperation among women that is tenuous but worldwide. Feminism was international—and antinational—during its 19th and early 20th century wave (known to this young country as the First Wave), and was also a contagion among many cultures during the centuries and various advances of the feminist revolution that were part of history long before this country was known as America.

The '70s were a decade in which women reached out to each other: first in consciousness-raising groups that allowed us to create a psychic turf (for women have not even a neighborhood of our own, much less a country), then in movement meetings and a women's culture that created more psychic territory; and finally across national and cultural boundaries. The '80s can build on these beginnings.

Ten years of our lives have passed—but they are also a map to the future. The images, mementos, and words that have been gathered here by a team of women editors are intended as a record, but not a whole picture. They are sense-memories; reminders of what has been.

We are all part of the spiral of history. The goal of this book is to evoke the unique part that lives in each of us.

—**Gloria Steinem, New York City, 1979**

The problem that has no name stirring in the minds of so many American women today is not a matter of loss of femininity or too much education, or the demands of domesticity. It is far more important than anyone recognizes. It is the key to these other new and old problems which have been torturing women and their husbands and children, and puzzling their doctors and educators for years. It may well be the key to our future as a nation and a culture.

—Betty Friedan, *The Feminine Mystique* (Norton), 1963.

Anne Dockery/LNS

. . .Our society, like all other historical civilizations, is a patriarchy. The fact is evident at once if one recalls that the military, industry, technology, universities, science, political office, and finance—in short, every avenue of power within the society, including the coercive force of the police, is entirely in male hands.

—Kate Millett *Sexual Politics* (Doubleday), 1970

NOW (National Organization for Women) Bill of Rights

Adopted at NOW's first national conference, Washington, D.C., 1967

I. Equal Rights Constitutional Amendment
II. Enforce Law Banning Sex Discrimination in Employment
III. Maternity Leave Rights in Employment and in Social Security Benefits
IV. Tax Deduction for Home and Child Care Expenses for Working Parents
V. Child Day Care Centers
VI. Equal and Unsegregated Education
VII. Equal Job Training Opportunities and Allowances for Women in Poverty
VIII. The Right of Women to Control Their Reproductive Lives

In fighting for our liberation we will always take the side of women against their oppressors. We will not ask what is "revolutionary" or "reformist," only what is good for women.

—Redstockings Manifesto, 1969

The first question from a male radical to a female liberationist is: "What about sex?" This seems strange. Apparently women can 'do their thing' as long as they don't cut off the sex supply, which is the major use men have for women. I usually answer by saying that it is not an important question; that women should have control of their own bodies, and never submit to sexual relations simply because they fear they might appear frigid or lose a friendship with a man. The response from the male radical is almost always that my attitude is *repressive*. It seems clear that the 'sex problem' is the man's problem, and he will have to take care of it. Women have been accepting the responsibility for it for far too long.

—Roxanne Dunbar, "Female Liberation as the Basis for Social Revolution," 1969

"Bitches are aggressive, assertive, domineering, overbearing, strong-minded, spiteful, hostile, direct, blunt, candid, obnoxious, thick-skinned, hard-headed, vicious, dogmatic, competent, competitive, pushy, loud-mouthed, independent, stubborn, demanding, manipulative, egoistic, driven, achieving, overwhelming, threatening, scary, ambitious, tough, brassy, masculine, boisterous and turbulent. A Bitch takes shit from no one. You may not like her, but you cannot ignore her."

—Joreen, "The Bitch Manifesto," 1969

WATCH OUT. MAYBE YOU'LL FINALLY MEET A *REAL* CASTRATING FEMALE.

—Female Liberation slogan, 1970

WITCH is an all-women Everything. It's theater, revolution, magic, terror, joy, garlic flowers, spells. It's an awareness that witches and gypsies were the original guerrillas and resistance fighters against oppression—particularly the oppression of women—down through the ages. . . . There is no "joining" WITCH. If you are a woman and dare to look within yourself, you are a Witch. . . . Your power comes from your own self as a woman, and it is activated by working in concert with your sisters. . . .

WITCH, 1969

It is a hidden fear that somehow, if they are only given a chance, women will suddenly do as they have been done by.

—Eva Figes, *Patriarchal Attitudes* (Stein and Day), 1970

Miriam Bokser

ACTIONS

Above—**Miss America Pageant Protest, 1968. Robin Morgan throws a bra into the Freedom Trash Can, where it joins girdles, curlers, false eyelashes, and wigs. (Bras were never burned at this protest or any other; bra-burning was an invention of the media.)**

Below—**An 11-hour sit-in at the "Ladies Home Journal" in 1970 protests the image of women in women's magazines. Protestors win joint control of a special supplement (published in August, 1970). John Mack Carter, editor-in-chief, sits on the desk; behind him just to the left is articles editor Leonore Hershey, who by the end of the decade becomes editor-in-chief. At the extreme left with glasses is Shulamith Firestone.**

"Mr. Mailer, in *Advertisements for Myself*, you said, quote, 'A good novelist can do without everything but the remnants of his balls.' For years and years I've been wondering, Mr. Mailer: When you dip your balls in ink, what color ink is it?"

—Cynthia Ozick questioning Norman Mailer during Town Hall debate, 1971

Tony Rollo/Newsweek

"Town Bloody Hall"/Pennebaker Inc.

Bettye Lane

Above—**Germaine Greer and Norman Mailer at the Town Hall Symposium of Ideas, 1971. The panel also includes Jill Johnston, Diana Trilling, and Jackie Ceballos.**
Far left—**Picketing the Playboy Club, New York City, 1970.**

Louise Brotsky

Above—**Chicago W.I.T.C.H. coven "hexing" the Transit Authority after a fare raise in 1970.** Below—**Fifty thousand women march down Fifth Avenue, August 26, 1970 in celebration of the 50th anniversary of suffrage—the largest women's demonstration up to that time.**

AS THE FBI SAW IT...

"Last week we pointed out that the so-called Women's Liberation Movement had its origin in Soviet Russia. This week, let's take a look at the red hot mommas of the '70's. A typical example of these females is Case Millett."

"The women, in general appeared to be hippies, lesbians or from other far-out groups. Most of them were very colorfully dressed, but the majority [sic] wore faded blue jeans. Most seemed to be making a real attempt to be unattractive. . . . One of the interesting aspects of the delegates' dress was the extreme fuzzy appearance of their hair. . . . Someone said this . . . was gotten by braiding their hair in tiny braids and leaving it that way while it was wet until it dried. Then they would take out the braids. From the looks of their hair they apparently really didn't bother to try and comb it out afterwards."

"__________ estimated that there are 150 to 200 small radical groups. . . . Several of the groups have no names. It is difficult to keep a record of the persons in the groups inasmuch as the women frequently switch according to possible changes in address, work place, movement affiliation, marital status, ideological analysis or whim. Radicals are increasingly finding success in the WLM as a vehicle through which to radicalize women."

—from F.B.I. files of the early seventies

William E. Sauro/NYT Pictures

WORK

Dale Bindheim/LNS

A job as a human right is a principle that applies to men as well as women. But women have more cause to fight for it. The phenomenon of the "working woman" has been held responsible for everything from male impotence to the rising cost of steak (because, according to one explanation, we are no longer staying home to prepare the cheaper, slower-cooking cuts, as good wives should). Unless we include a job as part of every citizen's right to autonomy and personal fulfillment, women will continue to be vulnerable to someone else's idea of what "need" is.

—Gloria Steinem, "Why Women Work," *Ms.*, March, 1979

42%—42.1 million—of the U.S. work force are women

Of the women in the workforce in March 1978, nearly 80% were in clerical, sales, service, factory or plant jobs

In 1977 full-time women workers had a median income of $6,256 less than men

On an average, women who work full-time earn 59 cents for every $1 earned by men

Three of every four divorced women and nearly half of all married women are in the labor force

More than half of all husband-wife families in 1978 had two or more wage earners

40% of mothers with children under the age of 6 are working

A secretary with 13.2 years of education earns 38% less than a truck driver with 9.0 years of education

4,173,000 men working in the private sector earn $25,000 a year. 140,000 women earn that much

By 1980, women's volunteer work may be worth more than $18 billion

Mariette Pathy Allen

Caroline Gooden on the job—and on lunch break—with construction co-workers.

BREAKTHROUGHS

United Airlines

By 1971, the Bell System—that is, the American Telephone & Telegraph Company, its subsidiaries, and 24 operating companies across the country—was the nation's largest employer of women. The Bell monolith was also "without doubt the largest oppressor of women workers in the United States," to quote the 1972 report of the Equal Employment Opportunity Commission. . . .

Goals and timetables [instituted in January, 1973] are nothing new in affirmative action plans, but the AT&T agreement dramatically expands their use by requiring that men be eligible for traditional "women's jobs." For example, about 10 percent of all new operators hired and 37.5 percent of new clerical workers must be male. These male hiring objectives—applied for the first time in this case—could have a major impact on sex stereotypes.

"This is a real image victory," said Whitney Adams, coordinator of NOW's task force on the FCC. "People will get a shock when they get a male operator and this will have a consciousness-raising effect on the whole society. This is essential to wiping out job ghettos."

—Lisa Cronin Wohl, "Liberating Ma Bell," *Ms.*, November, 1973

Bettye Lane

United Airlines

AT&T

Bettye Lane

An Urban Institute study of women on the Washington, D.C., force concluded that women made fewer arrests than men, but they tested better in "defusing" potentially violent situations. There was no difference in absenteeism or in ability to meet the physical demands of the job.

Policewoman: I understand the police wives' reactions to men and women on patrol. I'm a jealous wife too. But the bond between partners is unique. It's close, nonsexual and nonromantic. People think the only kind of closeness is love. But my partner and I are pulling together in life-and-death situations."

—*Ms.*, October, 1975

Cassie Mackin, one of the first floor reporters at the 1972 political conventions.

Jill Krementz

Betty Lou English/*Women At Their Work* (Dial)

Far left—**Madeline Lanciani, one of the first of the female hotel chefs.** Below—**Astronaut candidate Judith Resnik suits up.**

Annie M. Tiziou

"Talk of an American spacewoman makes me sick to my stomach."

—NASA spokesperson, quoted by the press, July, 1961

"We've never sent any women into space because we haven't had a good reason to. We fully envision, however, that in the near future, we will fly women into space and use them the same way we use them on Earth—and for the same purpose."

—James Lovell, astronaut, September, 1973

Current regulations require that preference for appointment to Astronaut Candidate positions be given to U.S. citizens when there is an adequate source of well-qualified citizens available. Qualified minority and women applicants are encouraged to apply.

—NASA recruitment press release, August, 1979

Cidne Hart/LNS

Center left—**Michelle Winston is first New York Mets ball girl, 1976.**

Bettye Lane

Cary Herz

Ann Dockery/LNS

Bettye Lane

Meeting the needs of the '80s: architect (*above*); nurse practitioner (*below*).

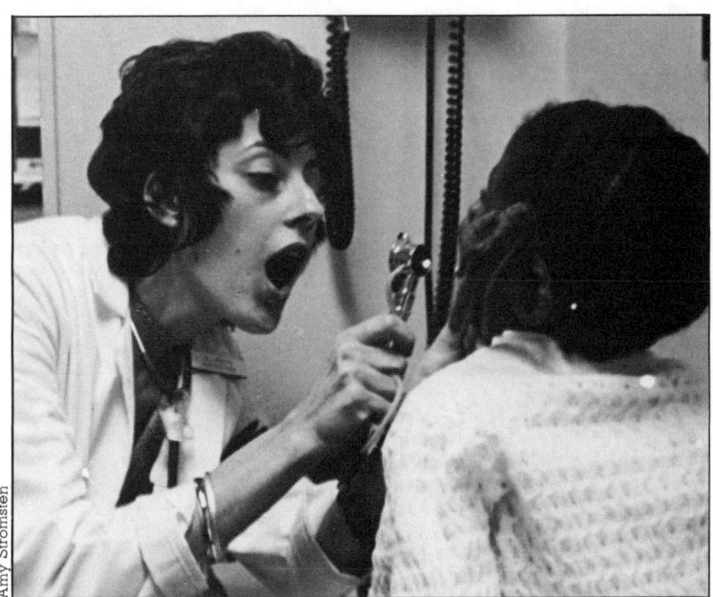

Amy Stromsten

Experts predict growth in the need for physician's assistants, health administrators, anesthesiologists, and X-ray technicians. The biggest demand is expected for mid-level health professionals—some of whom will be highly trained enough to provide competition to doctors for the patients of the 1980s.

The future looks brightest for women in nontraditional fields. Electronics, structural engineering, and the aerospace industry are among those that so far haven't been attracting enough women workers to satisfy affirmative action needs . . . jobs in commercial banking, auto sales, and restaurant and hotel management are increasing. The insurance industry is currently hiring more women—as actuaries and underwriters—than any other industry . . . the computer field promises to be the biggest employer in the coming decade.

—Milly Hawk Daniel, "What Are the Jobs of the 80s?" *Ms.*, September, 1979

AT THE TOP

"Among you students of Stockholm and among other students, at least in the Western world, women are represented in reasonable proportion to their numbers in the community; yet among the scientists, scholars and leaders of our world they are not. No objective testing has revealed such substantial differences in talent as to account for this discrepancy. The failure of women to have reached positions of leadership has been due in large part to social and professional discrimination. In the past, few women have tried and even fewer have succeeded. We still live in a world in which a significant fraction of people, including women, believe that a woman belongs and wants to belong exclusively in the home; that a woman should not aspire to achieve more than her male counterparts and particularly not more than her husband. Even now women with exceptional qualities for leadership sense from their parents, teachers and peers that they must be harder working, accomplish more and yet are less likely to receive appropriate rewards than are men.

"We cannot expect in the immediate future that all women who seek it will achieve full equality of opportunity. But if women are to start moving towards that goal, we must believe in ourselves or no one else will believe in us; we must match our aspirations with the competence, courage and determination to succeed."

—Nobel Laureate Rosalyn Yalow, addressing the students of Stockholm, October, 1977

UPI

"I will never know if it would have been the same with Harry Reasoner had my name been Tom Brokaw instead of Barbara Walters, and I don't want to know. Our careers are no longer intertwined, and we enjoy each other now as friends, and I think so much of what happened last year is leftover remnants of misunderstanding about women and of fear about women and fear about their world and communication."

—Barbara Walters, accepting the Matrix Award, Women in Communications, April, 1978

Above left—**Colleagues toast Dr. Rosalyn Yalow following announcement of her 1977 Nobel Prize for Medicine.** Above—**Incompatible anchors, Barbara Walters and Harry Reasoner.**

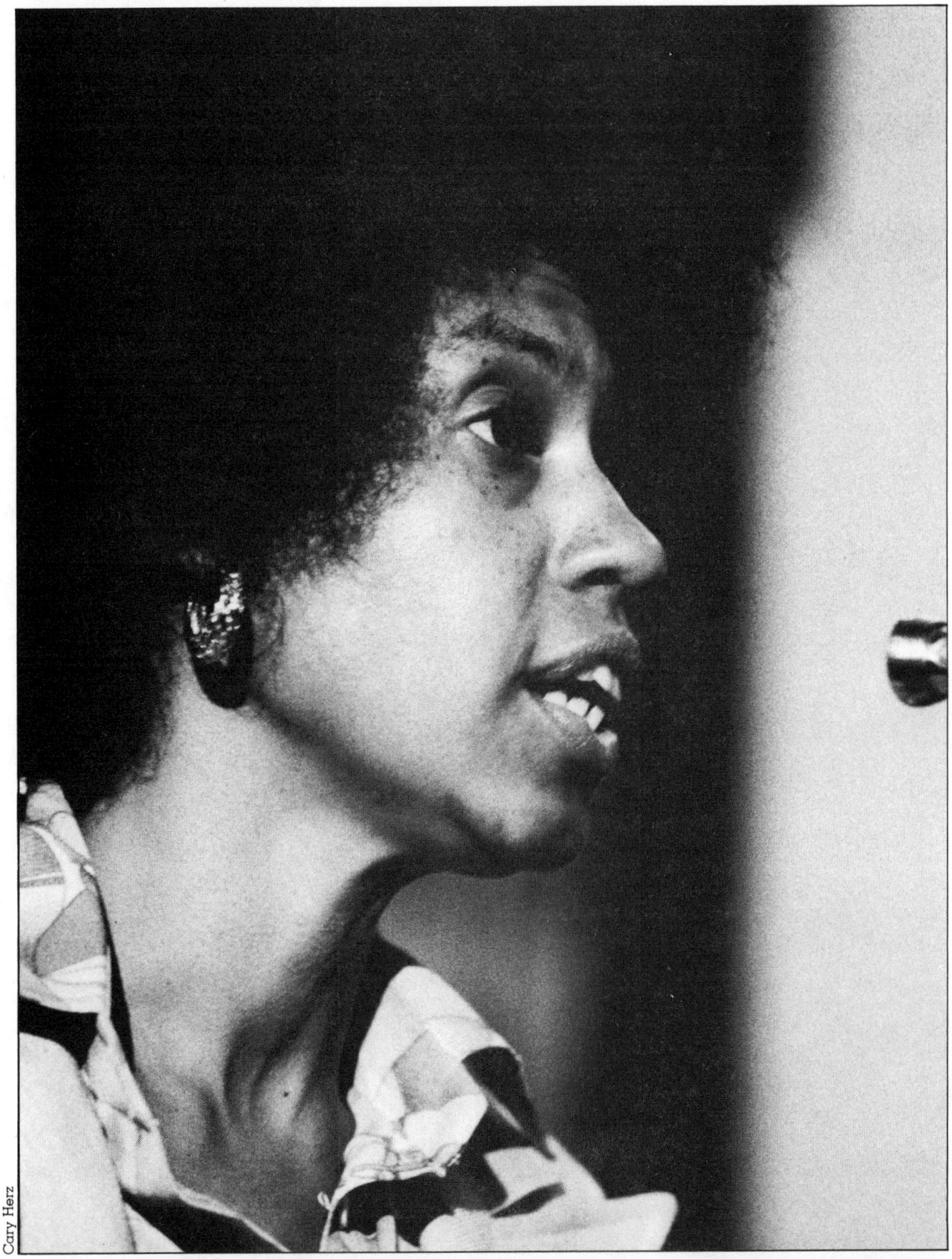

Cary Herz

Left—**Carter Administration's Chair of the Equal Employment Opportunity Commission, Eleanor Holmes Norton.**
Below—**Chief Justice of the California Supreme Court, Rose Bird.**

"A man has to be Joe McCarthy to be called ruthless. All a woman has to do is put you on hold."

—Marlo Thomas

"Katie Graham's gonna get her tit caught in a big fat wringer," John Mitchell said on hearing of the *Post*'s Watergate investigation. He was wrong. What she got instead was the esteem of much of the Western world, expressed through honorary doctorates, a Pulitzer prize, and plaques and awards.

—Jane Howard, "Katharine Graham: The Power That Didn't Corrupt," *Ms.*, October, 1974

Jill Krementz

Washington *Post* publisher Kay Graham enjoys visit from daughter, writer Lally Weymouth.

Top to bottom
Jane Cahill Pfeiffer, Chairman (sic) of the Board, National Broadcasting Company. **Gertrude Michelson,** director, General Electric. **Dr. Ruth Patrick,** director, E.I. du Pont de Nemours. **Margaret P. Mackin,** director, E.I. du Pont de Nemours.

Top to bottom
Patricia T. Carbine, director, New York Life Insurance. **Dr. Marina Whitman,** director, General Motors. **Sister Jane Scully,** director, Gulf Oil. **Lorene Rogers,** director, Texaco. **Eleanor B. Sheldon,** director, Mobil Oil.

Top to bottom
Kathryn D. Wriston, director, Union Carbide. **Catherine B. Cleary,** director, General Motors. **Martha Peterson,** director, Exxon. **Marian S. Heiskell,** director, Ford. **Anne L. Armstrong,** director, General Motors.

What do women really want? Louis Stangle feels he may have the answer in the "Talking Ms. Teddy Bear." Having successfully marketed the "Executive Teddy Bear" (which, not surprisingly, sports a business suit, tie, and vest), Stangle claims that he is introducing a female model in response to the countless requests he's received from disappointed women. Pull Ms. Teddy Bear's string, and she says such encouraging words as: "You can be whatever you want to be," "You've got what it takes," and "You're on your way to the top."

—*Ms.* "Gazette," July, 1979

"Every day, in this mostly male world, you have to figure out, 'Do I get this by charming somebody? By being strong? Or by totally allowing my aggression out?' You've got to risk failure. The minute you want to keep power—you've become subservient, somebody who does work you don't believe in. But it's all a learning process—this is the first generation who has stepped out and done it en masse."

—Paula Weinstein, vice-president, Warner Brothers, *Ms.*, December, 1977 (She is now vice-president, world-wide production, Twentieth Century Fox Corp.)

Rick Smolan/Contact

With the exception of Dolores [Huerta], there are no other women in the small, influential circle around [Cesar] Chavez; but nearly half of the union's organizers are women, and many of the UFW's important programs, like the credit union and clinics, are run by women. Huerta herself claims, "Women have one advantage over men—their egos aren't so involved. They can compromise to get what they want instead of forcing a showdown all the time." —Judith Coburn, "Dolores Huerta: La Pasionaria of the Farmworkers," *Ms.*, November, 1976

. . . We aren't used to being the boss, to giving direct commands or making direct demands. We confuse emotional intimacy with work relations. A bank teller named Helen told me about her resentment of one of the women managers: "Marlene is always very friendly; *too* friendly. She gets you into conversations that are like therapy; she sniffs out some vulnerable private area and gets you to talk about it. Then, when she has this intimate relationship established, she uses it to manipulate you into doing some job, you may not want to do. But it becomes a personal affront if you refuse."

This problem didn't come up as long as women were at home, or at work more or less equally confined to the secretarial pool— or any of the other traditional women's work groups. As far as the job was concerned, we were often interchangeable so that we could relate to one another as friends and equals. The bosses were mostly male. We did our work—we often shared it—and at lunch we talked about something else.

But when a woman identifies with the success of her own work, boundaries become important—and often clash with feelings.
—Signe Hammer, "When Women Have Power Over Women," *Ms.*, September, 1978

Above—**Sarah Caldwell, director of the Opera Company of Boston.**

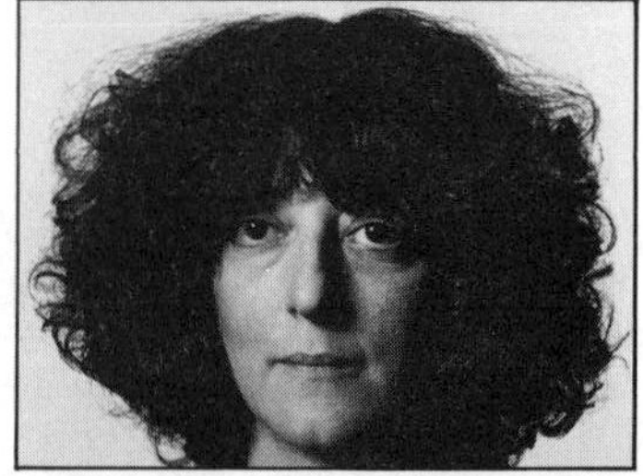

Column 1—***(top to bottom)* Joan Ganz Cooney, founder of Children's Television Workshop, creators of "Sesame Street." Lynn Salvage, president of The First Women's Bank of New York. Jean Nydetch, founder of Weight Watchers.**

Column 2—***(top to bottom)* Faye Wattleton, president of Planned Parenthood. Linda Wachner, president of Max Factor. Kathleen Nolan, first woman elected (1975) to head Screen Actors Guild.**

Column 3—***(top to bottom)* Marcia Tucker, director of The New Museum. Brig/Gen Jeanne M. Holm, U.S. Air Force. Charlotte Curtis, Op-Ed page editor, New York *Times*.**

TRADITIONAL

The fact that labor done in the marketplace—but not that carried on in the home—is rewarded by pay that presumably bears some relation to its value makes it difficult to calculate the net gain from women's growing contribution to market work. However, the important consideration is not the failure to measure the value of home work, but the tendency to impute a low market value to those services which, being customarily performed in the home, have commanded no price at all. Cleaning, laundry, and cooking have brought low wages in the labor market, reflecting the fact that in most instances these services bear no price tags. Not only has the buyer been conditioned to view these services as cheap; the women who do the work are conditioned to think of them in the same way. . . .

The big trade-off for the woman's market work is not a reduction in her home work, but a reduction in her free time. In one study, the total work load for the wife rose by an average of 13 hours per week as a result of her move into market work, while that of her husband actually dropped by an average of 1.5 hours per week.

—Juanita Kreps, "The Future for the Working Woman," *Ms.*, March, 1977

"There is no God-given law that says a secretary is making 'good money' when she earns $180 a week while a sanitation worker in New York City is earning entry-level pay at considerably over that. The difference is clear. He's organized in a powerful union. We are hopelessly and helplessly divided in most offices. Women *need* unions!"

—Margie Albert, organizer for District 65 of the Distributive Workers of America, *Ms.*, June, 1974

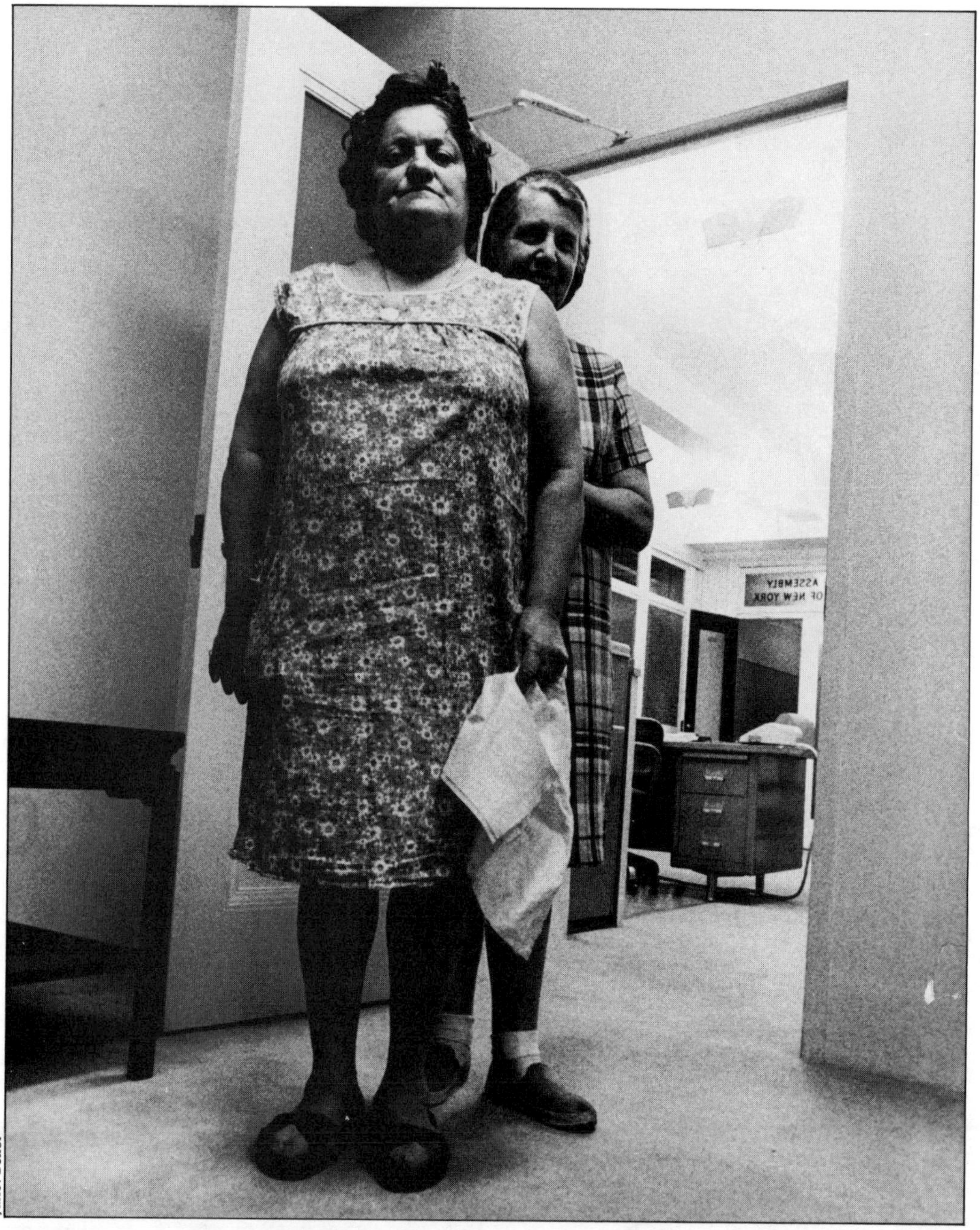

Janet Beller

The Department of Labor reports that more jobs are opening up in the secretarial field than in any of the other 299 work classifications on which it keeps tabs. Although there are already a record 3.6 million secretaries on public and private payrolls, new positions are being created at a rate of 440,000 a year. But while secretarial schools are filled, almost 20 percent of the jobs are going begging. . . .

In large part, the shortage is a side effect of the Women's Movement and equal opportunity programs. Now that they are encouraged to start out in management training programs or go on to study law, medicine, or business management, young women graduates are less apt to want to move from campus to a secretarial pool. Says Sheila Rather, an executive with the Manhattan office of Brook Street Bureau of Mayfair Ltd., a personnel agency: "Business has never accepted the fact that a secretary also wants a career path."

—*Time*, September 3, 1979

Chip Berlet/LNS

Cathy Cockrell/LNS

Cidne Hart/LNS

"I don't think of myself as a sex symbol or a servant. I think of myself as somebody who knows how to open the door of a 747 in the dark, upside down, and under water."

—12-year-veteran stewardess for TWA, *Ms.*, January, 1973

Western Airlines trainees practice survival exercise for emergency ditchings over water.

Wide World

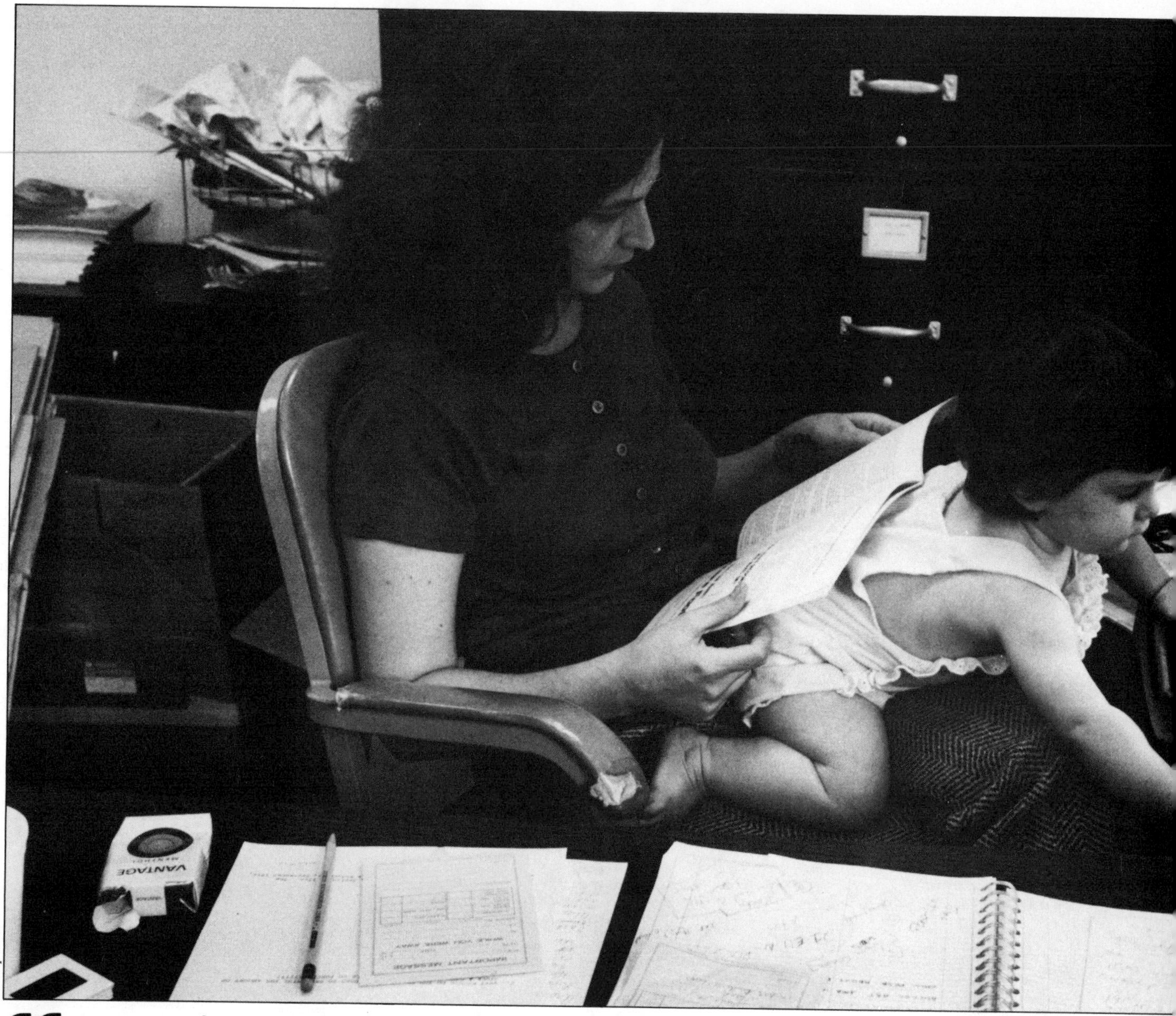

Maddy Miller

> "... what [two-year-old] Alix has taught me about work is that nothing is so important that it can't, in a pinch, be done with a child on one's lap. It's turned out to be a lot easier than I thought it would be. Most of our definitions of the circumstances under which business has to be conducted are far more rigid and artificial than necessary."
>
> —Karin Lippert, on working with children in the office, *Ms.*, March, 1975

> ... Men still escape an equal responsibility for children, home, and keeping up a relationship ... in a patriarchy having everything assumes that you start off with your basic stick-to-the-ribs wife/mother identity—and the rest is "liberated" gravy.
>
> —Letty Cottin Pogrebin, "Having It All: Should We?" *Ms.*, March, 1978

Above—**Phyllis Langer and daughter Alix work it out at *Ms.* magazine.** Right—**Firefighter Linda Eaton is banned by Iowa City officials in 1979 from nursing son Ian at firehouse.**

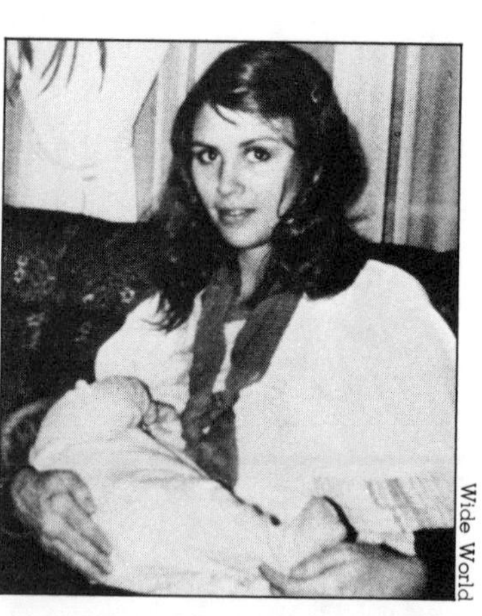

Wide World

Flextime is a proven innovation that's good for everybody, that raises productivity, creates more satisfied workers, gives people more chance to manage whatever outside responsibilities they have to manage, including their families. It's such a good idea and it's spreading practically at *no* speed at all!

It's possible that men simply don't perceive how changes such as flextime are going to improve their lives. However, I was intrigued by a University of Michigan survey which found that satisfaction with work schedules dropped dramatically in the 1970s, generally among men who wanted more time to be with their families.

Flextime also has revolutionary implications in terms of how people do their jobs, because people do have to be able to cover for one another, learn each other's jobs, and take on more responsibility.

—Rosabeth Moss Kanter, "Corporate Success: You Don't Have to Play by *Their* Rules—A Conversation with Rosabeth Moss Kanter," *Ms.*, October, 1979

BUCKING THE SYSTEM

More and more women are starting their own businesses—to find work in a tight job market, to find freer expression of their creative and management abilities, and to put into practice their own ideas of how the business world should operate. Whatever the motives, or combination of them, the self-employed woman is an idea whose time has come.

—Heidi Fiske and Karen Zehring, "How To Start Your Own Business," *Ms.*, April, 1976

Joan Saxe

Ede Rothaus

Above right—**Aileen Hernandez has opened an economic consulting firm, Hernandez Associates.** Right—**Publishing house, Daughters, Inc., is owned and operated by women.**

Bettye Lane

Margo St. James, first president of prostitutes union, COYOTE.

Crystal Lee Jordan fights to unionize J.P. Stevens in 1972.

Chie Nishio

The stakes are high. Secrecy is stringent. Using the most current figures available, there are an estimated 200,000 to 250,000 prostitutes in the United States today. Taking the lower estimate, at only six contacts a day and at the bottom price of $20 per trick, the millions of clients of prostitution contribute to the support of the underworld the incredible sum of between $7 and $9 *billion* annually. All of it untaxed.

Gail Sheehey, *Hustling* (Delacorte), 1973

Below—**Graphics are also anmmunition in the battle against job discrimination.**

Bettye Lane

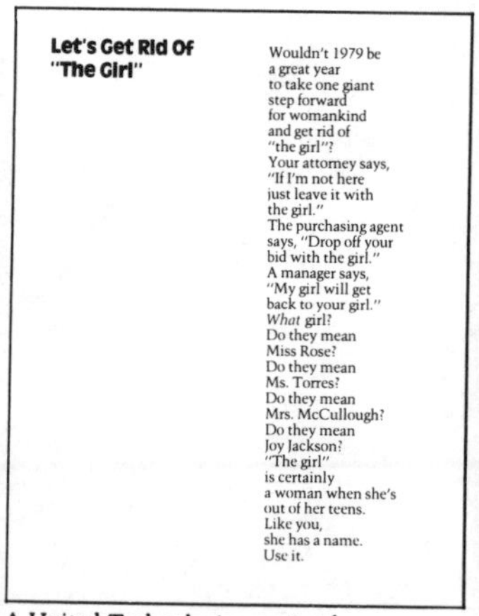

Let's Get Rid Of "The Girl"

Wouldn't 1979 be
a great year
to take one giant
step forward
for womankind
and get rid of
"the girl"?
Your attorney says,
"If I'm not here
just leave it with
the girl."
The purchasing agent
says, "Drop off your
bid with the girl."
A manager says,
"My girl will get
back to your girl."
What girl?
Do they mean
Miss Rose?
Do they mean
Ms. Torres?
Do they mean
Mrs. McCullough?
Do they mean
Joy Jackson?
"The girl"
is certainly
a woman when she's
out of her teens.
Like you,
she has a name.
Use it.

A United Technologies reprint from *The Wall Street Journal*

Welfare's like a traffic accident. It can happen to anybody, but especially it happens to women.

And that's why welfare is a women's issue. For a lot of middle-class women in this country, Women's Liberation is a matter of concern. For women on welfare it's a matter of survival.

That's why we had to go on welfare: survival. And that's why we can't get off now.

In fact, welfare was invented mostly for women. It grew out of something called the Mother's Pension Laws. To be eligible, you had to be female, you had to be a mother, you had to be "worthy." "Worthy" meant were your kids "legitimate," was your home "suitable," were you "proper"?

—Johnnie Tillman, first chairwoman of the National Welfare Rights Organization, 1972

Bottom—**Lawyer Harriet Rabb, successful in sex discrimination suits against *Reader's Digest* and *Newsweek*, moments after her 1978 court victory for women employees of the New York *Times*.**

Christina Thomson

Iris Schneider

In 1960, males were 1.62 times as likely as females to die of coronary heart disease; in 1976, males were 2.1 times as likely to die of heart disease. (Women, of course, are somewhat hormonally protected from heart attacks until after menopause.) Ulcer death rates are declining for both sexes, according to Dr. Lois Verbrugge of the University of Michigan, except that in this case the decline has been slightly more rapid for men. Overall, according to data analyzed by Dartmouth sociologist Allan Johnson, the story on gender and longevity has not changed since the 1920s: despite women's continuing influx into the work force, despite the "lifestyle" upheaval of the sixties and seventies (and—it should be added—despite all the unnecessary surgery performed on women, the reckless prescribing of estrogens and other hazardous drugs and devices), women live longer than men, and the gap continues to widen.

Leaving aside heart disease for more mundane ills, there's evidence that employed women actually have an edge over the women who work at home. According to national health surveys taken over the last two decades, employed women are less likely to report having been sick enough to go to bed within the last year, less likely to report chronic conditions such as arthritis, and less likely to complain of miscellaneous "pains and ailments."

—Barbara Ehrenreich, "Is Success Dangerous To Your Health?" *Ms.*, May, 1979

IN THE HOME

Eat, eliminate, prepare food, clean up, shop, throw out the garbage, a routine clear as a geometric form, a linear pattern that seems almost graceful in its simplicity. Despite computers and digit telephone numbers, nuclear fission, my life hardly differs from that of an Indian squaw settled in a tepee on the same Manhattan land centuries ago. Pick, clean, prepare, throw out, dig a hole, bury the waste—she was my sister. She would understand why there should be one day of total fast each week.

—Anne Roiphe, *Up the Sandbox* (Fawcett/World), 1973

The decisive contribution of women in the developed industrial society is rather simple—or at least it becomes so, once the disguising myth is dissolved. It is, overwhelmingly, to facilitate a continuing and more or less unlimited increase in consumption. . . . Just as production of goods and services requires management or administration, so does their consumption. The one is not greatly less essential than the other.

—John Kenneth Galbraith, "How the Economy Hangs on Her Apron Strings," *Ms.*, May, 1974

Still, running a household, after all, is not tantamount to death, anguish, or even waste. Decent and fulfilling lives have gone down that road, if fulfillment is counted in pies and sock-washings. And why not? Bureaucrats and dentists are equal drudges and fiddlers, jobs are cells of domesticated emotion, offices are repetitious and restrictive boxes. Both men and women practice housewifery, wherever they are. Hemingway's early tales are cookbooks. If only "the management of a house" were the whole story! But no: once invoke Nature and Destiny and you are inviting an intensified preoccupation with death. Death becomes the whole story.

This is simply because all the truth any philosophy can really tell us about human life is that each new birth supplies another corpse. Philosophy tells only that; it is true; and if the woman is seen only as childbearer, she is seen only as disgorger of corpses.

—Cynthia Ozick "The Hole Birth Catalog," *Ms.*, October, 1972

Dr. Jessie Hartline, a Rutgers University economist, suggests that housewives organize, pay each other the going rate for an exchange of household services, and receive the benefits of being "employed."

—*Ms.* "Gazette," December 1976

Despite the presence of myriad labor-saving devices in their homes, today's middle-class housewives spend as much time doing housework as did the women of 50 years ago who entirely lacked these conveniences. In 1966 the average full-time housewife spent about 55 hours per week at household tasks, while in 1924 her counterpart averaged 52 hours.

—*Scientific American*, April, 1976

Joan Roth

Bettye Lane

In Houston, Texas, a friend of mine stood and watched her husband step over a pile of toys on the stairs, put there to be carried up. "Why can't you get this stuff put away?" he mumbled. Click! "You have two hands," she said, turning away.
—Jane O'Reilly, "The Housewife's Moment of Truth," *Ms.*, Spring, 1972

Abigail Heyman/Magnum

The 1976 Federal inheritance tax reform increases the exemption allowed a surviving spouse, but otherwise a wife's labor on the farm does not legally earn her as much right as her husband to the capital they have accumulated.

CALIFORNIA DISPLACED HOMEMAKERS EQUAL OPPORTUNITY ACT, 1975

The legislature hereby finds and declares that there is an ever-increasing number of persons in this state who, having fulfilled a role as homemakers, find themselves "displaced" in their middle years through divorce, death of spouse, or other loss of family income. As a consequence, displaced homemakers are very often without any source of income; they are ineligible for categorical welfare assistance; they are subject to the highest unemployment rate of any sector of the work force; they face continuing discrimination in employment because they are older and have no recent paid work experience; they are ineligible for unemployment insurance because they have been engaged in unpaid labor in the home; they are ineligible for Social Security because they are too young, and for many, they will never qualify for Social Security because they have been divorced from the family wage earner; they have often lost their rights as beneficiaries under employers' pension and health plans through divorce or death of spouse, despite many years of contribution to the family well-being; and they are most often ineligible for Medi-Cal, and are generally unacceptable to private health insurance plans because of their age.

The legislature further finds and declares that homemakers are an unrecognized part of the work force who make an invaluable contribution to the welfare of the society as a whole. . . .

After decades of being one of the most stable, unchanging groups in American society, blue-collar wives—some 40 million women—are expressing dramatic changes in attitudes, according to a survey by Social Research, Inc., in Chicago.

"For years, research has shown that [the blue-collar wife's] life was captive of the triangle of husband, children, and home. . . . As late as 1965, we said that no important changes could be expected in her attitudes," said Dr. Burleigh B. Gardner, who chairs the study group. "Today, these women are rejecting such limitations. They feel women should have a choice of careers, homemaking, or both."

Among the more dramatic changes in attitude documented in the study are:

- **A new desire for independence—eight years ago, close to half of the women queried thought that a personal second car was just a luxury; today, the same number see it as a necessity.**
- **A desire for fewer children—in 1965, most blue-collar wives thought four children were an ideal family. Today, 71 percent in their early twenties say they plan to have two children, one—or none at all.**

—*Ms.* "Gazette," February, 1974

> **"**Isn't it ironic that the people who care for people's most valuable assets — their homes and their children—are treated so poorly in this country?**"**
>
> —Carolyn Reed, director, National Committee on Household Employment, *New York* Magazine, June 11, 1979

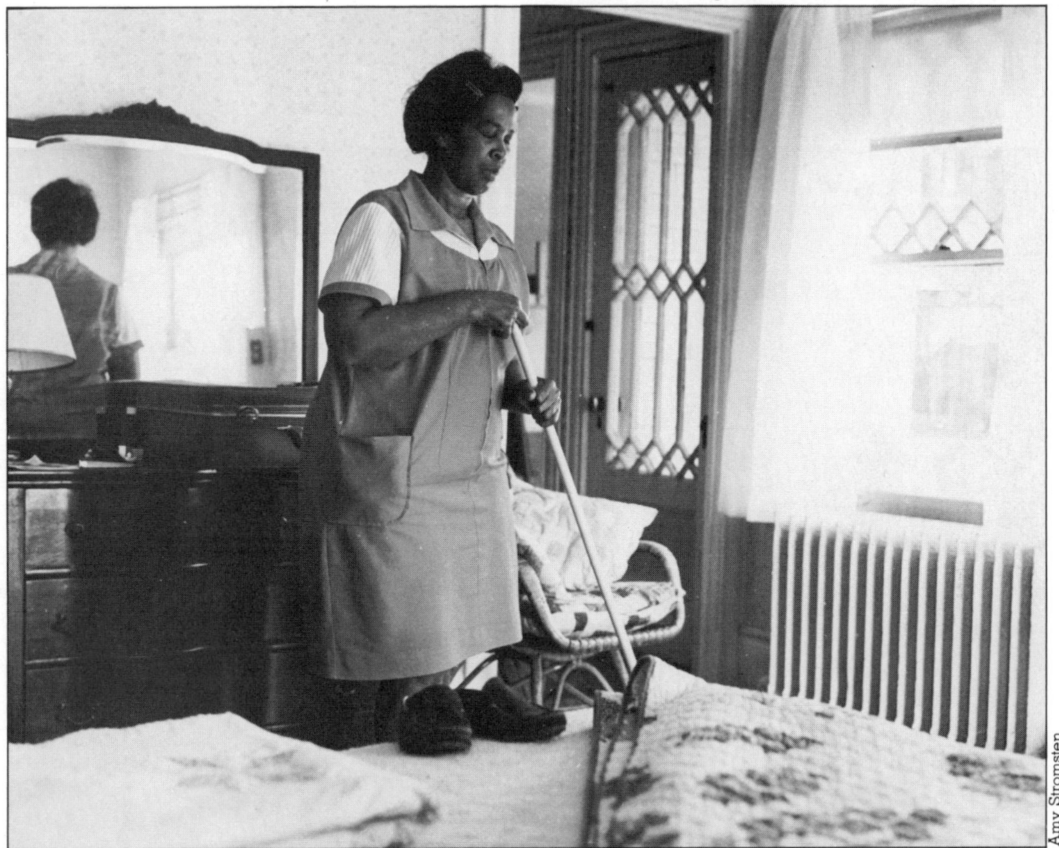

Amy Stromsten

A HOUSEHOLD EMPLOYMENT PLEDGE

I,__________, pledge to maintain and promote the Code of Standards of the National Committee on Household Employment as stated below. As an employer, I will not exploit any household worker employed by me. As an employee, I will pressure my employers and other household workers to establish these standards as a minimum code.

I. Wages

The hourly wage should be no lower than the minimum of $1.60 as stipulated in the federal Fair Labor Standards Act. Where the cost of living is higher than average, wages should be raised accordingly.

Higher wages should be paid for jobs requiring previously acquired training or skills.

Days upon which wages are to be paid should be agreed upon in advance.

Gifts of clothing and/or food should not be considered a part of the payment.

II. Hours

A. *Live-in workers.* Any hours in excess of 44 hours a week should be paid at 1½ times the regular hourly rate. Hours in excess of 52 hours a week should be paid at double the hourly rate.

B. *Live-out workers.* Day workers should receive overtime for hours in excess of eight hours a day.

Day workers employed on a full-time weekly basis by a single employer should be paid 1½ times the hourly rate for hours worked in excess of 40 hours a week.

III. Working relationships

Time schedules should be agreed upon in advance of employment.

If an employer does not require the services of a day worker for the agreed upon time, the employee must be notified at least a week in advance or else be compensated in full by the employer.

The employee has the responsibility of notifying the employer as soon as possible if she or he is unable to report to work.

A written agreement between employer and employee should clearly define the duties of the position, including specific tasks and frequency.

Rest periods, mealtimes, telephone privileges, and time out for private activities (such as church or recreation times for live-in employees) should be agreed upon in advance of employment.

The cleaning appliances provided by the employer should be efficient and safe. They should be used carefully by the employee.

Adequate provisions for maximum safety and health should be maintained at all times.

Work and work relationships should be periodically discussed with the intent of improving efficiency and understanding. Constructive and helpful evaluations of work should be encouraged.

Pleasant and private quarters should be provided for live-in employees.

A professional working relationship should be maintained by both parties. This includes equal and agreed upon forms of address for both employee and employer and their respective families

IV. Benefits

A. *Social Security.* Earnings should be reported and payments made in accordance with the law for Social Security credit toward old age, survivors', and disability insurance. Records of payment should be furnished annually to the employee in compliance with Social Security legislation.

B. *Sick leave.* Employees working one day a week in one home should receive a minimum of one day paid sick leave a year.

Full-time employees should receive a minimum of six days paid sick leave annually.

C. *Vacations.* Full-time day or live-in workers should receive two weeks' paid vacations after one year of service.

Employees working one day a week in one home should receive one day paid vacation for each six-month period worked.

For longer service, there should be an agreed upon increase in paid vacation time.

D. *Holidays.* Live-in workers should receive at least eight paid legal holidays a year.

Full-time live-out employees should receive six legal holidays with pay a year.

A day worker working one day a week in one home should receive one paid legal holiday a year, providing the holiday falls on one of the normal working days.

—National Committee on Household Employment, 1973

WAT

UPI

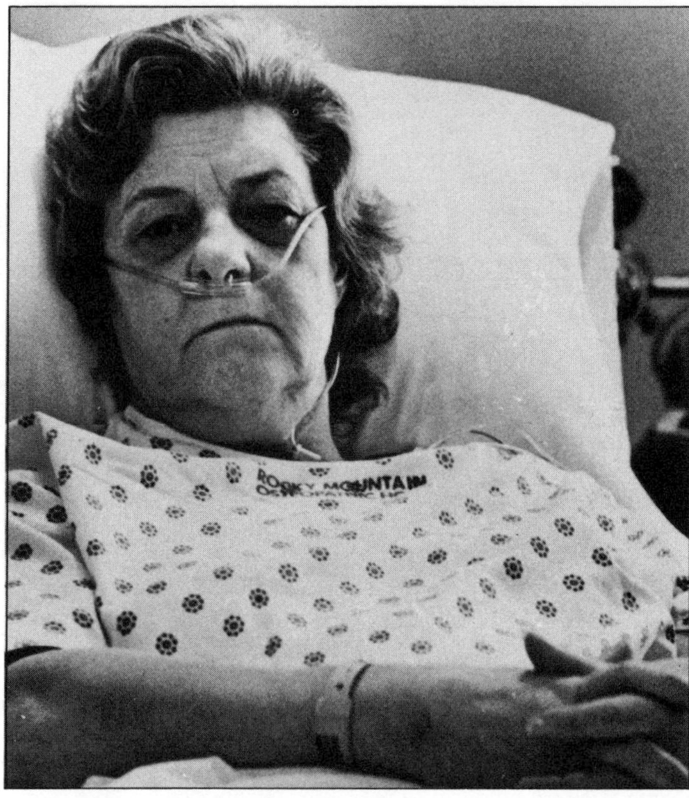

Wide World

Wide World

UPI

ERGATE

ON THE WATERGATE WOMEN

BY ROBIN MORGAN

Maureen Dean, wearing persimmon summer silk,
sits smiling, silent, in the Senate Hearing Room.

Her eyelids droop. She must not doze.
She bolts upright.
But if she cannot doze, she finds she thinks.
She is the second wife.
The first says that he never lied.
The musings of the second are inadmissible.

Martha Mitchell, Cassandra by extension,
nurses the bruises from her beatings,
nurses her mind from the forced commitments,
waits at home, alone, with the terror that all her truths
will be seen as comic relief.

Dita Beard
has disappeared,
clutching the heart she was permitted to keep
alive, in payment for her scandal's death.

Rose Mary would
if she could, but she can't;
lips sealed by loyalty (for which, read: fear),
a faintly ridiculous scapegoat
as any Good Friday girl could have predicted.

The Committee wives watch their husbands on TV,
alone, preferably, so they can smile to themselves
at the righteous purity of such judges.

All the secretaries hunch at their IBMs,
snickering at the keys.
What they know could bring down the government.

The maids, the governesses, the manicurists,
the masseuses avert their eyes.
What they know could bring down the family.

The mistresses wait for their phones to ring.
Afraid to miss the call, they hurry
through their vomiting.

None of these witnesses would be believed.
Some do not believe themselves.

And Dorothy, Mrs. Howard Hunt, tucked into her coffin,
could hardly testify
to the cash, nestled in her lap like a rapist,
to the plane's dive through a blue spring sky,
the taste of arsenic on her teeth,
the enormous dazzling wisdom that struck all her braincells
at the impact.
Her silence should bring down the nation.

But all the while, one woman, sitting alone
in rooms and corridors thick with deceit,
familiar, by now, with an unimaginable weariness,
having smiled and waved and hostessed her only life
into a numbness that cannot now recall
even the love
that was once supposed to make all this worthwhile—

having slept out summer in a wintry bed,
having borne children who were neither of them sons,
having, for years, stood at attention
so close to power, so powerless—

not, oh not
Thelma Catherine Patricia Ryan Nixon

blamed by the Right for her careful stupidity
blamed by the Middle for her cultivated dullness
blamed by the Left for her nonexistent influence
blamed by most men for being unbeautiful
blamed by some women for being broken
blamed by her daughters for their father
blamed by her husband for her memory of him
as a young Quaker—

not, oh not
Thelma Catherine Patricia Ryan Nixon

who, as a young girl, loved Scarlatti,
who wanted to become an actress playing Ibsen,
who lost her own name somewhere along the way,

who now sits alone in some oversized chair,
watching with detached interest
how her sedated visions do their best
to picket before so many defilements.

This is no melodrama.
Here is no histrionic pain.

Opposite page, clockwise from upper right—**In March, 1972 ITT's Dita Beard testifies from Denver hospital bed. Outspoken Martha Mitchell takes a joke. Rose Mary Woods shows how she might have erased 18 minutes of tape between Nixon and Haldeman when she pushed the record button by mistake as she turned to answer the phone. Maureen Dean at Senate hearings.** This page—**Pat Nixon bids farewell, August 9, 1974.**

Wide World

Call it a clan, call it a network, call it a tribe, call it a family. Whatever you call it, whoever you are, you need one. You need one because you are human. You didn't come from nowhere. Before you, around you, and presumably after you, too, there are others. . . . Even if you live alone, even if your solitude is elected and ebullient, you still cannot do without a clan or a tribe. —Jane Howard, *Families* (Simon & Schuster), 1978

FAMILIES

What we think of as the "traditional" nuclear family is actually a recent development, in its current form less than a hundred years old. Anthropology and history reveal a vast repertory of family forms that disappear, reappear, coexist, and differ within and across cultures, including: blood relationships, kinship systems, language alliances, loyalty groups, households, tribes, networks, clans, communes, the "stem" family, the "conjugal" family, the "extended" family, and still others.

—"Who is the American Family?" *Ms.*, August, 1978

Helen Nestor

Marcia, Ricardo, and Jennifer: a conventional nuclear family.

☐ 15.9 percent of all households include a father as the sole wage earner, a mother as a full-time homemaker, and at least one child.
☐ 18.5 percent include both the father and the mother as wage earners, plus one or more children at home.
☐ 30.5 percent of households consist of married couples with no children, or with no children living at home.
☐ 6.2 percent are headed by women who are single parents, with one or more children at home.
☐ 0.6 percent are headed by single-parent males, with one or more children at home.
☐ 2.5 percent consist of unrelated persons living together.
☐ 20.6 percent are single-person households. (Of these, almost a third are women over 65, more than a third of whom live below the federal poverty level.)
☐ The remaining 5.3 percent consist of female- or male-headed households that include relatives other than spouses or children.

—*U.S. Statistical Abstract, 1977*

Catherine Ursillo

Opposite page top—**Single man and his adopted daughter.** Bottom—**Joanne chose to be a single parent.**

"I don't like living alone in an apartment. You have no one to talk over the events of the day . . . No human contact."

—Florence Luscomb, 91, (above), member of The Cambridge Cooperative

Nancy Crampton

Jane Howard, who is single, with her extended family of niece and nephews.

. . . I had been told that nobody, *nobody* except my parents, my grandparents, and I, knew that I was adopted. I do not recall whether I was ever admonished *not* to tell anyone, but wise child that I was, I knew a Dirty Secret when I heard one, and I knew that D.S.'s don't get talked about either *in* the family, or out of it. So I was perfectly aware that I was breaking a tacit family rule by beginning to ask questions: "How old were my parents when they died?" "What did they die of?" "Why didn't anyone else in their families take me in?"

—Babette Dalsheimer, "Adoption Runs in My Family," *Ms.*, August, 1973

photos by Helen Nestor

"The agency assumed that something must be wrong with me. I was asked why I didn't just marry and have my own children. I was asked about homosexuality. And, of course, no one would believe that a single man is capable of cooking and cleaning and caring for a child." . . .

In November of 1965, the Los Angeles County Department of Adoptions placed the first child in this country in a single-parent home, after the California State Department of Social Welfare had passed a regulation stating that "single-parent applications may be accepted only when a two-family home has not been found because of the child's special needs." At the time, "special need" children were defined as "Negro and Mexican children, and those of all races and nationalities with severe medical problems." Today that definition includes racially mixed children, those with physical handicaps, and all children over five years of age.

—Gini Kopecky,
"Singles Who Adopt,"
Ms., June, 1977

Helen Nestor

Lesbian couple with son.

“I know of no evidence that homosexual partners are more apt to raise homosexual children. Most homosexuals are the children of conventionally heterosexual parents.”

—Dr. Benjamin Spock, *New Times*, July 23, 1976

Until recently American society has regarded the phrase *lesbian mother* as a contradiction in terms. Because lesbian relationships are between two women and are therefore nonprocreative, it was automatically assumed that there was no such thing as a lesbian mother.

Researchers who have done studies on female homosexuality have directed their attention primarily to sexual behavior. While they have noted that most lesbians have had some heterosexual experience before engaging in lesbian relationships, they have failed to recognize that a significant number of these women do have children. . . .

Lesbian women have in the past been deprived of their children or forced to live a deception. Only now, with a new consciousness and new honesty, are lesbian mothers beginning to emerge as individuals—strong in their concepts of motherhood and determined to fight for their children.

—Del Martin and Phyllis Lyon
"Lesbian Mothers,"
Ms., October, 1973

A great many of our contemporary problems have surfaced first, or in slightly different but acute form, in women's lives because they affect the family drastically. All too often they have been seen exclusively as family problems, personal dilemmas. The isolation of women from one another, each tucked away in her nuclear family, leaves a woman to grope with difficulties that may well have been thrust on her by society in the belief that she can solve them by herself. One real reward that the Women's Movement has brought us all is the increasing realization that a lot of family upsets are not unique, but instead the result of social dislocation. Understanding the nature of these upsets makes them easier to cope with because it not only brings in the social context, it gets rid of personal guilt.

—Elizabeth Janeway, *Man's World, Woman's Place: A Study in Social Mythology* (William Morrow), 1971

photos by Evelyn Hofer

A unique joint custody arrangement: the children stay put while their divorced parents divide the week living with them. Evelyn Hofer photographs family when mother moves out and father takes over for his Friday through Monday residency.

SPORTS

Despite the fact that the average man is larger, heavier, and stronger than the average woman, it is now clear that those differences are far less than it formerly appeared. Evidence shows that the difference in strength between trained male and female athletes is far less than that between average or untrained men and women. And it is equally clear that the differences of strength within either sex are far greater than the differences between them. . . .

—Ann Crittenden Scott,
"Closing the Muscle Gap,"
Ms., September, 1974

Abigail Heyman/Magnum

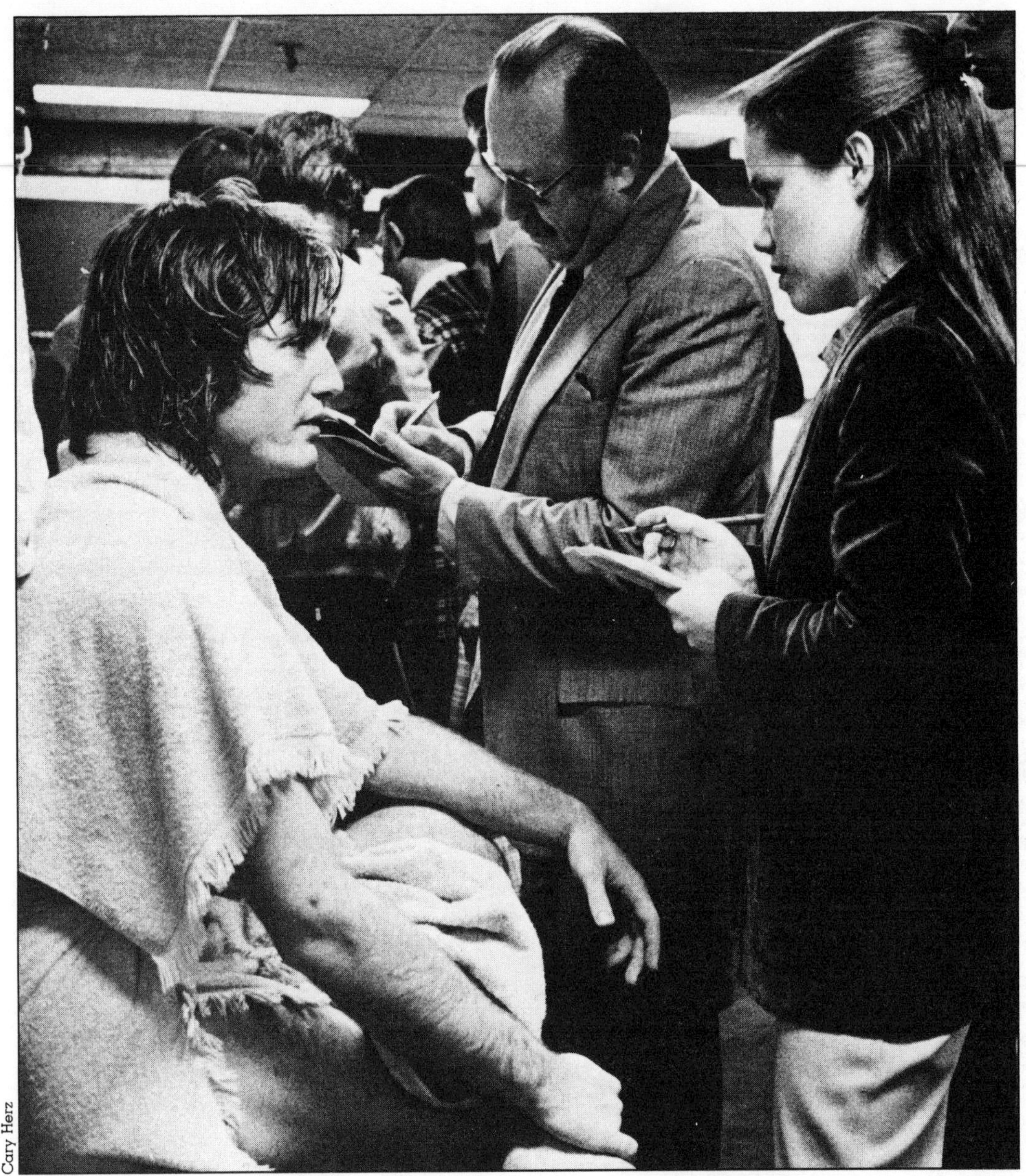

Cary Herz

The issue of female sportswriters confronting naked male athletes is an emotional one, but according to reporter Lawrie Mifflin, the locker room is "so grubby and smelly that it's totally unsexual."

In April, 1978 Judge Constance Baker Motley, in Federal District Court in New York, enjoined the Yankees from further exclusion of women from the Stadium clubhouses unless men were also excluded . . .

Bettye Lane

> "It is my understanding that Little League baseball is a monumentally successful operation . . . as American as the hotdog and apple pie. There is no reason why that part of Americana should be withheld from little girls. The sooner little boys begin to realize that little girls are equal and that there will be many opportunities for a boy to be bested by a girl, the closer they will be to better mental health."
>
> —Sylvia Pressler, hearing officer, ruling on the integration of Little League baseball, Hoboken, New Jersey, November 7, 1973

Ann Chwatsky

The Atoms track club of Brooklyn, New York, operates on the philosophy that young women can be independent and learn to compete on a man's level. "We were ahead of our time," says Fred Thompson (*coaching*), who founded the program in 1959. "The seventies are catching up to us."

Research on women who achieve and are successful in a wide range of endeavor demonstrates that most of them were tomboys. They were more independent, risk taking, adventurous, strong, achievement-oriented than their passive, conforming, dependent sisters. We're beginning to find out that muscle development and coordination go hand-in-hand with learning.

—Kathryn F. Clarenbach, addressing the Midwest Association for Physical Education of College Women, October, 1970

Our runners don't lift any weights because they're afraid of getting muscles. They knew their times weren't as good coming into ['76] Olympics, but now they know why.

—Wyomia Tyus, 1964, 1968 Olympic gold medalist in the sprint

Wide World

Evelyn Ashford beats East Germany's Marlies Gohr in the 100-meter run at the 1979 World Cup of Athletics meet.

Wide World

Left to right—**An official attempts to eject Kathy Switzer from the all-male Boston Marathon (1967) but is instead thrown to the sidelines by runner Thomas Miller. (In 1979, Joan Benoit completes the Marathon in record time of 2 hours, 35 minutes, 15 seconds.)**

Billie Jean King consoles Bobby Riggs after defeating him in straight sets to win the 1973 version of "the battle of the sexes."

UPI

Yeah, I watched *that* tennis match. Like a whole lot of people, I was anxious as hell—looking forward to it. Every time Bobby Riggs opened his mouth, I got madder. Sure, I know, most of his sounding was strictly promotion. But he was coming on too strong and uncool. So, after all this nonsense, when it comes time for the match, I'm on the edge of my seat . . . digging Billie Jean's cool and ready for her to cream this cat. Now I got to admit that, deep down, there's that little doubt—can she really do it? After the first set—man, no more doubt. I'm yelling at the television. Real kicks! Billie Jean wins the second set, and I'm wild—shouting for a love set to really finish Mr. Riggs.

—*Mel W.*

—Letter to the editors, *Ms.*, December, 1973

ABC Sports

Left—**Billie Jean King wins a record 20th title at Wimbledon by taking the 1979 doubles.** Below—**Sixteen-year-old Tracy Austin, 1979 (and youngest ever) U.S. Women's Open tennis champion.**

Wide World

Billie Jean didn't scream until May of 1970, when she arrived at Il Foro Italico for the Italian Open. First prize for the women's singles was $600 compared to $7,500 for the men. "That's when I began thinking *boycott*. So did Rosie Casals, Esme Emanuel, Ceci Martinez, and some others.

"There was no alternative. By the time we got to Forest Hills four months later, we were boiling. Everywhere the ratio was insulting; worst of all in the U.S. at the Pacific Southwest Open in Los Angeles where it was ten to one. We decided we wouldn't play the Southwest. Gladys Heldman provided the alternative through Virginia Slims, with a tournament in Houston where the money was about five times as good. That was the start."

—Bud Collins, "Billie Jean King Evens the Score," *Ms.*, July, 1973

Lisa Ebright

"I see no reason why a woman can't throw as effectively as a man. There are a lot of statements about anatomical differences, but there is not much documented evidence. Maybe we're really talking about poorly skilled people. People with poor athletic skills tend to throw poorly."

—Linda Zwiren,
director of Human Performance Laboratory, Hofstra University,
Ms., April, 1976

Cary Herz

Cary Herz

Above—**Jane Frederick, the U.S.A.'s number one pentathlete.** Upper right—**Women's rugby is five years old in 1979 with 150 teams at play nationwide.** Bottom right—**Ace softball pitcher Joan Joyce.**

Cary Herz

I am in the ninth grade and on the girls' varsity basketball team at our school. I'm captain of the team and lead it in scoring, steals, and assists. I love basketball.

During our whole season this year we had only five games: we had to furnish rides to the games ourselves; we had to play in our gymsuits because we had no uniforms in which to play; we were able to use the gym only when the boys were through with it; and we had a grand total of about 30 spectators at all our games combined. Our principal did not announce any of our games, and did not provide a late bus so that kids could stay and watch. One time I asked if it would be possible to get uniforms for our team. I was told to earn the money through car washes, dances, and bake sales. Yet each of the boys received brand-new $30 uniforms this year.

Everyone seems to think that girls playing basketball is a big joke, but I am dead serious. If we are good enough to be called varsity, aren't we good enough to be respected? —*Jane L.*

—Letter to the editors, *Ms.*, June, 1973

Without Title IX our basketball team would be ten steps behind where we are today. [Her team is Old Dominion University, the 1979 intercollegiate champions, and she is perhaps the best female player in the country.] I couldn't have come to Old Dominion without a full scholarship, which is now equivalent to what the men get, and if we didn't have the money from Title IX to travel and play the best teams just as our men do, we wouldn't have won the championship [O.D.'s first].

—Nancy Lieberman, (above), *Ms.*, September, 1979

Cary Herz

UPI

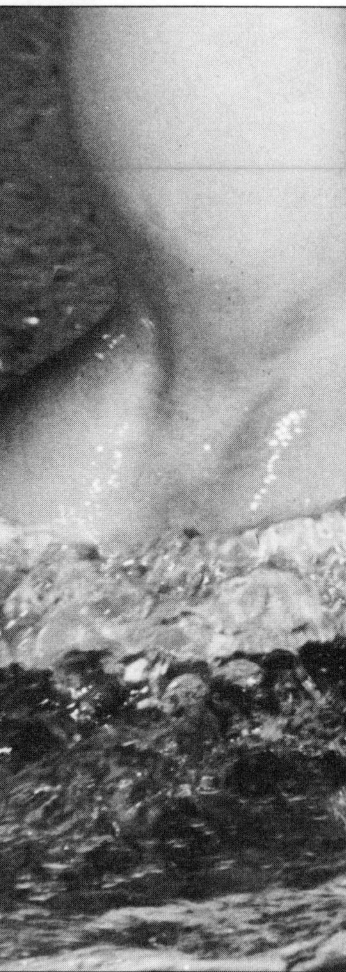

Ken Regan/Camera 5

Left—**Marion Tyger Trimiar applies for a New York State boxing license in 1974, is granted one in 1978.** Right—**Nadia Comaneci scores a perfect 10 and the gold medal for women's gymnastics at the 1976 Montreal Olympics.**

The real issue is the strength of the human will and the ability to focus that will under the most unimaginable of circumstances. . . . It isn't that every painful experience offers ultimate awareness of life's intrinsic values. It's that the most extreme conditions require the most extreme response, and for some individuals, the call to that response is vitality itself. . . . The integrity and self-esteem gained from winning the battle against extremity are the richest treasures in my life. —Diana Nyad, *Other Shores* (Random House), 1978

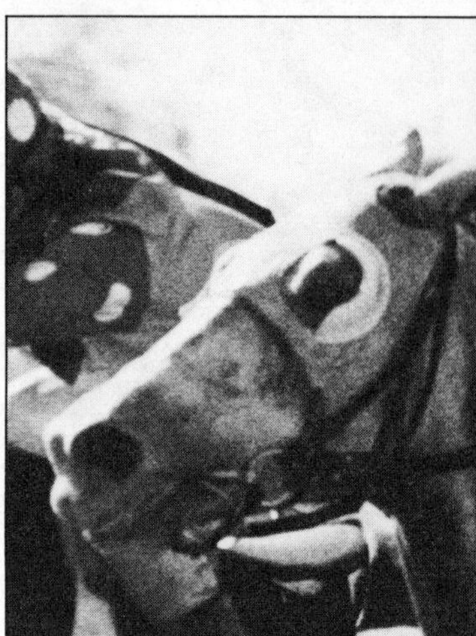

Bettye Lane

UPI

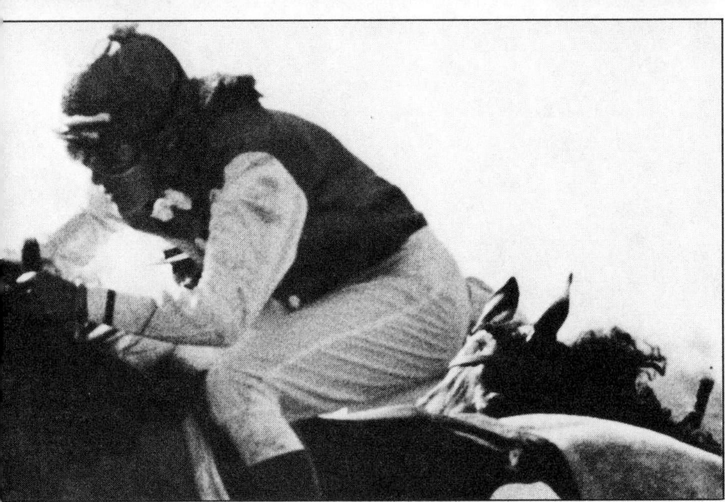

UPI

Clockwise from upper right—**Janet Guthrie, first woman to qualify for and race in the Indianapolis 500, takes 8th place in 1977. Beverly Johnson is the first woman to climb (1978) the face of Yosemite's 3,000-foot El Capitan. In 1973, Robyn Smith finishes in the money on half her mounts even though she usually rides long shots. Diana Nyad is in the water 27 hours and 38 minutes to become the first person to swim from the Bahamas to Florida (1979).**

CAMPUS

"You are the women who will take your place in the world where *you* can decide who shall flourish and who shall wither; you will make distinctions between the deserving poor and the undeserving poor; where you can yourself determine which life is expendable and which is indispensable. Since you will have the power to do it, you may also be persuaded that you have the right to do it. As educated women the distinction between the two is first order business. . . . Women's rights is not only an abstraction, a cause; it is also a personal affair. It is not only about 'us'; it is also about me and you. Just the two of us."

—Toni Morrison, commencement address, Barnard College, May, 1979

When women's studies began a decade ago, many of us hoped and expected that it would "wither away" as the curriculum became truly coeducational. What has been accomplished in 10 years is important, but the agenda for the rest of the century is still full if we are to develop institutions not only free of sex-bias, but fully committed to the equal education of women. For such tasks, the base and "networks" provided by women's studies seem more useful than ever.

—Florence Howe,
Ms. "Gazette,"
September, 1979

Between 1970 and 1977, the number of women students aged 22 to 34 increased by 133 percent to about 2 million. Those women students who are 35 and older constitute the second-fastest-growing group of returnees, having increased 94 percent from 1972 to 1977. By 1978, both groups together constituted 25 percent of all post-high school students and, according to Census Bureau estimates, by 1985, 40 percent of all college students will be over 25.

—Elizabeth Stone,
"The New Kid in Class is Your Mother,"
Ms., September, 1979

When I ask my female college students about their futures, the typical response is an *ambitious life program*: "Sure I want to get married and have kids," comes the reply, "but after I've gone to school, got a career going, traveled around . . . I'm not going to miss out on anything! I'll start my family when I'm thirty-five or so. . . ."

—Anita L. Micossi,
"Having It All: Will We?"
Ms., March. 1978

Constantine Manos/Magnum

Bob Kalmbach

Richard Carpenter

Top—**The University of Michigan Marching Band is integrated in 1972.** Above—**For the first time in history, the presidents of all the Seven Sister Colleges are women. (*Front row, left to right*) Mary Patterson McPherson, Bryn Mawr; Barbara Newell, Wellesley; (*center row*) Jill Conway, Smith; Matina Horner, Radcliffe; (*back row*) Elizabeth Kennan, Mount Holyoke; Virginia Smith, Vassar; Jacquelyn Mattfield, Barnard.**

Women in [a] Tufts program encouraged the director to apply for funding so that they could help other women returning to school by writing down their experience and recommendations. The administration went ahead and wrote a proposal calling for a paid "professional" researcher to assist each of the women. But the students, who were for the most part black, had gone to college explicitly so they wouldn't have to play second fiddle to "experts" any more.

They felt that institutions in general branded them unfairly as being somehow afflicted simply because they did not fit comfortably into programs designed for young, single, middle-class people.

Their advantages, they felt, came largely from intense experiences in coping with the real world. Many of them had borne heavy responsibility for the lives of others; for younger brothers and sisters, and crippled or aging relatives. Parenthood had brought even more responsibility. Their vast work experience, much of it concerned with community issues such as housing and health care, gave them a unique knowledge of urban problems, and skills in organizing and public speaking as well.

Convinced of what they had to offer, they demanded some major reforms in the philosophy of college education; they urged their own schools and others to grant credit for work and life experience, to devise examinations to arrive at such credit, and to cut out nonessential course requirements.

In so doing, the women placed themselves in the forefront of educational innovation—and helped their own college to do the same.

Jan Riddell and Sam Bingham, "Continuing Education: The Older, Wiser, Student," *Ms.*, September, 1973

"Math anxiety is an 'I can't' syndrome, and whenever it strikes . . . it creates the same symptoms and response. 'I can't do this. No amount of practice or trying will make it work for me. I never really understood math. I always memorized and got away with it. Now I've hit the level I always knew was there. I can't do it.' "

—Sheila Tobias, author of *Overcoming Math Anxiety* (W.W. Norton), 1978

WEAL and other civil rights groups won a significant victory with the settlement of three suits charging the government with failure to enforce laws barring sex and race discrimination in education.

Under the terms of the agreement, which has the effect of a court order, the government is required to make a major nationwide effort to end all forms of discrimination at all levels of education which receive federal tax dollars. HEW is commited to hire 898 additional OCR employees, to eliminate a backlog of 3,000 unresolved complaints of discrimination by September 30, 1979, and to begin broad civil rights compliance reviews of schools and universities. WEAL President Eileen Thornton hailed the court order as "a meaningful breakthrough." She said, "As a result of negligence and mismanagement, HEW has allowed a huge number of cases to pile up and then used the resulting logjam as an excuse for government inaction."

—WEAL Washington Report, February, 1978

"As an historian of feminism, I am convinced that the major reason why recurring waves of feminist concern have borne such modest fruit in modern society has been the lack of institutions which could foster the study of central questions relating to the position of women in society beyond the life-time of a particular feminist generation. . . . Smith College could serve an important function if it could become the home of such a research institute . . . ."

—Jill Conway, president of Smith College, *Ms.*, May, 1979

(Half of the 300 women's colleges that were open in 1970 have folded, or become coeducational or "coordinate" with other institutions.)

If times are tough for all academics, they're toughest for the one in four scholars who are women.

"I have a fantasy," says Janet [an assistant professor of anthropology]. "All the administrators have a big meeting about the woman problem. 'Let's allow a few women on campus,' they say. 'We'll put them on every committee so they're hopelessly overextended. Let's make them very aware of how tough the competition is so they feel vulnerable. Keep telling them they're lucky to be here. Then we'll appoint a director of women's studies. They can all bitch to her. We'll look as though we're really concerned with women—don't we put them on all the committees, don't we have a women's studies program? They'll wear themselves down, take the heat off us, and eventually we can fire them for not getting anything accomplished.'

"Of course I know there isn't any plot. These men aren't diabolical fiends. But when I came to this campus I was greeted like the Messiah. The women were spread so thin they were desperate. I've come to feel desperate, too. Everything to do with women is dumped on a few women, so the administration can forget about us. And it's destroying us."

—Mary Crawford, "Climbing the Ivy-Covered Walls," *Ms.*, November, 1978

If by some obvious fluke I had landed in a girls' school, well, then, I thought, unpacking my Scribner's first edition Hemingway and Hogarth Press books, I would lend Vassar my legitimacy.

—Michael Wolff, "The Making of a Vassar Man," *Ms.*, September, 1974

Bettye Lane

FACT SHEET

PUBLIC AFFAIRS OFFICE
UNITED STATES MILITARY ACADEMY
WEST POINT, NEW YORK 10996
Tel: (914) 938-2006

WOMEN AT WEST POINT

Second Year Report

ATTRITION

Class of 1980 - 119 women entered. At the end of Cadet Basic Training, the eight-week summer's training program, 102 remained, for an attrition rate of 14%. As of January 31st, 1979, 64 women remain for an attrition rate of 46%. The attrition rate for men at the end of the first summer was 9 % and, as of 31 January 1979, it was 38%.

Class of 1981 - 104 women entered with 94 remaining at the end of Cadet Basic Training, an attrition rate of 9%. The men's attrition rate for the same period was 6%. As of January 31, 1979, 74 women remain, for an overall attrition rate of 29%. The men's overall attrition rate is 26%.

Class of 1982 - 124 women entered and, of that number, 111 completed Cadet Basic Training, for an attrition rate of 10%. The male attrition rate for Cadet Basic Training was 11%, marking the first time the women's rate was below that of the men. As of 31 January 1979, 100 women remain; overall attrition rate is 19%, as opposed to 17% for the men.

With a total of 238 women in the Corps of Cadets (out of an aggregate total of 4131), integrated into all 36 companies, coeducation is coming of age at West Point. Vestiges of male resentment remain, but, on the whole, the women cadets have made a place for themselves at West Point and are daily bringing credit to themselves and their alma mater.

-30-

Bettye Lane

We therefore declare a state of emergency for the National Organization for Women in which we turn all our resources to the ratification effort and to extension of the ratification deadline for an additional seven years.

By taking this action, we emphatically state that the extension of the deadline is necessary. . . . We are not willing to accept the false hope of reintroduction . . . that erases 55 years of work.

Rather, we recognize that a vote against extension of the deadline is a vote *against* equality for women in this century.

We are determined to be victorious because we will not tolerate the possibility of living lives in which there is no realistic hope of sisters and brothers, wives and husbands, mothers and fathers, women and men, living together, working together as equals.

WE HAVE PASSED THE POINT OF NO RETURN!

—NOW declaration, February, 1978

ERA

". . . Twenty-four words have never been so misunderstood since the four words 'One size fits all.' "

—Erma Bombeck, humorist, *Ms.*, June, 1978

Wide World

Congresswomen Martha Griffiths (*left*) and Bella Abzug await House vote on Equal Rights Amendment, 1971. (Griffiths sponsored the amendment.)

Bettye Lane

"Opponents say women will become like men. I think women will have to work overtime to catch up with men at evildoing."

—Father Theodore Hesburgh, *Ms.*, January, 1976

"Father, forgive them, they know not what they do. . . . American womanhood [will be] crucified on a cross of dubious equality and specious uniformity."

—Senator Sam Ervin (D.-N.C.), March 22, 1972, acknowledging defeat as the ERA is passed by the Senate, 84-8

Bettye Lane

Ann Chwatsky

Carol Kitman

Above left—**Activist Flo Kennedy gives support.** Above—**Actor Alan Alda (*left*) with *Redbook* editor-in-chief Sey Chassler. Alda lobbies State legislators for passage; Chassler organizes publication of ERA articles in July, 1976 issues of 35 magazines.**

Right—**Abzug, Marlo Thomas, Carol Burnett, who donates $25,000, mobilize Hollywood.**

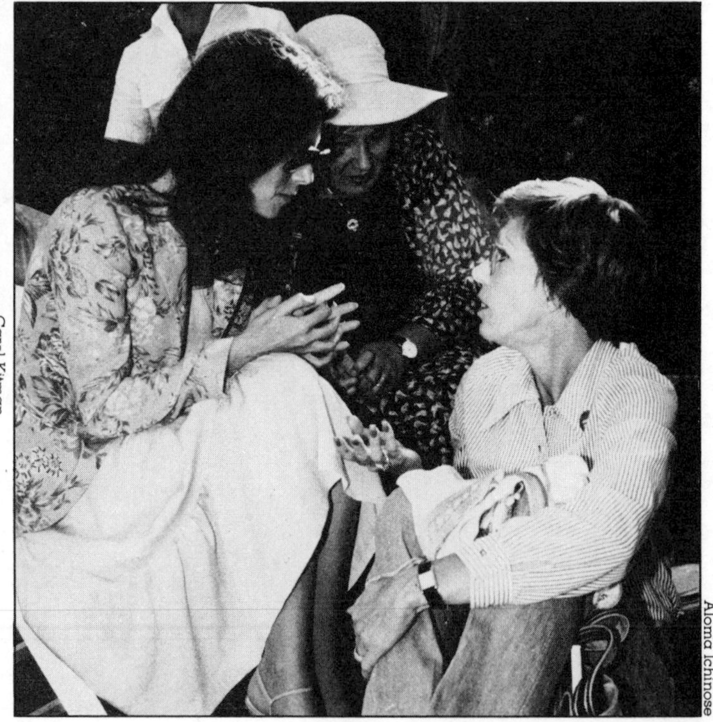

Aloma Ichinose

"A handful of willful and mischievous men—two in Florida, two in North Carolina, five in South Carolina, seldom more than a dozen anywhere, are blocking passage of ERA—using fun and games to maneuver it, deciding to stall justice toward women as the expendable issue which can be used to barter for political mischief."

—Liz Carpenter,
ERAmerica co-chair,
in testimony before the
House Subcommittee on
Civil and Constitutional
Rights, May 17, 1978

If in 1970 women who worked had earned the same amount per hour as men who worked, it would have cost employers an additional $96 billion in payroll alone. . . . If women had earned the same as men and worked the same number of hours, the addition to the payroll would have been $303 billion . . . the significance of the figures, I think, is plain enough. The Equal Rights Amendment and the traditional role of women in the capitalist economy are incompatible.

—Elinor Langer,
"Why Big Business
Is Trying To Defeat the ERA,"
Ms., May, 1976

Joan Roth

"The claim that American women are downtrodden and unfairly treated is the fraud of the century. The truth is that American women have never had it so good. Why should we lower ourselves to 'equal rights' when we already have the status of special privilege?" —Phyllis Schlafly, quoted in "The Sweetheart of The Silent Majority," *Ms.*, March, 1974

"When I began to work for ERA, I was appalled at the laws regarding the married woman. The law essentially regards the married woman as the property of her husband. Well, ERA is not going to send policemen into everybody's house to make sure that everything is being done equally. It is just a legal situation that will recognize that the wife, under law, will be a partner in the family enterprise."

—Ann Follis, president of Homemakers Equal Rights Association,
"Woman Alive!" April, 1977

Housewives for ERA

"I'd be damned if I'd pay some son-of-a-bitching man alimony. What's important to the average woman is home, husband, and church, but the Women's Movement has disrespect for family relationships. You never hear them talk about the construction of a family, and what's really important to women: being a mother. After the vote, I heard some women at a meeting I went to talking about what kind of a stupid ass would vote against her own rights, but I noticed that all of them were divorced or not married. They're not living like I'm living and they're not doing what I'm doing!"

—Ann Giordano, a 43-year-old community worker quoted in "What The Hell Happened in New York? The 400,000 Vote Misunderstanding," Lindsy Van Gelder, *Ms.*, March, 1976

Bettye Lane

The New York State ERA is defeated, November, 1975.

Chie Nishio

Nearly 100,000 marchers—wearing white and carrying purple and gold banners to comemmorate the colors of the suffragists—descend on Washington, D.C., July 9, 1978, to support Extension. (*Left to right*) Midge Costanza, Bella Abzug, Katie Pottinger, Gloria Steinem, Dick Gregory, Betty Friedan, Liz Holtzman, Barbara Mikulski. Opposite page—**Ellie Smeal is jublilant over October 6, 1978 vote by Congress to extend ratification.**

"This national boycott campaign urges organizations and groups that support the ERA not to hold their conventions and meetings in unratified states. This campaign has special significance because it is an example of a civil rights movement of the 1970s successfully employing a traditional political tactic dating back to the Boston Tea Party and used in major human rights campaigns throughout American history."

—Eleanor Smeal,
president of NOW,
March, 1978

Christine Jones

The separation of sex from emotion is at the very foundations of Western culture and civilization. If early sexual repression is the basic mechanism by which character structures supporting political, ideological, and economic serfdom are produced, an end to the incest taboo, through abolition of the family, could have profound effects. Sexuality would be released from its straitjacket to eroticize our whole culture, changing its very definition.

—Shulamith Firestone, *The Dialectic of Sex* (Morrow), 1970

SEXUALITY

. . . In a recent survey of 52,000 *Psychology Today* readers, many respondents assumed that, in general, their friends' sex lives were better than their own. In particular, although some 22 percent of the men and 21 percent of the women were virgins, they estimated that only 1 or 2 percent of their friends were inexperienced.
. . . As sex researchers keep raising the ante on what the normal body can enjoy, these sexy times surround us with hints, often false, that every other body is doing more than we are. We know that once is not enough, but we don't know when more has become too much.

—Carol Tavris and T George Harris, "Keeping Up with the Joneses," *Ms.*, November, 1976

Whenever female orgasm and frigidity are discussed, a false distinction is made between the vaginal and the clitoral orgasm. Frigidity has generally been defined by men as the failure of women to have vaginal orgasms. Actually the vagina is not a highly sensitive area and is not constructed to achieve orgasm. It is the clitoris which is the center of sexual sensitivity and which is the female equivalent of the penis.

—Anne Koedt, "The Myth of the Vaginal Orgasm," *Notes From the Second Year*, 1970

But what precisely is the female orgasm (which may or may not be developed by a given culture) and where does it take place? A woman knows when she's had one (if she doubts it, she hasn't), but since her orgasm is not punctuated by the sure sign of ejaculation, men have felt free to develop lunatic theories about it, and women have not learned to trust their own bodies.

—Barbara Seaman, *Free and Female, The Sex Life of the Contemporary Woman* (Coward, McCann & Geoghegan), 1972

The hullabaloo over the female clitorally stimulated orgasm has further done nothing to liberate women, because male domination of all women has not changed. Men are heard gloating over the power trip of "I can make my girl go off like a machine gun"—this decade's version of scalps and bedpost notches.

—Laura X, "On Our Sexual 'Liberation,' " paper presented at Breaking the Shackles of Women conference, University of California, January 1970

We make love for hours and I cannot come. The next time we meet, I tell him, with shyness, pauses, and a voice barely audible, what might make it easier for me. Now he cannot stay hard.

"Christ, I don't believe it!" he says. "For years I've wanted a woman to do what you've done. I've asked them to tell me what they like, but they haven't and now I know why. I feel threatened, like I'm being asked to perform."

—Sara Davidson "What Am I Doing Here?" *Ms.*, October, 1975

Pat Field

Young people should have the right of a sense of ownership of their own bodies, and the right to whatever bodily pleasures we are endowed with. They need experiences that heighten their bodily awareness—swimming, sensuous experiences, dancing. They must know that sex is for pleasure as well as for procreation so that at appropriate times they can express what they want to say other than in words—but at all times responsibly.

. . . Sexual variety should not focus on technique because, after all, there are just so many ways one can have intercourse. Yet, I truly feel that there are as many ways of loving as there are people in the world and as there are days in the lives of those people.

—Dr. Mary Calderone,
Founder of sex information and Education Council of the United States (SIECUS),
Impact Magazine, October, 1978

Women have never been asked how they felt about sex. Researchers, looking for statistical "norms," have asked all the wrong questions for all the wrong reasons—and all too often wound up telling women how they should feel rather than asking them how they do feel. Female sexuality has been seen essentially as a response to male sexuality and intercourse. There has rarely been any acknowledgment that female sexuality might have a complex nature of its own which would be more than just the logical counterpart of (what we think of as) male sexuality.

—Shere Hite,
The Hite Report
(Macmillan), 1976

Bettye Lane

Melissa Shook

Wide World

Perhaps the most intriguing finding is not about homosexuals, but about heterosexuals. As Masters and Johnson tell it, heterosexuals are generally bumblers in their lovemaking: they hurry sex, misread signals, and communicate poorly. Men usually assume, wrongly, that lubrication of the vagina means that the woman is ready for intercourse. Many women have no idea how men like to be touched sexually, and most men massage the female genitals in a straightforward gung-ho style that women find harsh. And enjoyment of sex is clouded by the fear of not reaching orgasm.

—"Masters and Johnson on Homosexuality," *Time*, April 23, 1978

Masturbation has been a continuous part of my sex life since the age of five. It got me through childhood, puberty, romantic love, marriage, and it will, happily see me through old age.

—Betty Dodson, "Getting To Know Me," *Ms.*, August, 1974

A woman's life was made for fantasy. All those idle hours, the boring repetitive jobs. . . . We were born to stay at home. . . . Daydreams are often as close as [we] get to what [we] really want.

—Nancy Friday, *My Secret Garden . . . Women's Sexual Fantasies* (Trident), 1973

Flo Fox

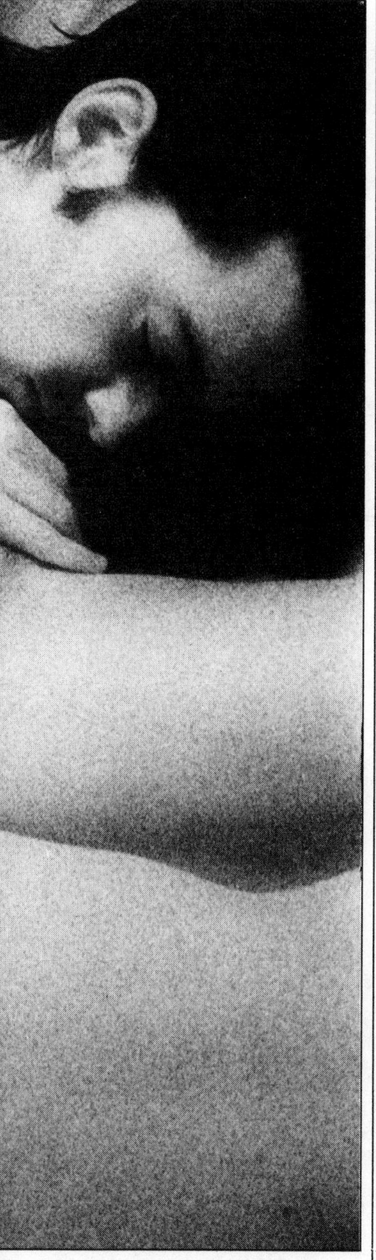

Neither history nor literature has left us any worthwhile evidence on the sexuality of old women. It is an even more strictly forbidden subject than the sexuality of old men.

—Simone de Beauvoir
The Coming of Age, 1972

By the time I met the woman with whom I had the most intense sexual experiences of my life, I had been having perfectly satisfying sex with men for 15 years. I had also already had an affair with a woman which, while important to me in many ways, was far less physically charged than any of my heterosexual relationships. If I'd never hooked up so passionately with the second woman, I might consider myself a confirmed heterosexual today. . . . My dreams and fantasies could remain bisexual; I could continue to be sometimes equally attracted to the male and female star at the movies; still, the world would define me not by my own sexuality but by my lover's gender. . . .

I have known, or know of, other male and female bisexuals who may have a distinct sexual preference but are committed to a specific person of the nonpreferred gender; who have no sexual preference but feel a social or political pull toward either the "gay" or "straight" world; who derive very different sexual and/or emotional satisfaction from men and women, and need both; who have a definite sexual preference but "make do" with the nonpreferred gender; who like sleeping with both sexes but only fall in love with one; who are fundamentally homosexual or heterosexual but enamored of the idea of bisexuality; whose sexual preference seems to go in cycles at different times of their lives; or whose only bisexual experience is within group sex.

—"Orlando," "Bisexuality: A Very Personal Confession,"
Ms., October, 1978

The zipless fuck is absolutely pure. It is free of ulterior motives. There is no power game. The man is not "taking" and the woman is not "giving." No one is attempting to cuckold a husband or humiliate a wife. No one is trying to prove anything or get anything out of anyone. The zipless fuck is the purest thing there is. And it is rarer than the unicorn. And I have never had one.

—Erica Jong,
Fear of Flying
(Signet), 1973

"I stayed celibate for about a year and a half. Oddly, it was a very sexual period for me. I became sensitive to my body, to its rhythms and contours and textures. It was the same sort of heightened awareness I used to experience during a fast, that (interim) denial of my hunger in service to myself. I even began to enjoy the low-level sexual tension; it had a vitality and excitement of its own."

—Ziva Kwitney,
Ms., October, 1975

I started a consciousness-raising group in my neighborhood. One night we talked of our feelings about women. Four women had spoken—words about mothers, sisters, friends, but no sexual feelings—and it was my turn. I drew my breath in sharply and then told of my feelings about E. I talked for too long, afraid to stop because I didn't know what response I would get. Finally, the woman next to me spoke: "I think it took guts to talk about that. I once felt attracted to my best friend, but I didn't feel I could bring that up here." Nothing more happened. I was relieved. But when the group disbanded after a year, I found myself saying at our final meeting that one of the ways in which the group had disappointed me was our failure to deal with really difficult or taboo feeling. "Like what?" someone challenged. "Lesbianism," I said. I thought of it merely as an example.

—Joan Larkin,
"Coming Out,"
Ms., March, 1976

Prostitutes are accused, even by feminists, of selling their bodies; but prostitutes don't sell their bodies, they rent their bodies. Housewives sell their bodies when they get married—they cannot take them back—and most courts do not regard the taking of a woman's body by her husband against her will as rape. And I am inclined to think that the right to get up and go home afterward might almost be worth sleeping with strangers for money, instead of going out to work in a laundry or whatever.

—Flo Kennedy,
Color Me Flo: My Hard Life and Good Times
(Prentice-Hall), 1976

Many [homosexuals] could very well serve as models of social comportment and psychological maturity. Most are indistinguishable from the heterosexual majority with respect to most of the nonsexual aspects of their lives, and whatever differences there are between homosexuals and heterosexuals' social adjustment certainly do not reflect any malevolent influence on society on the part of the homosexuals.

—Alan P. Bell and Martin S. Weinberg,
Homosexualities: A Study of Human Diversity
(Simon & Schuster), 1978

Opposite page—***(left to right)* Episcopal priests Allison Cheek, Carter Heyward, and Jeannette Piccard celebrate mass at Riverside Church, New York City, October, 1974.**

The biblical and popular image of God as a great patriarch in heaven, rewarding and punishing according to his mysterious and seemingly arbitrary will, has dominated the imagination of millions over thousands of years. The symbol of the Father God, spawned in the human imagination and sustained as plausible by patriarchy, has in turn rendered service to this type of society by making its mechanisms for the oppression of women appear right and fitting. If God in "his" heaven is a father ruling "his" people, then it is in the "nature" of things and according to divine plan and the order of the universe that society be male-dominated. Within this context a mystification of roles takes place: the husband dominating his wife represents God "himself." . . . The emerging creativity in women is by no means a merely cerebral process. In order to understand the implications of this process it is necessary to grasp the fundamental fact that women have had the power of *naming* stolen from us. We have not been free to use our own power to name ourselves, the world, or God.

—Mary Daly,
Beyond God the Father: Toward a Philosophy of Women's Liberation
(Beacon Press), 1973

RELIGION

Cary Herz

"And so I must remove myself from the leadership structure of the Episcopal Church as a protest against the inhumane treatment of women, especially the 11 women priests. To carry out the unjust laws of this church which do not affirm the right of females to be priests and bishops is to visit oppression upon women."

—Dr. Charles Willie, top-ranking lay person in the Episcopal Church, in his letter of resignation, August, 1974

The first woman to become a rabbi, Sally Priesand, conducts Sabbath service.

Betty Lou English/*Women At Their Work* (Dial)

In the past few years many Jewish women have come to question the ugly stereotypes foisted upon them by male Jewish literati and comedians; they have also rejected the strict sex-role division within the Jewish tradition. They are searching testimony and their own past for the heroines ignored within Jewish culture—and finding them. Admiring the strengths of their mothers and grandmothers, they seek new ways to express their own talents . . . and are beginning to demand positions of communal leadership, full equality within the synagogue, and full partnership in Jewish life.

—Paula Hyman, "Is It Kosher To Be Feminist?" *Ms.*, July, 1974

Dayenu

If Eve had been created in the image of God and not as a helper to Adam, **dayenu** (it would have sufficed).

If she had been created as Adam's equal and not been considered a temptress, **dayenu.**

If she were the first woman to eat from the tree of knowledge and had been recognized as bringing knowledge to us, **dayenu.**

If Lot's wife had been honored for compassion in looking back at the fate of her family in Sodom; and had not been punished for it, **dayenu.**

If our mothers had been honored for their daughters as well as for their sons, **dayenu.**

If our fathers had not pitted our mothers against each other, like Abraham with Sarah and Hagar, or Jacob with Leah and Rachel, **dayenu.**

If the Just Women in Egypt who caused our redemption had been given sufficient recognition, **dayenu.**

If Miriam were given her seat with Moses and Aaron in our legacy, **dayenu.**

If women had been among the writers of the Tanach and had interpreted our creation and our role in history, **dayenu.**

If women had written the Haggadah and placed our mothers where they belonged in history, **dayenu.**

If every generation of women together with every generation of men would continue to go out of Egypt, **dayenu, dayenu.**

—E.M. Broner and Naomi Nimrod, from "A Woman's Passover Haggadah," *Ms.*, April, 1976

When the last politician has murdered the last son and
The last child has starved for the last grains of
Rice and the last absolution has bloodied the
Last Holy Land and the last prayer leaves
The last bullet-punctured heart neatly
I'll turn my head on my pillow and
Salute *that power that exists*
In all of us in the form
Of Illusion Reverence
All Reverence to
Her Reverence
Reverence to
Her all
Rever-
ence
to
H
e
r

from "All Reverence to Her" by Barbara Chase-Riboud, *From Memphis and Peking* (Random House, 1974)

Mary Beth Edelson

Although statistical information on the witchcraft persecutions is very incomplete, the most reasonable estimate of the number executed on the whole of the Continent and the British Isles from 1484 until the end of the 17th century would seem to be 9 million. It may well have been more. The ratio of women to men executed has been variously estimated at 20 to 1 and 100 to 1. Witchcraft was a woman's crime. . . . The magic of the witches was an imposing catalog of medical skills concerning reproductive and psychological processes, a sophisticated knowledge of telepathy, auto- and hetero-suggestion, hypnotism, and mood-controlling drugs. Women knew the medicinal nature of herbs and developed formulas for using them. The women who were faithful to the pagan cults developed the science of organic medicine, using vegetation, before there was any notion of the profession of medicine.

—Andrea Dworkin,
Woman Hating
(E. P. Dutton), 1974

Graffiti on a Madrid street: "There is no liberation of women without revolution." Added below is the slogan: "nor revolution without the liberation of women."

National cultures vary greatly according to the degree of the suppression of the female culture. The veil and seclusion of women and their almost total segregation in Arab culture make for differences between them and, for example, Swedish women. A Swedish woman may not be able to tolerate the suppressed life of Arab women but she also, if she is sensitive, may not be able to tolerate her suppression as a female in Sweden. We cannot, like James Baldwin, even temporarily escape from our caste role to Paris or another country. It is everywhere; there is no place to escape.

—Barbara Burris, The Fourth World Manifesto, 1971
(First published in *Notes From the Third Year.*)

Kappa/Liaison

WORLD

Chadori in training,
April, 1979

Abbas/Liaison

> “We have faced the tanks of the Shah. Do you think we can be stopped by boys with knives?”
>
> —Iranian woman protester

Iranian women march through Teheran to protect women's rights against threats from religious extremist followers of Ayatollah Khomeini, March, 1979.

Duhamell/Sygma

Iranian women in chadors mourn the sudden death of Ayatollah Taleghani, more moderate than Ayatollah Khomeini. Teheran, September, 1979.

C. Spengler/Sygma

Right—**Betty Williams *(left)* and Mairead Corrigan, founders of the women's peace movement in Northern Ireland, accept the Nobel Peace Prize in 1977, but their movement declines at the end of the decade.**

Peter Marlow/Sygma

Below—**Indira Gandhi, first woman prime minister of India, 1966 to 1977, makes a bid to regain power at the end of the decade.**

Top Right—**Sirimavo Bandaranaike, first woman prime minister of Sri Lanka (until 1972 called Ceylon), 1970 to 1977. She hosts the 1976 conference of nonaligned countries.**

Bottom—**Simone Veil, formerly French Minister of Health, is elected in July, 1979, as first woman president of the European parliament.**

Dilip Mehta/Contact

United Nations

Gisèle Freund

"I'm not an activist, but I am greatly concerned with women's problems and the conditions of women's lives. My role is to try to do my job in the Ministry as well as I can and thereby demonstrate that women can fulfill such functions just as well as men can. . . . In the long run, I believe, people will come to say: 'After all, women can be trusted.'

—Simone Veil
French Minister of Health,
Ms., February, 1976

Samuel Iavelberg/Gamma

Gamma

Far Left—**Maria de Lourdes Pintassilgo, first woman prime minister of Portugal in 1979.**
Left—**Chiang Ch'ing, member of Politburo, People's Republic of China, leader during the Cultural Revolution, is denounced and arrested in October, 1976 as one of the "Gang of Four," a month after the death of her husband Mao Tse-tung.**

Israeli Consulate

Fallaci: Okay. At last we've reached Golda Meir as a personality. Shall we therefore talk of the woman Ben Gurion termed "the best man in my cabinet"?

Meir: That's just a legend that has arisen around me. It's also a legend I've always found irritating, although men repeat it as a great compliment. You think it is? I don't.

—Oriana Fallaci interview with Golda Meir, *L'Europeo*, 1973

Above—**Golda Meir, first woman prime minister of Israel, 1969 to 1974, at the Wailing Wall, after the Six Day War. She died at the age of 80 in December, 1978.**

Wide World

Left—**Margaret Thatcher, addressing supporters on May 4, 1979, upon winning the election that made her Britian's first woman Prime Minister.**

I am *not* suggesting that, were we British subjects, we should vote for Thatcher—but I don't think we should narrow our idea of the participation of women in politics to the notion that women are going to create new or ideal types of candidates. We're going to have candidates of every political coloring. The more the better, I think, especially since the first ones who actually get a modicum of power are likely to oppose, or deny, connections with feminism.

—Susan Sontag addressing National Women's Political Caucus meeting, June, 1978.

Nadine Markova

Nadine Markova

Bettye Lane

Nadine Markova

The opening ceremony in Mexico City, June 19, 1975. The official UN World Conference for International Women's Year approved a World Plan of Action, the Declaration of Mexico on the Equality of Women and their Contribution to Development and Peace, and 34 resolutions. Feminists, many of whom were meeting at nongovernmental Tribune sessions, were often critical of the official government appointed delegates for debating regular UN issues with too little regard for the needs of women.

Top—**Pen Tsung, a revolutionary committee vice chair of a prefecture in the Tibetan Autonomous Region, an alternate on the People's Republic of China delegation.**
Center—**Shirley Field-Ridley, Guyanan Minister of Information and Culture.**
Above—**Laura Allende, sister of Chile's slain president Salvador Allende, and Le Thi Xuyen, representative from North Vietnam, at a women in solidarity with Chile rally during the conference.**

The International Tribunal on Crimes Against Women, Brussels, Belgium, 1976; a meeting of the Coordinating Committee: *(left to right)* Nicole Van de Ven, Diana Russell *(leaning forward)*, Marguerite Russell, Elizabeth Natland, Lydia Horton, Grainne Fanen *(hidden)*, Miriam Bazzanella, Erica Fisher, Moni Van Look, and Lily Boeykens.

P. Bolsius

photos by Nadine Markova

Above—**Two U.S. women, Ann Bleaden (*left*) and Sally Withers, with her son, tune in to Tribune proceedings.**
Below—**Informal exchange outside the meeting rooms of the Tribune, IWY sessions sponsored by nongovernmental organizations: Margaret Ford (*left*) of the United States, Chandrike Guttal of India, and Mitsu Tanaka of Japan.**

"I hold this meeting to be a great historic event. . . . Women coming from all over the world will become conscious of the scandal of their condition. . . . Talk to one another! Talk to the world! Bring to light the shameful truths that half of humanity is trying to cover up. . . . I salute this tribunal as being the start of a radical decolonization of women."

—Simone de Beauvoir,
opening statement, International Tribunal on Crimes Against Women, Brussels, Belgium, March, 1976

Rosette Coryell/LNS

"Solidarity with Iranian women in their Struggle"—More than 2,000 women march through Paris, March 16, 1979. Demonstrators also march in major American cities, and in Mexico City, London and Copenhagen to protest regressive laws imposed by Ayatollah Khomeini.

Gamma/Liaison

French women demonstrate in Paris for free abortion and contraception, April, 1974.

Gilda Grillo

Gilles Peress/Magnum

At the end of *The Second Sex*, I said I wasn't a feminist because I thought that the solution to women's problems must depend on the socialist evolution of society . . . but I have come to realize that we must fight for an improvement in woman's actual situation before achieving the socialism we hope for. . . . That is why I have now joined the MLF [Mouvement de Liberation des Femmes].

—Simone de Beauvoir (Shown wearing band that reads "Abortion and Contraception, available and free.") interview by Alice Schwartzer, *Ms.*, July, 1972

"Enough./It is time to cry: enough./And form a block with our bodies."

—New Portuguese Letters, Spring, 1972

Above—***(left to right)*** **"The Three Marias": Maria Teresa Horta, Maria Isabel Barreno, Maria Fatima Velho da Costa. *New Portuguese Letters*, their anthology of feminist writing published in 1972 and banned by the government as an "outrage to public decency," results in a prolonged trial and protests of solidarity around the world. Just after the military dictatorship in Portugal was overthrown in 1974, and under the new regime, the Three Marias are acquitted.**

Wide World

Women in Rome make the symbol of the uterus as they march for abortion on demand, April, 1976. In 1978 Italian feminists win an abortion reform bill after their protests help force new elections on a recalcitrant government.

Prostitutes in Lyons go on strike and "sit in" in St. Nizier Church, June, 1975. French feminists organize in support of their demands for social security and pensions.

Alain Nogues/Sygma

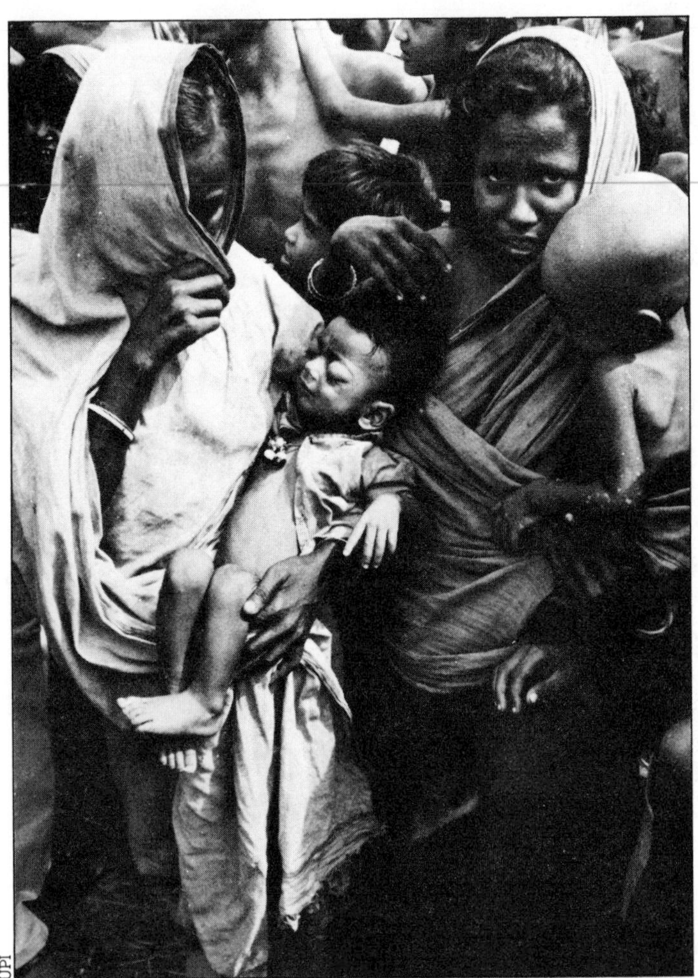

UPI

I forcefully created for myself, under extremely hostile conditions, my ideal life. I took an obscure and almost unknown village in the Southern African bush and made it my own hallowed ground. Here, in the steadiness and peace of my own world, I could dream dreams a little ahead of the somewhat vicious clamor of revolution and the horrible stench of evil social systems. . . .But nothing can take away the fact that I have never had a country; not in South Africa or in Botswana where I now live as a stateless person.

—Bessie Head,
South African novelist,
Ms., November, 1975

The war was over; East Pakistan became a new nation called Bangladesh; the newspapers were full of "return to normality" articles. It was in one of these, that I found a reference to "the heartbreaking reports that as many as 200,000 Bengali women, victims of rape by West Pakistani soldiers, had been abandoned by their husbands, because no Moslem will live with a wife who has been touched by another man."

—Joyce Goldman
"Women of Bangladesh,"
Ms., August, 1972

"The population of Bangladesh is 50 percent female and almost all family planning methods are related to women. Men cannot understand the specific problems and side effects of the pill, injectables, IUD, or tubectomies. Men do not have menstruation, and they do not get pregnant. But unfortunately, it is men who are in charge of the family planning services of this country."

—Gita Chakravarty,
paramedic,
Bangladesh, 1976

Above—**Bangladesh refugees in a camp near Calcutta, November, 1971.**
Right—**Gita Chakravarty, director of a people's health center in Bangladesh, 1976.**
Below—**A "Bench School" in the slums of Cartagena, Columbia, 1978. These informal classrooms serve as childcare centers, and as sources of training and employment for housewives.**

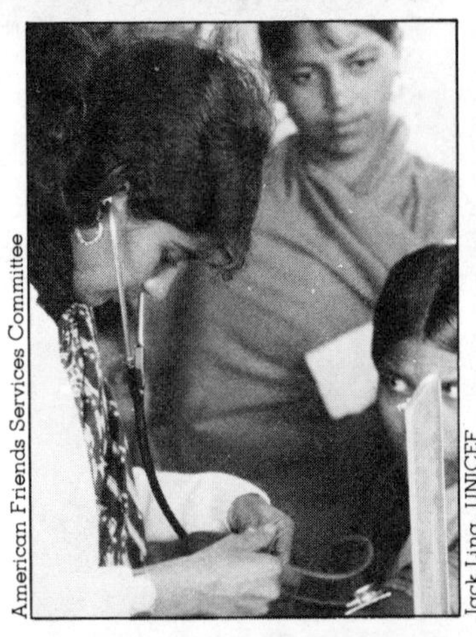

American Friends Services Committee

Jack Ling, UNICEF

Horst M. Cerna/UNICEF

if you want to build a house
come together and work
with us
but if you want to work alone
don't bother to come near us

if you want to work hard
by all means join us
but if you are lazy
be kind enough to stay
away from us . . .

—"Mabati" Work Chant

Opposite page—**Women's work crew in Lesotho. In Africa, 60 percent to 80 percent of agricultural workers are women. But since they labor in family fields, official records list women as only 5 percent of the work force.**
Above—**Women of a "Mabati" group in rural Kenya, 1976. By replacing traditional thatched roofs with corrugated iron ones (called "mabati" in Swahili), women both improve their homes and develop work cooperatives.**

National Archives

The "new man" in the White House.

> "No one better typified Mr. Middle America. Twenty years ago, if [Gerald Ford] had helped with the dishes, he would have pulled the shades down. To me, that picture [in his shirtsleeves in the kitchen] was a marvelous indicator of change."
>
> —Rena Bartos, market research specialist, *Ms.*, December, 1978

MEN

I *think* of C as an equal, no questions about it in my mind as we dine with a mutual woman friend in London. I try not to make decisions for C, try to ask what she wants to do, try not to impose, but—bullshit!—the old urge to dominate, the simple, crass desire to have my own way still rises, the male chauvinist's power erection, so linked to the sexual one that it is sometimes hard to separate sex from power or to guess which it is that a man really wants.

Across from us, at a banquette, a group of noisy gentlemen on the verge of drunkenness are staring at us—at C, to be exact, who is beautiful and tanned and has her back to them. I, on the other hand, am facing them. Ponderously and inaccurately, they toss a few pieces of bread in C's direction to attract her attention. She ignores them. A few minutes later the waiter appears with a silver platter bearing a card, accompanied by the expectant giggles of our neighbors. Before C can reach it, I pick it up and turn it over. It is one of those printed trick cards you can buy at fun fairs or in novelty shops—

I want to sleep with you!
Tick off your favorite love position from the list below,
and return this card with your telephone number

. . . I tear the card up, then, suddenly transfixed by the stupid, sniggering stare of the man who sent the card, I pick up the ashtray from our table and hurl it straight at his face. . . .

Well, it's a scene, we've lived through them before, but afterward, outside on the street I find C in tears, as furious as she is miserable. What did I expect? That she'd be *grateful*? That she'd thank me for defending her honor? I have made her into an object, *my* object, I wasn't avenging an insult to C, I was avenging an insult to *me*—and with what stupidity and low-grade violence! C, who can after all look after herself, lashes out at me in the rainy street: "If you ever do that again, I'll leave you! Do you think I couldn't have handled that, or *ignored* it?"

—Michael Korda
Male Chauvinism! How It Works
(Random House), 1973

The Lord giveth and the Lord taketh away. The American Psychiatric Association has now listed male chauvinism as a certifiable psychiatric illness. Dr. Sherwyn M. Woods defines the effects of this syndrome in an article in *Archives of General Psychiatry* called "Some Dynamics of Male Chauvinism." "Male chauvinism refers to a . . . blind allegiance and simple-minded devotion to one's maleness that is mixed with open or disguised belligerence toward women." But lest women feel vindicated, Woods suggests: "it was more often their mothers" who were responsible for the male chauvinism of their sons and that a number of wives had "chosen male chauvinists in order to meet their own emotional needs."

—*Ms.* "Gazette," June, 1976

Ten years ago, the rising young executive with 2.4 children and a captive wife stood ready to go anywhere, anytime, for advancement. "Now I rarely see that man," says Robert Booth, head of Corporate Recruiters, which scouts personnel for the country's top corporations. "The new executive draws the line at uprooting the family." In a recent survey of 758 companies by Atlas Van Lines, 66 per cent reported that some employees were turning down transfers—nearly twice the 1973 percentage.

—*Newsweek*, "How Men Are Changing," January 16, 1979

Joyce Ravid

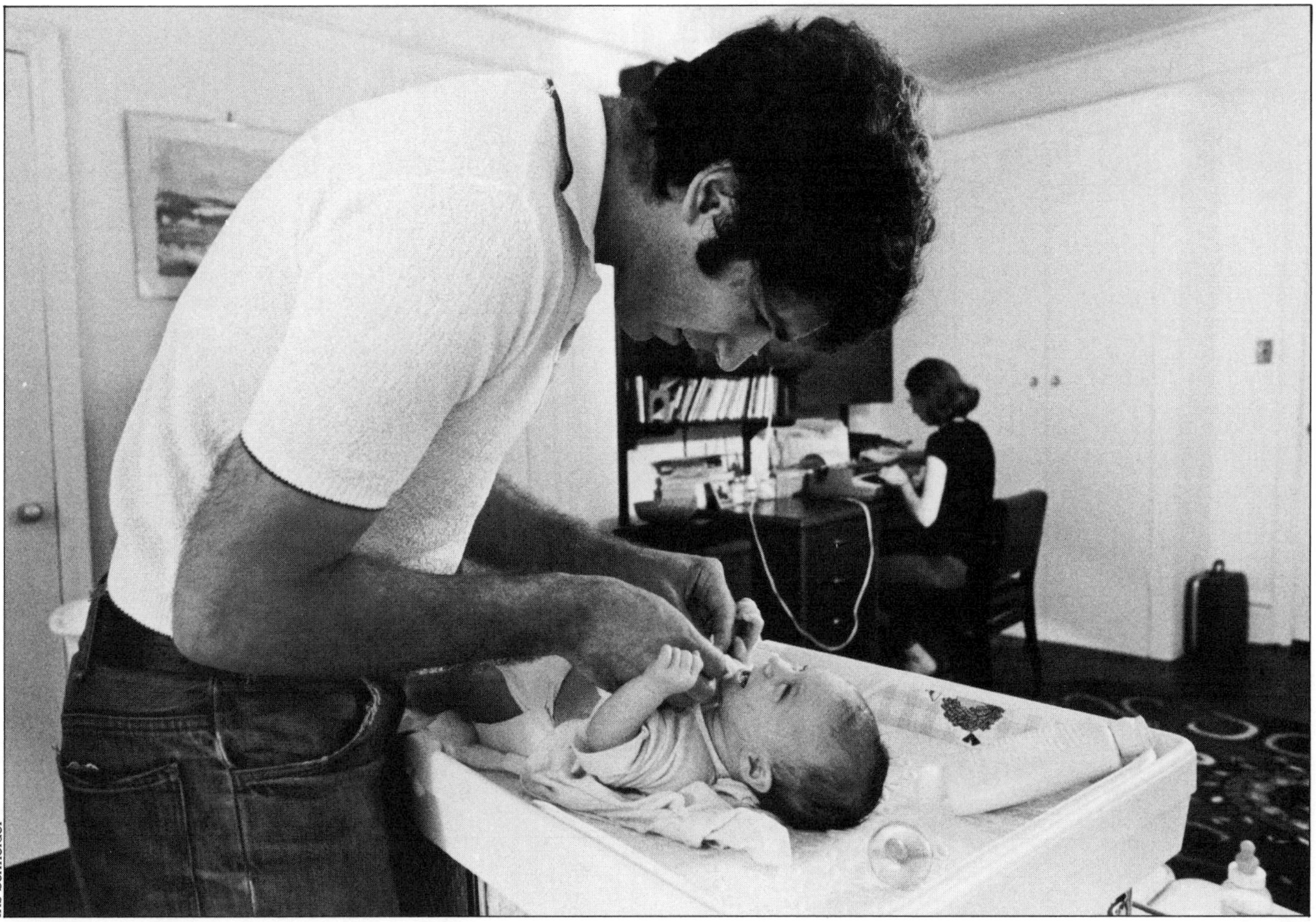

Iris Schneider

> . . . it was simply understood that I was going to take on roughly half of the domestic chores so that she could do the other work she needed to do.
>
> There was something of a shock for me in discovering the sheer quantity of the housework, and my standards of acceptable cleanliness fell rapidly.

—Joel Roache, "Confessions of a Househusband," *Ms.*, November, 1972

Bettye Lane

TESTOSTERONE POISONING

Everyone knows that testosterone, the so-called male hormone, is found in both men and women. What is not so well known is that men have an overdose.

Until now it has been thought that the level of testosterone in men is normal simply because they have it. But if you consider how abnormal their *behavior* is, then you are led to the hypothesis that almost all men are suffering from *testosterone poisoning*.

The symptoms are easy to spot. Sufferers are reported to show an early preference (while still in the crib) for geometric shapes. Later, they become obsessed with machinery and objects to the exclusion of human values. They have an intense need to rank everything, and are obsessed with size. (At some point in his life, nearly every male measures his penis.)

It is well known that men don't look like other people. They have chicken legs. This is symptomatic of the disease, as is the fact that those men with the most aviary underpinnings will rank women according to the shapeliness of *their* legs.

The pathological violence of most men hardly needs to be mentioned. They are responsible for more wars than any other leading sex.

Testosterone poisoning is particularly cruel because its sufferers usually don't know they have it. In fact, when they are most under its sway they believe that they are at their healthiest and most attractive. They even give each other medals for exhibiting the most advanced symptoms of the illness.

But there is hope. Sufferers can change (even though it is harder than learning to walk again). They must first realize, however, that they are sick. The fact that this condition is inherited in the same way that dimples are does not make it cute.

Eventually, of course, telethons and articles in the *Reader's Digest* will dramatize the tragedy of testosterone poisoning. In the meantime, it is imperative for your friends and loved ones to become familiar with the danger signs.

Have the men you know take this simple test for—

THE SEVEN WARNING SIGNS

1. *Do you have an intense need to win?* When having sex, do you take pride in always finishing before your partner? Do you always ask if this time was "the best"—and gnaw on the bedpost if you get an ambiguous answer?

2. *Does violence play a big part in your life?* Before you answer, count up how many hours you watched football, ice hockey, and children's cartoons this year on television. When someone crosses you, do you wish you could stuff his face full of your fist? If so, you're in big trouble, fella, and this is only question number two.

3. *Are you "thing" oriented?* Do you value the parts of a woman's body more than the woman herself? Are you turned on by things that even *remind* you of those parts? Have you ever fallen in love with a really great doorknob?

4. *Do you have an intense need to reduce every difficult situation to charts and figures?* If you were present at a riot, would you tend to count the crowd? If your wife is despondent over a deeply felt setback that has left her feeling helpless, do you take her temperature?

5. *Do you tend to measure things that are really qualitative?* Are you more impressed with how high a male ballet dancer can leap than with what he does while he's up there? Are you more concerned with how long you can spend in bed than you are with how you or your partner feels while you're there?

6. *Are you a little too mechanically minded?* Would you like to watch a sunset with a friend and feel at one with nature and each other, or would you rather take apart a clock?

7. *Are you easily triggered into competition?* When someone tries to pass you on the highway, do you speed up a little? Do you get into contests of crushing beer cans—with the beer still in them?

If you've answered yes to three or fewer of the above questions, you may be learning to deal with your condition. A man answering yes to more than three is considered sick and not someone you'd want to have around in a crisis—such as raising children or growing old together.

WHAT TO DO

1. *Don't panic.* Your first reaction may be that you are sicker than anyone else—or that you are the one man in the world able to fight it off—or, knowing that you are a sufferer, that you are the one man ordained to lead others to health. These are all symptoms of the disease. Just relax. First, sit back and enjoy yourself. Then find out how to enjoy somebody else.

2. *Try to feel something.* (Not with your hands, you oaf.) Look at a baby and see if you can appreciate it. See if you can get yourself to cry by some means other than getting hit in the eye or losing a lot of money.

3. *See if you can listen while someone is talking.* Were you the one talking? Perhaps you haven't got the idea yet.

4. *Practice this sentence:* "You know, I think you're right and I'm wrong." (Hint: it is useful to know what the other person thinks before you say this.)

FOR WOMEN ONLY: IF YOU ARE LIVING WITH A SUFFERER

1. Remember that a little sympathy is a dangerous thing. The sufferer will be inclined to interpret any concern for him as appropriate submissiveness.

2. Let him know that you expect him to fight his way back to health and behave like a normal person—for his own sake.

3. Only after he begins to get his condition under control and has actually begun to enjoy life should you let him know that there is no such thing as testosterone poisoning.

—*Alan Alda, "Ms.",* October, 1975.

Men without women frequently become the "single menace" and tend to live short and destructive lives—destructive both to themselves and to the society.

—George Gilder, *Naked Nomads: Unmarried Men in America* (Quadrangle), 1974

Jon Voight and Burt Reynolds in *Deliverance*.

Women at Dartmouth were given a nickname: cohogs. The men serenaded them with obscenities.

Bob Adelman

Our cohogs, they play one.
They're all here to spoil our fun,

Chorus:
With a knick-knack, paddy-whack,
Send the bitches home,
Our cohogs go to bed alone.
Our cohogs, they play three,
They all have to squat to pee,

(chorus)

Our cohogs, they play seven,
They have ruined our masculine heaven,

(chorus)

Carroll W. Brewster, then dean of the college, judged this song one of the most creative and original in the contest. (Brewster left that year to become president of a women's school in Virginia.)

—Andy Merton, "Hanging On (By a Jockstrap) To Tradition at Dartmouth," *Esquire*, June ,1979

Warren Farrell (*dark beard*), author of *The Liberated Man*, leads a C-R group, 1973. Participants hold hands to overcome phobia of touching other men. To control male tendency to dominate conversation, each man receives two toothpicks, which he places in center after each contribution. He then speaks only to ask questions.

Paul Suidzinski

As a man, my conditioning and problems are not only different, but virtually the inverse of those of most women. We've been taught that "real men" are never passive or dependent, always dominant in relationships with women or other men, and don't talk about or directly express feelings; especially feelings that don't contribute to dominance. . . . There is nothing among men that resembles the personal communication that women have developed among themselves. We don't know very much about ourselves, and we know even less about each other.

—Marc Feigen Fasteau, "Why Aren't We Talking?" *Ms.*, July, 1972

It was the boy who had to ask the girl for a date, a frightening enough prospect until it occurred to me that she might say no! That meant risking my ego, which was about as substantial as a toilet-paper raincoat in the African rainy season.

—Julius Lester, "Being a Boy," *Ms.*, July, 1973

Now it seems to me [men] do not care so much about the novels and the buildings, but they do care a great deal about whether or not *they* have written or built them. Ambition, in other words, is directed inward rather than outward, is preoccupied with self rather than things. . . .

Life seems to be punctilious about dividing men into winners and losers. . . . The winners in life do not forget their old friends; the old friends withdraw. They all but back out of the winner's lives, not from envy or bitterness but almost apologetically, in order to escape a sense of awkward inadequacy more intense than anything else this side of adolescence.

—Thomas Powers, "Can Friendship Survive Success?" *Ms.*, January, 1975

Each of us has in his inmost self wrestled with this greatest male fear of all—that "changing ourselves" can only mean one thing ultimately: the freezing up of our sexuality. Yet this very fear may be part of a strategy we have developed to resist change, even when we think we welcome it. Central to that strategy are five basic lies about male sexuality which men tell women (and ourselves, and other men).

—Kenneth Pitchford, "Lies We Tell Ourselves About Sex," *Ms.*, April, 1978

I'm a part-time college student, and I made a remark in a class to the effect that I agree with the Women's Liberation Movement. One of the students who knew my age (I am 76) said, for the benefit of all, that at his age he was still chasing women. I answered that I was not trying to catch any women, nor was I trying to chase any away. What I was doing was following them—for they are the only group on the horizon today heading toward a better world, and that is why I am giving them my wholehearted support.

—Joe L.
—letter to the editors
Ms., September, 1975

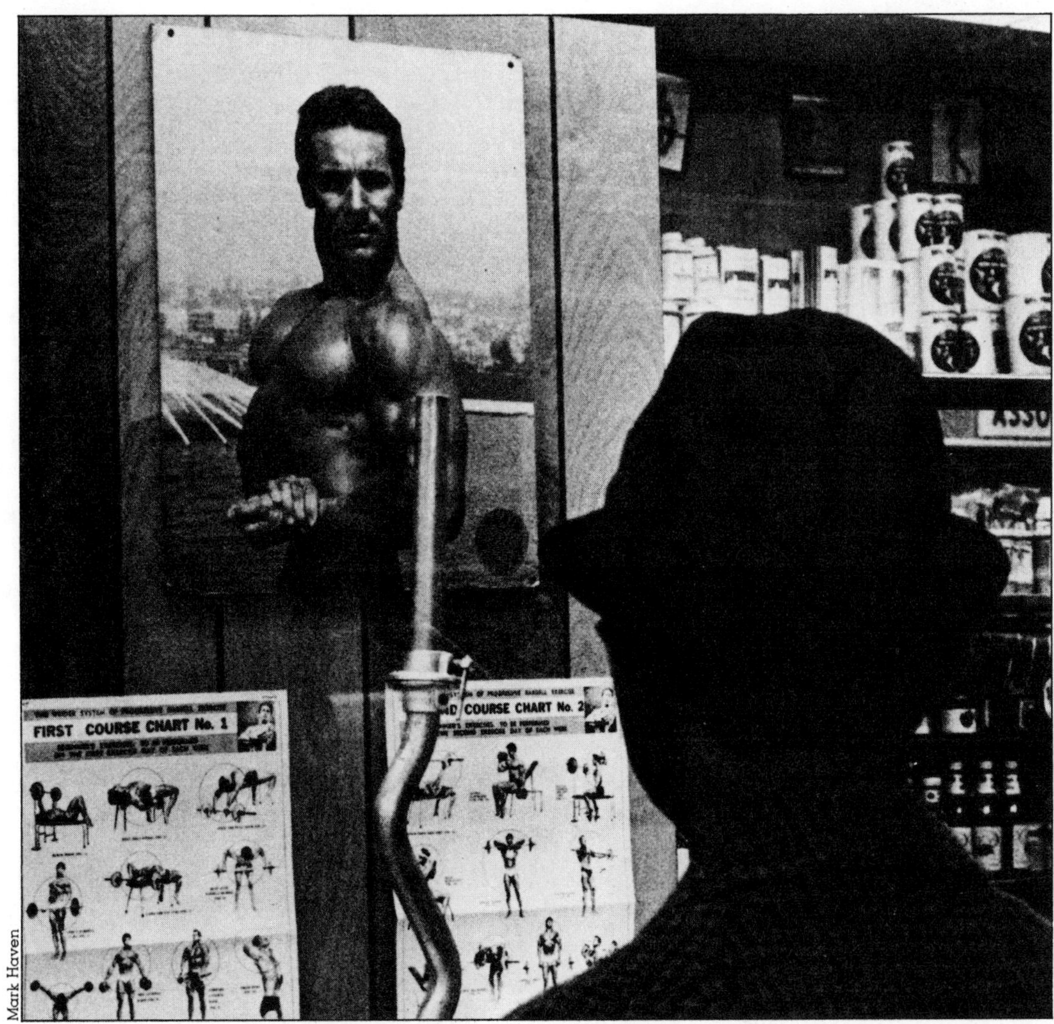

Mark Haven

. . . men are deprived of a knowledge of their own bodies, perhaps even more severely than women . . .

—Venable Herndon, "Some Surprises About Male Nudity," *Ms.*, March, 1978

So let woman be what she would, and what she could. Let her cohabit on elephants if she had to, and fuck with Borzoi hounds, let her bed with eight pricks and a whistle, yes, give her freedom and let her burn it, or blow it, or build it to triumph or collapse. . . . he would agree with everything they asked but to quit the womb, for finally a day had to come when women shattered the pearl of their love for pristine and feminine will and found the man, yes that man in the million who could become the point of the seed which would give an egg back to nature, and let the woman return with a babe who came from the root of God's desire to go all the way, wherever was that way.

—Norman Mailer
"The Prisoner of Sex,"
Harper's, March, 1971

The majority of older men have barely modified their views of male-female roles. Nor have the winds of change ruffled blue-collar communities, where wives have been working for years just to make ends meet and a man's home—however humble—is still his castle. . . .

Even among the college males she interviewed for her book, *Dilemmas of Masculinity*, sociologist Mirra Komarovsky found the majority were a study on contradictions. Typically, they would endorse the idea of working wives, then add the proviso that a wife's career should not rival her husband's or interfere with the smooth functioning of the home. They approved of women entering the professions, then disapproved of "aggressive, ambitious" women students.

—*Newsweek*,
"How Men Are Changing,"
January 16, 1978

Under the male supremacist system that now blights our planet, women are defined first by their reproductive capacities. They produce babies. They are the first producers of the first product. A product is that which is made by human labor. Even though in actuality not all women can produce babies, all women are defined as the producers of babies. That is why radical feminists regard women as a class of persons who have in common the same relationship to production (reproduction).

The raw materials out of which babies are formed are the mother's flesh and blood, the nutrients that nourish her, the very stuff of her own physical existence. An embryo literally feeds from and is formed out of the mother's body.

Once the baby is born, this product of the mother's labor, made from the raw materials of her body, does not belong to her. It belongs to a man. It belongs to one who did not and cannot produce it. This ownership is systematized in law, theology, and the national mores; it is sanctioned by the State, sanctified in art and philosophy, and endorsed by men of all political persuasions. A baby who is not owned by a man does not have a legitimate civil existence.

—Andrea Dworkin, "Phallic Imperialism," *Ms.*, December, 1976

BODY & MIND

Marcia Resnick

Bettye Lane

By the spring of 1972 there was a new development or perhaps just an extension of health courses and conferences—women's body courses. Here there was much greater emphasis on actual demonstration with the body, self-help and direct discussion of sexuality. Instead of continuing the split between book learning and real experience, or what we know in our heads and what we feel in our bodies—a split which corresponds to the separation of gynecology and psychiatry—women decided that the only way to get to know and feel comfortable with our bodies was by using our bodies as the starting point in our courses. The best time, it was felt, to learn about anatomy is when our bodies are being examined.

—Ellen Frankfort,
Vaginal Politics
(Quadrangle), 1972

We have lived through the era when happiness was a warm puppy, and the era when happiness was a dry martini, and now we have come to the era when happiness is "knowing what your uterus looks like."

—Nora Ephron,
Crazy Salad (Knopf), 1975

Opposite page—**Unique as we are, two women who look extraordinarily alike meet one another in San Juan, Puerto Rico.** Left—**In November, 1972 members of the Los Angeles Feminist Health Center demonstrate vaginal self-examination to New York City women.**

MEDICINE

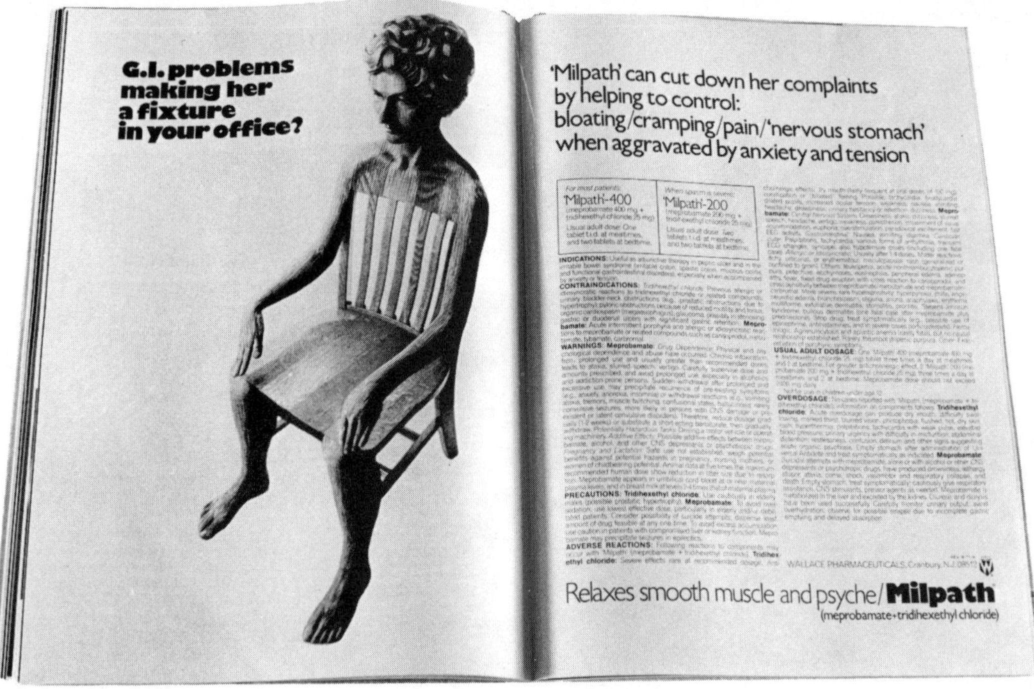

A 1972 advertisement running in several medical magazines.

A physician has the duty to inform a patient of "material" risks inherent in a surgical procedure, and to disclose "feasible" alternative methods of treatment, the Oregon supreme court has ruled.

—*Surgical Advances*, January–February, 1972

In June of 1972, hearings on "liberalization" of the California insurance code drew attention to a provision allowing insurance companies to refuse disability payments for injuries resulting from calamities such as "war, suicide, hallucinatory drugs, and organs peculiar to females." A threatened class action suit by a local chapter of the National Organization for Women caused the California code to be cosmetically amended to substitute "reproductive organs"—peculiar to both men and women—for "organs peculiar to women."

—Susanne Stoiber, "Insured: Except in Case of War, Suicide, and Organs Peculiar to Females," *Ms.*, June, 1973

In the beginning we called ourselves "the doctors group." We had all experienced similar feelings of frustration and anger toward specific doctors and the medical maze in general, and initially we wanted to do something about those doctors who were condescending, paternalistic, judgmental, and noninformative. . . . So we decided on a summer project—to research those topics which we felt were particularly pertinent to learning about our bodies. . . .

As we developed the course we realized more and more that we really were capable of collecting, understanding and evaluating medical information. . . . We were equally struck by how important it was for us to be able to open up with one another and share our feelings about our bodies. The process of talking was as crucial as the facts themselves. Over time the facts and feelings melted together in ways that touched us very deeply, and that is reflected in the changing titles of the course and then the book—from *Women and Their Bodies* to *Women and Our Bodies* to, finally, *Our Bodies, Ourselves*. [As of 1979, the book had sold 2 million copies.]

—Boston Women's Health Book Collective, *Our Bodies, Ourselves* (Simon & Schuster), 1973

A [University of California at San Diego] study team audited medical records of 52 married couples to determine doctors' responses to five common medical complaints: back pain, headache, dizziness, chest pain and fatigue. . . . "The only variable that correlated with the extent of workup was the sex of the patient," the report said. "In fact, men received a more extensive workup than women for all complaints studied. . . .

"Finally and most controversially," said the report, "the data may bear out what many critics already claim: namely, that the physicians—who in this study were all male—tend to take illness more seriously in men."

—Harold M. Schmeck, Jr., "Study Backs Charge of Sexism in Medicine," *New York Times*, June 5, 1979

"A certain type of woman becomes a nurse. She is different from a girl who becomes a poetry major at Yale. Most nurses don't have a strong ego: they're mellow and on the meek side. They're often 'yes-men' who don't stand up for what they think is right: they prefer following orders to directing orders. It becomes a glorified housewife's role."

—Junior Resident, quoted in "Doctors Diagnose Nurses," by Lucinda B. Fleeson, *Ms.*, August, 1973

"You will never know how hostile I become every time I hear a feminist berate a woman because she is a nurse," says a black R.N. from New York. "What can possibly be more liberating than an opportunity to earn money? Or, does liberation mean we have to be doctors? I thought it meant being able to make choices." . . .

"I remember the first time I saw the cheerful binding on our medical-surgical nursing text," recalls a Ph.D. "My first thought was that it was abducted from a sixth-grade social studies classroom. I glanced at the medical text which lay near it—dignified and scholarly. It had no cover illustrations of smiling interns and calm chiefs-of-staff poised mannequin-like against the background scenes of medical-surgical experience. I was already beginning to feel quite inferior to persons who read those regal medical books."

Today, more and more nurses are studying alongside doctors and sharing their austere texts. Nurses are hopeful that this will educate doctors about the intelligence and basic humanity of nurses. But a lot more than classroom exposure may be necessary.

—Tricia Kusher, "Nurses! Nurses! Nurses!," *Ms.*, August, 1973

Keith Madden/LNS

Washington, D.C. nurses strike, June, 1978.

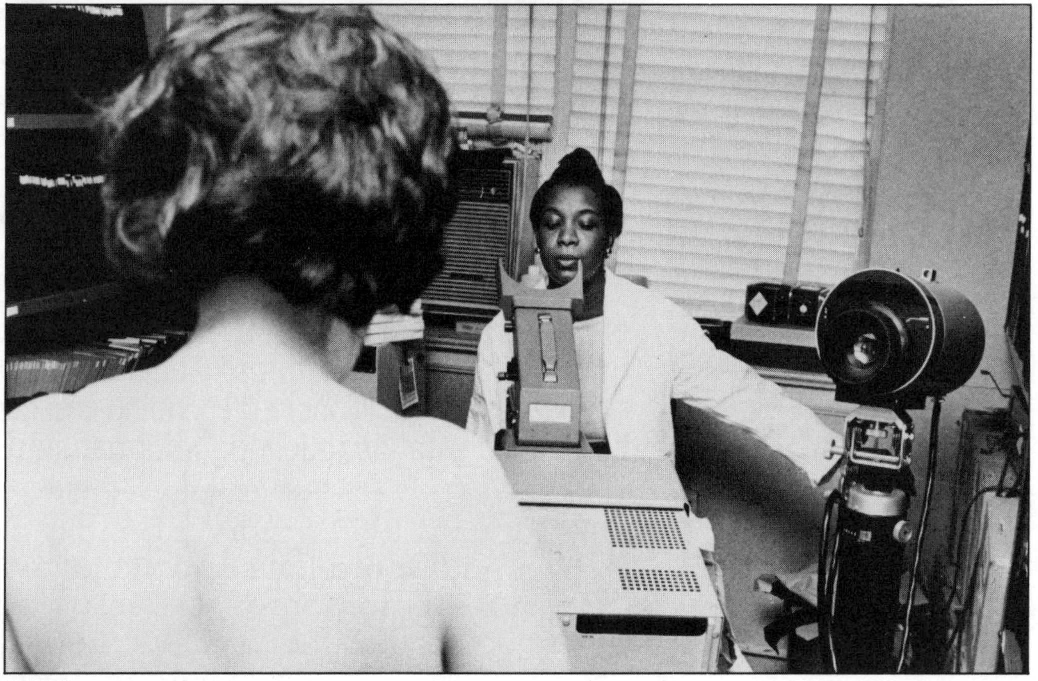

Breast exam is shown as the media recognizes the reality of women's health needs and care in "ABC News Closeup on Women's Health: A Question of Survival," January, 1976.

CONTRACEPTION

More than 4 million American women now use intrauterine devices. Another 4 million women have worn IUDs over the past decade—most since the "Pill scare" of 1970. Yet only recently have American women begun to realize that in using IUDs—devices of varying sizes, shapes, and materials that prevent pregnancy when inserted in the uterus—they have unwittingly been taking part in a vast experiment. It does not resemble what one normally thinks of as an experiment—seldom are the patients asked for their "informed consent," seldom are they told of the benefits and risks, seldom are control groups provided or strict scientific protocols followed—but an experiment it is.

Through a process of trial and error that has as its major "testing method" the passage of time, unsuspecting women in this country and around the world have provided drug companies and the scientific community with the bulk of the data that now exists on IUDs—and even that is full of holes.

Dr. Russel J. Thomsen, a private physician in Walla Walla, Washington, who has testified before a number of government committees investigating IUDs, argues that most researchers and manufacturers traditionally underestimate the seriousness of side effects associated with IUDs.

"When an IUD-user gets a perforated uterus, it's not a simple surgical procedure to resolve the problem," he explains. "It often requires dangerous, life-threatening surgery. And when a woman gets pregnant wearing an IUD and then miscarries, it isn't something that just happens at home over a toilet. It usually requires hospitalization, blood transfusions, and difficult surgical procedures. Then we've got massive pelvic infections on top of all this. So we're talking about major complications endangering the life or physical well-being of patients. But these complications are usually glossed over in IUD studies. If a woman has a disastrous pregnancy, most studies simply list it as a pregnancy—not as the disaster it is."

—Barbara J. Katz, "The IUD: Out of Sight, Out of Mind?" *Ms.*, July, 1975

"We also think—and I'm sorry, gentlemen, if this disturbs any of your egos—that condoms should be marketed in three sizes, because the failures tend to occur at the extreme ends of the scale. In men who are petite, they fall off, and in men who are extra well-endowed, they burst. Women buy brassieres in A, B, and C cups and panty hose in different sizes, and I think if it would help condom efficacy, we should package them in different sizes and maybe label them like olives: jumbo, colossal, and supercolossal, so that men don't have to go in and ask for the small."

—Barbara Seaman, testifying before the Select Committee on Population, March, 1978

Cigarette smoking increases the risk of serious cardiovascular side effects from oral-contraceptive use. This risk increases with age and with heavy smoking (15 or more cigarettes per day) and is quite marked in women over 35 years of age. Women who use oral contraceptives should be strongly advised not to smoke.
The use of oral contraceptives is associated with increased risk of several serious conditions, including thromboembolism, stroke, myocardial infarction, hepatic adenoma, gallbladder disease, hypertension. Practitioners prescribing oral contraceptives should be familiar with the following information relating to these risks.

Not until 1963, when a Senate Committee on Government Operations subcommittee, headed by Senator Hubert Humphrey, investigated the FDA, was it revealed that the 1960 decision to approve Enovid was based on clinical studies of only 132 women who had taken the Pill continuously for a year or longer. [Not until 1970 was a warning required in Pill packaging.]

—Barbara Seaman, "The New Pill Scare," *Ms.*, June, 1975

[Since 1970] about 200 young women have been admitted to American hospitals with a rare type of vaginal or cervical cancer that was almost unknown before 1970. The only thing they had in common was that while they were still in the womb, their mothers had been administered diethylstilbestrol (DES), a synthetic estrogen, to prevent possible miscarriage. Between 1945 and 1965, the drug's peak period of use, DES was given to several million women despite the fact that its effectiveness in preventing miscarriage was questioned.

It wasn't until 1971 that the FDA warned physicians against the use of DES in pregnancy. In August, 1971, the *New England Journal of Medicine* also stated that "there should no longer be doubt that synthetic estrogens are absolutely contraindicated in pregnancy." Yet the June, 1972, issue of the *American Journal of Obstetrics and Gynecology* still advocated the use of DES for acne in pregnancy. (Besides the "antimiscarriage" uses, DES has long been prescribed for acne and thinning hair, for premenstrual tension, as hormone replacement for aging women, and to dry up the breast milk of new mothers who did not intend to nurse.) And in 1972, sales of DES by Lilly, the major supplier, totaled nearly $2 million.

This rise in use is partly due to the fact that DES is the only ingredient in a new drug, the "morning-after pill," which, when taken within 72 hours after intercourse, is supposed to slough off the uterine lining in such a way as to prevent implantation of a fertilized ovum . . . .

Ironically, while prescriptions for the morning-after pill—although then unapproved for this use by the FDA—were reaching an all-time high, American scientists, journalists, and interest groups were engaged in a national outcry against the use of DES as an additive in cattle feed. The FDA was permitting DES to be fed to cattle because it made the animals fatten on less grain, thereby saving cattlepeople $90 million yearly. For nearly 10 years, scientists had been protesting this use of DES, because in animals given 20 milligrams a day, DES causes cancerous tumors.

—Kay Weiss, "Afterthoughts on the Morning After Pill," *Ms.*, October, 1973

Eleven Mexican-American women filed a class-action suit against one of the largest and most prestigious teaching institutions: The USC–Los Angeles County Medical Center. Ten of the plaintiffs claim that they were sterilized against their will or after being pushed into agreeing to the operation while under the stress of labor. The eleventh plaintiff was about to be sterilized, but the operation was postponed; the delay let her change her mind. . . .

Guadalupe Acosta, age 35, who gave birth to a stillborn daughter at L.A. County in August, 1973, was sterilized after her delivery. "I never signed for that operation," she asserts. "The hospital told me my common-law husband signed, but *he* told me that he only signed for the cesarean. It's true, because he sent me for the Pills the next month—he wouldn't have done that if he'd known I was sterile."

—Claudia Dreifus, *Ms.* "Gazette," December, 1975

General Motors of Canada prohibits fertile women from working in its battery plant because of fear that the lead-oxide emissions in the plant could hurt unborn children, a fear partially substantiated by Johns Hopkins University in Baltimore. (Other medical studies show that the male as well as the female reproductive system can be affected by lead and chemical emissions.)

Recently, six women were told they must prove that they could not bear children or be transferred to another department. One of them, Norma James, had herself sterilized because of her need for the job.

—*Ms.* "Gazette," June, 1976

CHILDBIRTH

Abigail Heyman/Magnum

It was the most incredible, wonderful, terrifically joyful, sexual, sensual, loving time of our lives. It was so intensely personal that it's hard to believe we didn't discover it all by ourselves. But it is as common as dying, or making love, or being born. It's what the hospitals categorize as "normal childbirth," and it was extraordinary for us because we did it together.

—Donald Sutherland,
"Childbirth Is Not for Mothers Only,"
Ms., May, 1974

Preventive interferences are the doctor's ways of turning sloppy old nature into a clean, safe science. They may explain that obstetrical science is simply a "just-in-case" game of playing the odds in the woman's favor: "just in case" you hemorrhage, we'll give you simulated hormones before you expel the placenta; "just in case" your perineum tears, we'll make a nice clean incision before delivery; "just in case" labor tires you out, we'll give you an early sedative; "just in case" you need a general anesthesia (for an emergency cesarean), we'll keep a vein open and stop you from eating and drinking throughout labor, even if it takes 24 hours; or "just in case" you totally lose control, we'll knock you out right now. Hearing this, the pregnant woman cannot help but believe that normal birth is loaded with unpredictable horrors that only her doctor can prevent. . . . But the truth is that in at least 90 percent of all births, these interferences are unnecessary, costly, and in many cases damaging to either mother or child, or both.

—Suzanne Arms,
Immaculate Deception: New Look at Women and Childbirth in America
(Houghton Mifflin), 1975

Since 1970, the "C-section" statistics have edged upward at a steady rate of nearly 1 percentage point a year. Large teaching hospitals, particularly on the East Coast, report rates of 16 to 20 percent. Dr. Graham Hawkes, professor of obstetrics and gynecology at the New York Hospital-Cornell Medical Center, told a *Daily News* reporter that within five years he expected the ratio to be closer to one in every three deliveries.

"There are times when a cesarean is unquestionably advisable, and lifesaving for mother or child or both," says Dr. Murray W. Enkin, associate professor of obstetrics and gynecology and a member of the board of the International Childbirth Education Association. "Most of the time, however, the indications for the operation are less definite, and depend largely on a judgment call [subjective judgment]. How long is prolonged labor? At what point should it be terminated by cesarean? How great is the risk of a breech birth to the baby? Is the change in a baby's heart rating the real distress which demands that the baby be delivered immediately, or is it just the response of the baby to the normal stress of labor? There is no easy answer to these questions. Despite a great deal of research, there is a lot of opinion and little fact." Nevertheless, most physicians concur: cesarean section has changed from an operation of necessity to one of choice.

—Deborah Larned
"Why Cesarean Births are Up 100 Percent," *Ms.*, October, 1978

For industrial countries, the population-per-obstetrician ratio, and the population-per-pediatrician ratio unexpectedly significantly relate in a negative way to the infant mortality rate. The population-per-nurse and the nurse-and-midwife ratios are, interestingly, positively related to the infant mortality rate. It is not clear what *these statistical relationships* mean, but they *offer little support for the importance of medical care as distributed by physicians in reducing infant mortality.*

—Irvin Emanuel, M.D., *Birth Defects; Risks and Consequences,* edited by Sally Kelly, *et al.* (Academic Press)

"Midwifery is in the midst of a renaissance throughout the United States, although it is growing fastest in California and the West," said Dr. Lewis Mehl, coordinator of Psychophysiological Research at the Center for Research on Birth and Human Development, Berkeley, California.

He cites these reasons for the renaissance:

Questioning of the role of technology in childbirth. Many couples say that childbirth has been dehumanized because of such obstetrical pratices as the use of drugs and surgical incisions of the vagina. They believe that midwives, because they have been exposed to less technology in their training than have physicians, tend to use it more sparingly.

Increased demand for women practioners as a result of the Women's Movement.

Better training for midwives. Unlike the midwives of the past, who had no background in physiology or psychology, today's midwife is apt to be a nursing school graduate who has also completed a one-year course in midwifery at one of 24 schools approved by the American College of Nurse Midwives. There are now about 2,500 nurse midwives in the United States who have passed the rigorous examination of the college. About 250 graduates become certified each year.

Acceptance by the federal government. The Air Force has used nurse midwives at its base hospitals across the country, and the Department of Health, Education, and Welfare has encouraged institutions it funds to employ nurse midwives.

Changes in the laws that license midwives.

—Sharon Johnson, "Midwives: Acceptance Is Growing Nationwide," *New York Times,* June 19, 1979

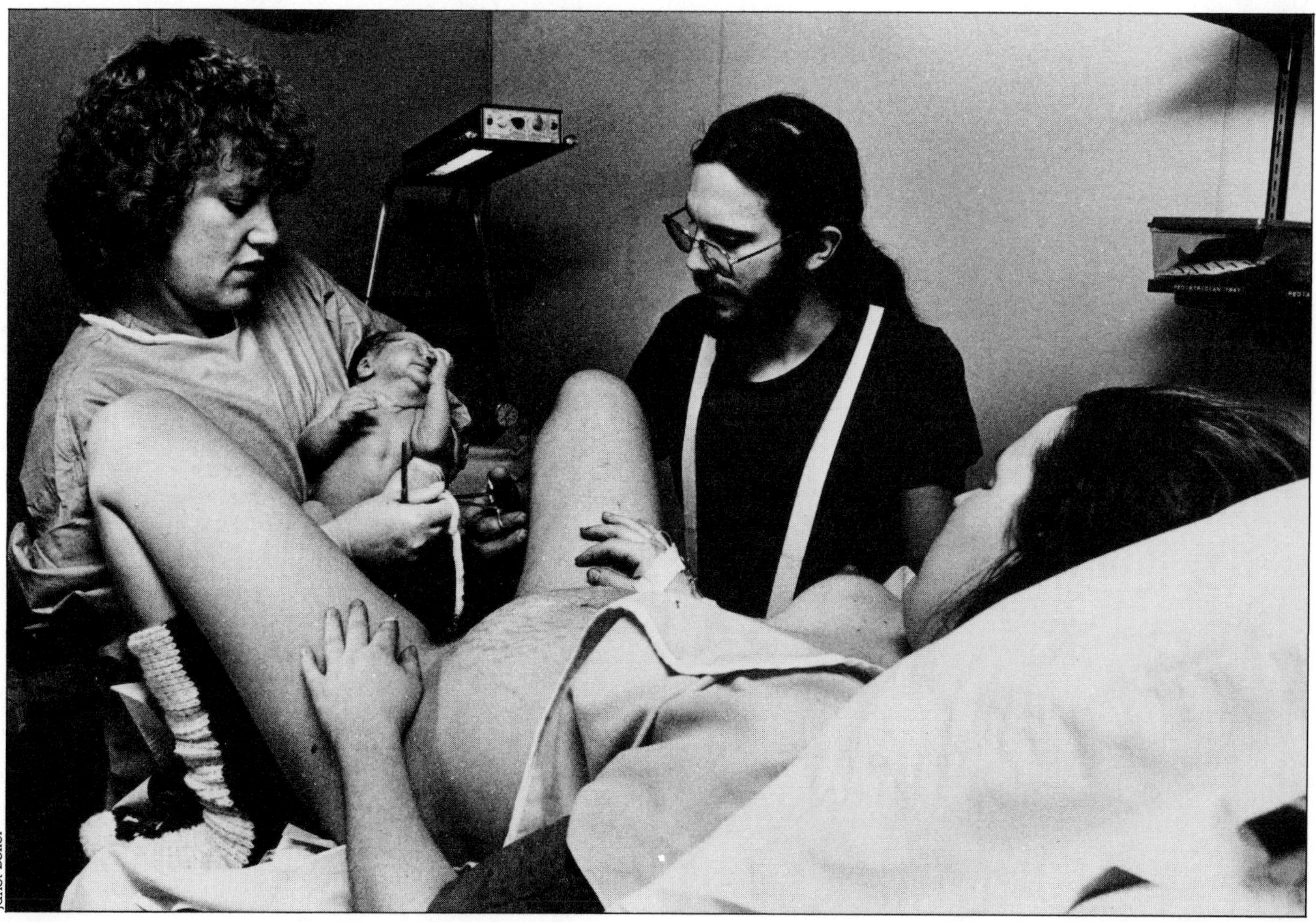

Janet Beller

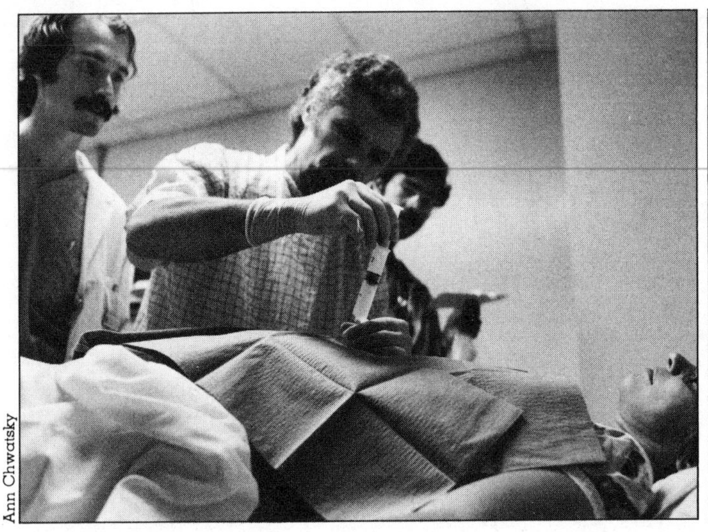

Ann Chwatsky

[To perform amniocentesis, a test for genetic defects,] the doctor guides a four-inch needle through the belly wall into the peritoneal cavity, through the uterine wall, and lastly into the amniotic sac. All this must be done without nicking a blood vessel or any of the blood-filled sinuses that are laced around the uterus. Once you get the needle inside the sac, it mustn't penetrate the fetus itself or any portion of the umbilical cord, which may be looped in any position. You don't push the needle in blindly, however, trusting to luck. You must know how the baby is lying, you locate the placenta so you can avoid it, and you push that needle in with the greatest caution, testing as you go. Still, it's a great relief when you get a clear tap—amniotic fluid and no blood.

—*Dr. Anonymous,*
The Confessions of a Gynecologist
(Bantam), 1972

It is possible that this technology would mean still another way that women's bodies would be used—as temporary havens for other people's children. One could imagine a flourishing "rent-a-uterus" business. One British doctor has even suggested a "reasonable" price for such a service—2,000 pounds (or about $4,000). It wouldn't be the first time that poor women found that their bodies are their one salable commodity.

How far should we go in manipulating embryos? There has been speculation that in the future we may be able to change the sex, the hair color—even the intelligence of embryos. The most outrageous fantasy is that of "designing" people—a legless astronaut for a life in space or a human being with gills to live in the oceans.

—Caryl Rivers,
"Genetic Engineers: Now That They've Gone Too Far, Can They Stop?"
Ms., June, 1976

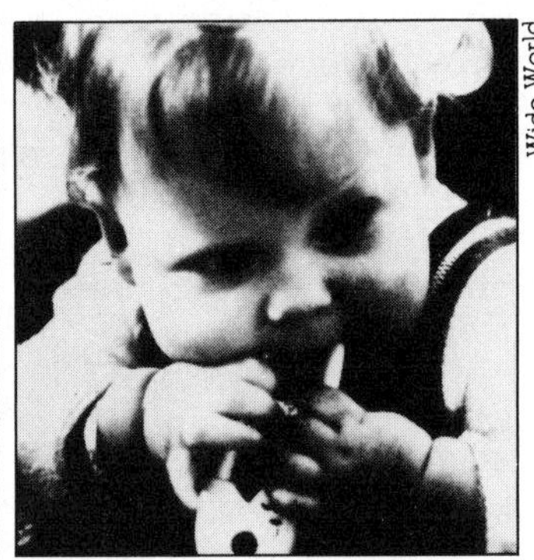

Wide World

Left—**Louise Brown, first baby to be successfully conceived in a test tube, is a year old, July, 1979.** Below left—**Erica Jong is 36 when she gives birth in August, 1978 to daughter Molly.**

Christina Thomson

In the human female the ages 15 to 44 are called the *reproductive life span*, although in the United States the average age of menarche (onset of menstruation) is 13, and only half of all women reach menopause by 50.

The reproductive capacity of women—and men—deteriorates with advancing age. But physically, there is no ideal time to have a baby, for mother and baby do not operate on the same trajectory of risk. Maternal risk is lowest in the late teens and twenties, rises slowly but steadily through the thirties, and after 40 may be as much as 10 times higher than for women in their twenties.

Infant mortality, on the other hand, is lowest when mothers are in their late twenties and only rises again very slowly thereafter. The infant mortality rates for mothers aged 35 to 39 are the same as the rates for mothers aged 20 to 24, while the rates for mothers over 40 are comparable to those aged 15 to 19.

A most dangerous time to have a baby, in terms of risk to *both mother and child*, is in the early teens, the years just after menarche. It's as if the female reproductive system were warming up, but is not yet ready to go the distance.

—Barbara Seaman,
"How Late Can You Wait To Have a Baby?"
Ms., January, 1976

☐ Nearly 1 million teenagers become pregnant each year.
☐ Teenagers accounted for one fifth of all 1974 births, 53% of the out-of-wedlock births, and one third of the abortions in the United States.
☐ Almost two and a half times as many teenagers gave birth as there were reported cases of venereal disease among teenagers of both sexes.
☐ Out of 608,000 births to teenage women in 1974, nearly 13,000 were to women aged 14 or younger.
☐ The number of mothers under 16 years of age has increased 80% since 1960.
☐ Only one in five sexually active teenage women use contraception consistently.
☐ Of the approximately ten million females aged 15 through 19, as many as 20% will experience a premarital pregnancy before they are out of their teenage years.
☐ Three-fourths of all first pregnancies to teenage women are begun premaritally.
☐ Half of the brides in the U.S. who are younger than 18 years old are pregnant.
☐ Almost one fourth of women who have their first child in their teenage years have three more within a seven-year period.
☐ Only 26 states explicitly permit teenagers to obtain contraception without parental consent, although all 50 permit abortion without consent.

—The Population Institute, 1979

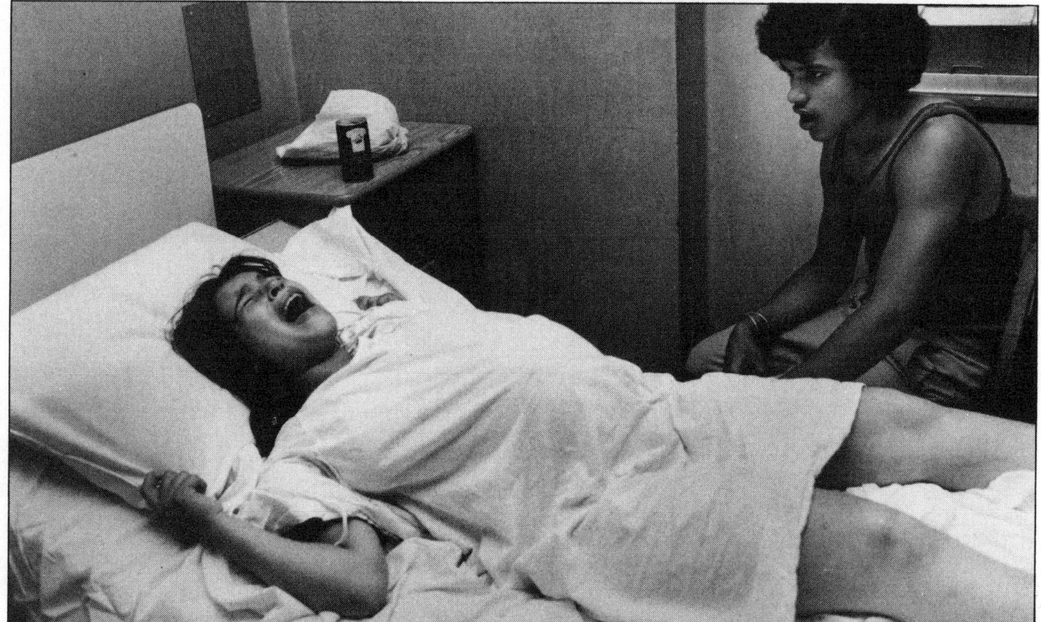

photos by Mary Ellen Mark/Magnum

Top to Bottom—
Jeannette Alejandro is 15, Victor Orellanes, 14, when their baby Chastity is born in September, 1978.

SELF IMAGE

Transsexualism just may be the most fervent and radical testimony to the power of sex roles in this gender-based political system called patriarchy. If our humanity was really a shared and common ground, would sex roles be such prisons that some people feel they must mutilate themselves in order to set their personalities free? . . .

In a landmark doctoral thesis at Boston College, Jan Raymond, a specialist in medical ethics, has analyzed in-depth interviews with transsexuals. She concluded that they might have acted as critics of this sexually stereotyped society; critics who are now silenced by the reduction of a simple and physical way out of their struggle.

—Gloria Steinem,
"If the Shoe Doesn't Fit, Change the Foot,"
Ms., February, 1977

They say it's worse to be ugly. I think it must only be different. If you're pretty, you are subject to one set of assaults; if you're plain you are subject to another. Pretty, you may have more men to choose from, but you have more anxiety too, knowing your looks, which really have nothing to do with you, will disappear. Pretty girls have few friends. Kicked out of mankind in elementary school, and then kicked out of womankind in junior high, pretty girls have a lower birthrate and a higher mortality. It is the beauties like Marilyn Monroe who swallow twenty-five Nembutals on a Saturday night and kill themselves in their thirties.

—Alix Kates Shulman,
Memoirs of an Ex-Prom Queen
(Knopf), 1972

I had an uncle who loved to tell the following joke: Why is it bad to be a grandpa? No one was supposed to be able to imagine the answer, though this joke was told at least eight times in the course of my girlhood. The answer was because you have to sleep with Grandma. My aunt usually laughed at that answer. Like most women then, she either thought the storyteller meant some other grandma or she had learned to laugh in hopeful identifying bawdiness.

He means you! He means you! I wanted to cry out. And of course, now, finally, as I guessed it would be, the joke is at me and my friends.

I am in my kitchen. This was always a room for hospitality, slavery, and family pleasure. Nowadays—another time of life—it's old friends who sit at the table. We talk lots of politics, talk about our lives—look at the pile of new books creasing the tablecloth. This week Rosetta Reitz's book is on top. *Menopause: A Positive Approach.* **Question:** What does she mean "positive"? **Answer:** Simply that most books on menopause have been written by male gynecologists and have been viciously negative—describing the condition of our female lives after 45 as "equivalent of a eunuch," "living decay," "common aberration," or "a curable and preventable deficiency disease. . . ."

Rosetta Reitz has researched the literature, interviewed medical practitioners, and, perhaps most important, talked honestly and sympathetically with women—*and listened.* So my friends found the information they were searching for—its biological explanation put into sensible and proper proportion: hot flashes don't mean you're a sick woman and being sad doesn't mean you're crazy. . . . Reitz is unequivocal in describing estrogen replacement therapy as carcinogenic.

—Grace Paley,
reviewing *Menopause: A Positive Approach,*
by Rosetta Reitz
(Chilton Books, 1977),
Ms., February, 1978

B.C. (Before Consciousness): There we were, pre-feminism, denying there was any problem, solitarily certain that each of us was herself the problem: "I self-loathe, therefore I am." There was no question about this, yet we knew the answer—appearances mattered, after all. Therefore we curled, plucked, dieted, bleached, straightened, shaved, uplifted, and otherwise adorned. One day we compared notes, went into a painful but hilarious labor, and gave birth—to ourselves, we thought.

A.D. (After Defiance): There we were, feministically aware of how political the issue of appearance always had been—which meant that now it *really* mattered. Sometimes our eager solidarity slid into the old conformism: edicts declaring that short hair equals long consciousness, for instance. One day we noticed that we had given birth perhaps more to a litter of identical siblings than to our own difficult selves.

—Robin Morgan,
"The Politics of Body-Image,"
Ms., September, 1977

Wide World

The right of Renee Richards, formerly Richard Raskind, to play on the women's tennis circuit is challenged in 1976, but she's soon accepted as fair competition.

In March, 1975 Julie Roy wins suit against psychiatrist Dr. Renatus Hartogs, who seduced her as part of therapy.

Wide World

"There is definitely more patient-therapist sex than in the past," opines the chairman of a local APA ethics committee. How much is there? In a celebrated 1973 California study, 51 percent of the 85 male psychiatrists surveyed admitted to sexual intercourse with patients. One might have expected the inflammatory 1975 trial—in which Julie Roy, a 31-year-old *Esquire* secretary, successfully sued psychiatrist Renatus Hartogs for malpractice—to have had some inhibiting impact on Casanovas of the Couch. Apparently it didn't. Another survey, published a year ago, polled 1,000 Ph.D. psychologists (703 responded) and found that 5.5 percent of the males admitted to intercourse with patients, while 10.9 percent indulged in "erotic contact" (defined as "that which is primarily intended to arouse or satisfy sexual desire"). As expected, female Ph.D.s had a hands-off policy (.6 percent admitted to intercourse). Less expected was the rampant recidivism: 80 percent of all males admitting to intercourse did so with more than one patient.

—Jonathan Black,
"Pelvic Therapy,"
New Times,
December 1, 1978

"Well, the desire to fail comes from some deep psychological conviction that the consequences of failure will be *satisfying*. These girls [tested] were motivated by the opposite; they were positively anxiety-ridden over the prospect of success. They were not simply eager to fail and have done with it, they seemed to be in a state of anxious conflict over what would happen if they succeeded. It was almost as though this conflict was inhibiting their capacity for achievement."

—Matina Horner,
quoted in
"Why Women Fear Success,"
by Vivian Gornick,
Ms., Spring, 1972

I'm really alone—in good solitude—in those rare moments I can only describe as pure present. They resemble grace. They are gratuitous. Suddenly, I become alone. My self is undivided. I don't stand back, critically, and take aim at me in the second person—"You're too fat, lazy, haven't had an idea in weeks, can't write. . . ." There is no such static from my body, my ambitions, obligations, guilts, objects, from things I have left imperfect or undone. Seeing becomes simple.

—Judith Thurman,
"Living Alone,"
Ms., July, 1975

"The Movement taught women about anger—about how they were using it against themselves. Now the question of power brings up the problem of anger in a new way. How are you going to use power if you're angry? There is fear you will retaliate for old wrongs; that if you have power you will be destructive. There is also the fear you will be retaliated against for the misuse of power. I've found that as my patients start expressing their anger, their wish for power increases."

—Dale Bernstein,
quoted in "When Women Have Power Over Women,"
by Signe Hammer,
Ms., September, 1978

Psychologists have set about describing the true nature of women with an enthusiasm and absolute certainty which is rather disquieting. . . . I don't know what immutable differences exist between men and women apart from differences in their genitals; perhaps there are some other unchangeable differences; probably there are a number of irrelevant differences. But it is clear that until social expectations for men and women are equal, until we provide equal respect for both men and women, our answer to this question will simply reflect our prejudices.

—Naomi Weisstein,
"Kinder, Küche, Kirche as Scientific Law: Psychology Constructs the Female," 1969

For whether Freud's constructs are assumed to represent people's actual fantasies or (as Shulamith Firestone would have it) a system of metaphors or (as Kate Millett seems to think) just euphemisms, what really concerns feminists is the relation between those constructs and "real life." Why should a little girl assume that everyone is supposed to have a penis? Suppose she has never seen one? How can a little boy fantasize penetrating his mother if he has never observed intercourse or seen a vagina close up? Is it, perhaps, the adult who in retrospect attaches a specific meaning to the child's inchoate desires?

—Ellen Willis,
"Feminists vs. Freud: Round Two,"
Ms., August, 1974

When we hear jokes against women, and we are asked why we don't laugh at them, the answer is easy, simple, and short. Of course we're not laughing, you asshole. Nobody laughs at the sight of their own blood.

I know of no . . . traditions of women's humor. By women's humor, I don't mean women being funny. I mean a humor which recognizes a common oppression, notices its source and the roles it requires, identifies the agents of that oppression.

—Naomi Weisstein,
introduction to *All She Needs*,
drawings by Ellen Levine
(Quadrangle), 1973

We clamor to rehearse personal examples of *saying no to unfair demands*. Mary and "Dan" act out a familiar situation:
"DAN": Gee, I would like some coffee. Mary, would you make some?
MARY: Well, I'd like a cup, too, but frankly, I feel uncomfortable being the only woman here with all you men and being asked to make the coffee.
"DAN": But I didn't ask you because you're a woman; I asked you because you make damn good coffee.
MARY: Nevertheless, I'd prefer not to make it.

—Jean Withers,
"Don't Talk While I'm Interrupting . . ."
Ms., March, 1975

The physical castration of the female in some parts of Africa finds its analogical counterpart in the psychological castration of the European and American female.

—Betsy Luthuli,
The Female State, 1970

Are the women who continue to outnumber men in American psychiatric facilities (479,167 women to 478,088 men in 1964; 615,112 women to 564,749 men in 1968) really "crazy"?

And why are so many women seeking help, viewing themselves and being viewed as "neurotic" or "psychotic"?

There is a double standard of mental health—one for men, another for women—existing among most clinicians. According to a study by Dr. Inge K. Broverman, clinicians' concepts of healthy mature men do not differ significantly from their concepts of healthy mature adults. However, their concepts of healthy mature women do differ significantly from those for men and for adults. For a woman to be healthy, she must "adjust" to and accept the behavioral norms for her sex—passivity, acquiescence, self-sacrifice, and lack of ambition—even though these kinds of "loser" behaviors are generally regarded as socially undesirable (i.e., nonmasculine).

What we consider "madness," whether it appears in women or in men, is either the acting out of the devalued female role or the total or partial rejection of one's sex-role stereotype. When and if women who fully act out the female role (who are maternal, compassionate, self-sacrificing) are diagnosed or hospitalized, it is for "depression," "suicide attempts," "anxiety," and "paranoia." When and if women who reject the female role (who are angry, self-assertive, or sexually aggressive) are diagnosed or hospitalized, it is for "schizophrenia," "promiscuity," or "lesbianism." A woman who curses, or is competitive, violent, or successful; a woman who refuses to do housework is "crazy"—and "unnatural." A woman who cries all day, who talks to herself in low, frightened tones, or a woman who is insecure, timid, filled with self-contempt is a more "natural" woman—but she too is "crazy."

—Phyllis Chesler,
Women and Madness
(Doubleday), 1972

Betty Ford tosses football to her husband one week after undergoing a mastectomy in September, 1974.

HARD DECISIONS

Breast cancer is curable only when it is treated early. If you suspect you have cancer, don't delay treatment because you are afraid that the treatment will mutilate your body. Modern methods of treatment are not mutilating. . . . If your surgeon refuses to consider anything but a radical mastectomy, find one who will.

Since the results of the various treatments of breast cancer are much the same in terms of your chances of survival or cure, you have a right to join in the decision as to how you will be treated.

—George Crile Jr., M.D., *What Women Should Know About the Breast Cancer Controversy* (Macmillan), 1973

I throbbed with feelings I knew I shouldn't have: rage, self-pity, fear, frailty. I didn't like myself for having them. I liked myself in the hospital better. I liked that phony in the hospital, that Sleeping Beauty. She was good. She was cheerful. She was brave, a good sport. Everyone loved her. Who would love her now? Even her own husband was (understandably) turning against her. Where did she go, that Good Betty? I stood at the sink and thought about her. I also thought about the other Good Betty—Mrs. Ford, waving gamely with her bad arm from the White House balcony—and those other brave, good ladies. "Just fine," Happy Rockefeller had said, when a reporter asked her how she felt after her mastectomy.

And what of those other good, smiling, brave, famous ladies? Fine, they were all fine. "I'm happier than I've ever been in my life," beamed Marvella Bayh on syndicated television after her operation. What was the matter with me? I was one of the lucky ones, after all. No bad stuff in the nodes. Why was I being such a lousy sport all of a sudden?

—Betty Rollin, *First, You Cry* (Lippincott), 1976

National Archives

DOUBLE JEOPARDY

All women suffer oppression, even white women, particularly poor white women, and especially Indian, Mexican, Puerto Rican, Oriental, and black American women whose oppression is tripled by any of the above mentioned. But women do have female oppression in common. This means that we can begin to talk to other women with this common factor and start building links with them and thereby build and transform the revolutionary force we are now beginning to amass. This is what Dr. King was doing. We can no longer allow ourselves to be duped by the guise of racism. Any time the white man admits to something you know he is trying to cover something else up. We are all being exploited, even the white middle class, by the few people in control of this entire world.

—Mary Ann Weathers, "An Argument for Black Women's Liberation As a Revolutionary Force," *No More Fun & Games*, #2, 1969

Barbara Johns

Rosemary Quesada Weiner

Billie Nave Masters, Mariki Tse, Sandy Sewell, and Coretta Scott King (*left to right*) line up to read minority plank at Houston conference.

I was born in the Congo
I walked to the fertile crescent and built the Sphinx
I designed a pyramid so tough that a star
that only glows every one hundred years falls
into the center giving divine perfect light
I am bad

I sat on the throne
drinking nectar with Allah
I got hot and sent an ice age to europe to cool my thirst
My oldest daughter is Nefertiti
the tears from my birth pains
created the nile
I am a beautiful woman

—from "Ego-Tripping," by Nikki Giovanni, 1970

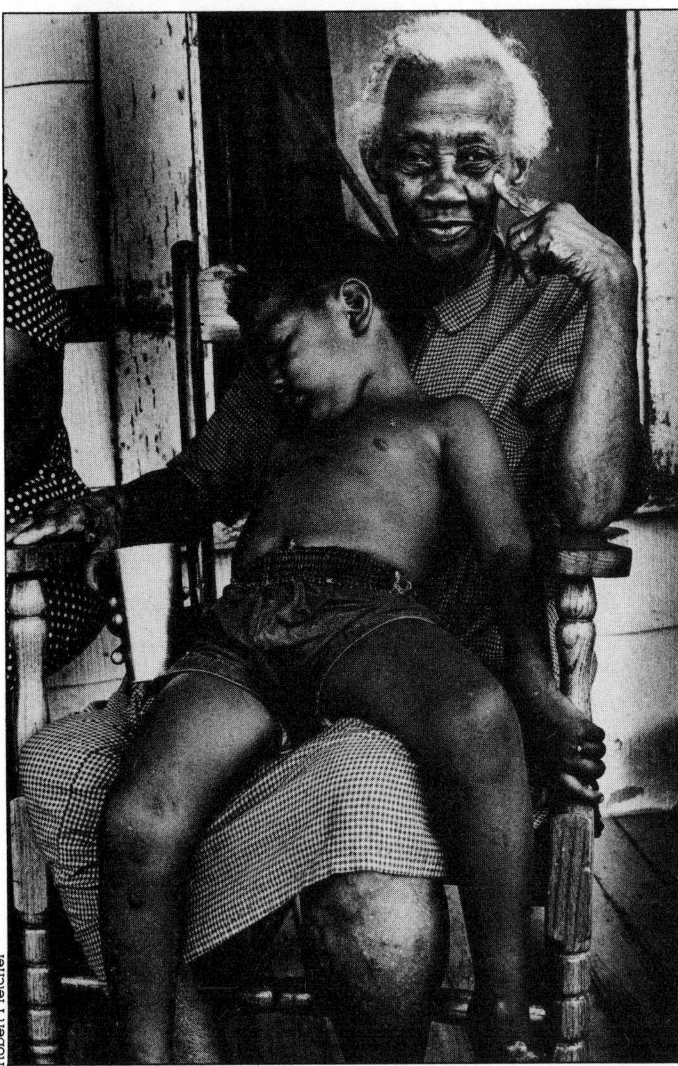
Robert Fletcher

But when, you will ask, did my overworked mother have time to know or care about feeding the creative spirit?

The answer is so simple that many of us have spent years discovering it. We have constantly looked high, when we should have looked high—and low.

For example: in the Smithsonian Institution in Washington, D.C., there hangs a quilt unlike any other in the world. In fanciful, inspired, and yet simple and identifiable figures, it portrays the story of the Crucifixion. It is considered rare, beyond price. Though it follows no known pattern of quiltmaking, and though it is made of bits and pieces of worthless rags, it is obviously the work of a person of powerful imagination and deep spiritual feeling. Below this quilt I saw a note that says it was made by "an anonymous Black woman in Alabama, a hundred years ago."

If we could locate this "anonymous" Black woman from Alabama, she would turn out to be one of our grandmothers—an artist who left her mark in the only materials she could afford, and in the only medium her position in society allowed her to use.

As Virginia Woolf wrote further, in *A Room of One's Own:*

"Yet genius of a sort must have existed among women as it must have existed among the working class. [Change this to *slaves* and *the wives and daughters of sharecroppers.*] Now and again an Emily Brontë or a Robert Burns [change this to *a Zora Hurston or a Richard Wright*] blazes out and proves its presence. But certainly it never got itself on to paper. When, however, one reads of a witch being ducked, of a woman possessed by devils [or *Sainthood*], of a wise woman selling herbs [our rootworkers], or even a very remarkable man who had a mother, then I think we are on the track of a lost novelist, a suppressed poet, of some mute and inglorious Jane Austen. . . . Indeed, I would venture to guess that Anon, who wrote so many poems without signing them, was often a woman. . . ."

—Alice Walker,
"In Search of Our Mother's Gardens,"
Ms., May, 1974

". . . black people, having been deprived of the ability to follow the pattern of American family life, have a chance to start anew, to build a different kind of life where men and women are equal."

—Eleanor Holmes Norton,
"The Black Family and Feminism,"
by Cellestine Ware,
Ms., Spring, 1972

Though originally it was the white man who was responsible for the black woman's grief, a multiplicity of forces act upon her life now and the black man is one of the most important. The white man is downtown. The black man lives with her. He's the head of her church and may be the principal of her local school or even the mayor of the city in which she lives.

She is the workhorse that keeps his house functioning, she is the foundation of his community, she raises his children, and she faithfully votes for him in elections, goes to his movies, reads his books, watches him on television, buys in his stores, solicits his services as doctor, lawyer, accountant.

The black man has not really kept his part of the bargain they made in the '60s. When she stood by silently as he became a "man," she assumed that he would finally glorify and dignify black womanhood just as the white man had done for the white woman. But he did not. He refused her. His involvement with white women was only the most dramatic form that refusal took.

—Michele Wallace,
Black Macho and the Myth of the Superwomen
(Dial), 1979

Michele Wallace adds a new chapter to the sexual politics of black women and men.

Ellie Thompson

"Our role is to support anything positive in black life, and destroy anything negative that touches it. You have no other reason for being. I don't understand art for art's sake. Art is the guts of the people."

—Elma Lewis, *Ms.*, May, 1977

Peter Southwick

Elma Lewis, founder of the Elma Lewis School of Fine Arts, Roxbury, Mass.

Official and unofficial attempts to blunt the effects of the egalitarian tendencies between the black man and woman should come as no surprise. The matriarch concept, embracing the "female castrator" cliché is a weapon of open ideological warfare. Black men and women alike remain its potential victims—men unconsciously lunging at the woman, equating her with the myth; women sinking back into the shadows, lest an aggressive posture resurrect the myth. . . .

—Angela Davis, "On Black Women," *Ms.*, August, 1972

Furthermore, since every one of these movements calls for liberation of some kind, it has become necessary to try and define what liberation apparently signifies to the Black Movement, the Third World Movement, and the Women's Movement, respectively. In this effort. . . I have met with rigid formulations and stifling analyses such that membership in one movement must seem to discredit your support of any other.

—June Jordan, "Second Thoughts of a Black Feminist," *Ms.*, January, 1977

"Being head of the [Black Panther] party is hard work. I'm honored and proud to carry out our program, but I don't like the position because it leaves me vulnerable. I'm not happy being a target."

—Elaine Brown, *Ms.*, March, 1976

There is a lot of speculation about the uniqueness of black women's economic progress. It has been said that black women have benefited doubly, both as blacks and as women; that we have outpaced black men in obtaining the available jobs; that we earn more than other women; and that our economic position is to be envied rather than deplored.

These popular myths do not consider the statistical evidence: black women are still economically disadvantaged. While there have been singular outstanding achievements, they are the exception. The yardstick for measuring how far black women as a group actually have come must be applied to their employment and unemployment status, occupational distribution, earnings, education, and incidence of poverty. If we examine changes that have taken place in the 1970s, when efforts resulting from legislation to help eliminate sex and race bias were under way, we see that black women wage earners still are relatively low on the economic yardstick, and this status penalizes not only black women, but their families and in fact, the entire black community.

—Alexis M. Herman, "Still . . . Small Change for Black Women," *Ms.*, February, 1979

Be it resolved . . . That we, as *Chicanas*, will promote *la hermanidad* [sisterhood] concept in organizing *Chicanas*. As *hermanas*, we have a responsibility to help each other in problems that are common to all of us. . . . That *Chicanas* be represented in all levels of *La Raza Unida* party and be run as candidates in all general, primary, and local elections. . . . That *Chicanas* receive equal pay for equal work; working conditions be improved; *Chicanas* join unions and hold leadership positions; *Chicanas* be given the opportunity for promotions and be given free training to improve skills; there be maternity leaves with pay. . . . That we endorse legalized medical abortions in order to protect the human right of self-determination. Be it also resolved that *Chicanas* are to control the process to its completion. In addition, we feel that the sterilization process must *never* be administered without full knowledge and consent of the individual involved.

—Demands of Women of *La Raza Unida*, 1972

"We have applied to the United Nations for sovereignty. We want recognition from the United States. [We] believe the white man is destroying the land. . . . The Indian believes man is only equal to all living things. All are part of the Great Spirit. We can take a lesson from the animals who never kill more than they can eat. The white man breaks the rules of nature. He will destroy himself."

—Lorelei Means, *Ms.*, July, 1976

"Lie to Americans. Tell them you were born during the San Francisco earthquake. Tell them your birth certificate and your parents were burned up in the fire. Don't report crimes; tell them we have no crimes and no poverty. Give a new name every time you get arrested; the ghosts won't recognize you. Pay the new immigrants twenty-five cents an hour and say we have no unemployment. And, of course, tell them we'reagainstCommunism."

—Maxine Hong Kingston, *The Woman Warrior: Memoirs of a Girlhood Among Ghosts* (Knopf), 1976

The sensitive woman from a colonized people also recognizes that many times it has been easier for her economically than for the men of her group. Often she can get a job where a man cannot. She can see the damage done to the men as a result, and feels reluctant to risk threatening their self-respect even further. This may be a short-range viewpoint involving false definitions of manhood, but it is created by immediate realities whose force cannot merely be wished away. It is also a fact that in many Chicano families, the woman makes many of the important decisions—not just consumer decisions—though the importance of her role will be recognized only privately. This may seem hypocritical or like a double standard, but the knowldege of having real influence affects how the Chicana feels.

—Elizabeth Sutherland, Introduction to "Colonized Women: the Chicana" *Sisterhood Is Powerful* (Random House), 1970

LNS

Chinese-American sign carrier at International Woman's Day, March, 1975.

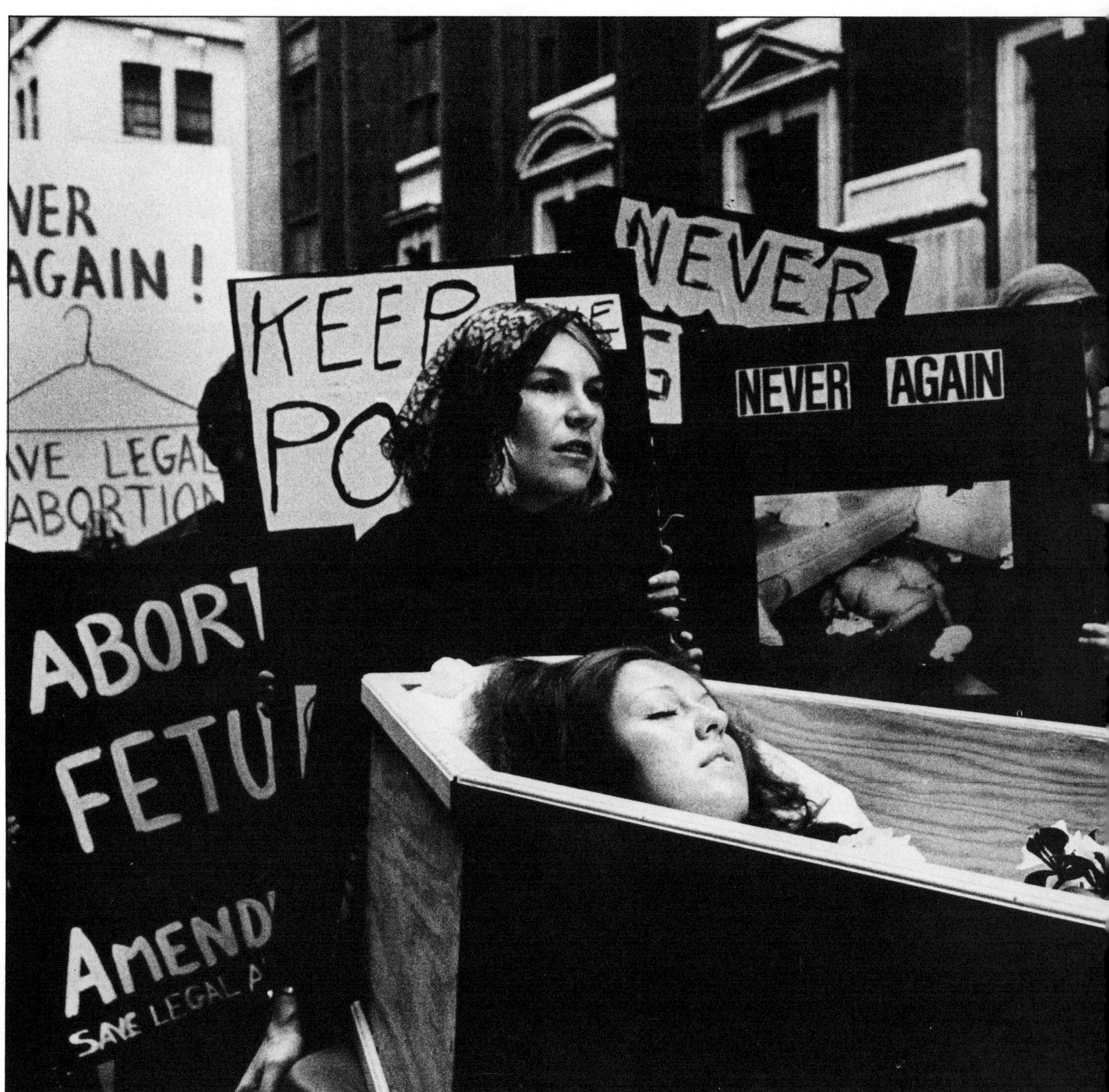
VER
AGAIN !
AVE LEGAL
ABORTION
KEEP
PO
NEVER
NEVER AGAIN
ABORT
FETU
AMEND
SAVE LEGAL

REPRODUCTIVE FREEDOM

Bettye Lane

1973 "street theater" demonstration dramatizes the death of a woman from an illegal abortion ("Never Again" placard).

On Monday morning, January 22, 1973, the Court handed down the decision in the Texas case (Roe v. Wade) that stated: the right to privacy "is broad enough to encompass a woman's decision whether or not to terminate her pregnancy."

Justice Harry A. Blackmun, writing for a majority of seven of the nine justices, summarized the opinion of the Court as follows:

"1. A State criminal abortion statute of the current Texas type, that excepts from criminality only a *life saving* procedure on behalf of the mother, without recognition of the other interests involved, is violative of the Due Process Clause of the Fourteenth Amendment.
(a) For the stage prior to approximately the end of the first trimester, the abortion decision and its effectuation must be left to the medical judgment of the pregnant woman's attending physician.
(b) For the stage subsequent to approximately the end of the first trimester, the State, in promoting its interest in the health of the mother, may, if it chooses, regulate the abortion procedure in ways that are reasonably related to maternal health.
(c) For the stage subsequent to viability, the State, in promoting its interest in the potentiality of human life, may, if it chooses, regulate, and even proscribe, abortion except where it is necessary, in appropriate medical judgment, for the preservation of the life or health of the mother."

In addition, the Supreme Court's opinion in the Georgia case (Doe v. Bolton) invalidates the following requirements contained in the Georgia statute:

1. The requirement that the abortion be performed in a hospital accredited by the Joint Commission on Accreditation of Hospitals.
2. The requirement that the abortion be approved by a hospital committee.
3. The requirements of confirmation by two Georgia licensed physicians in addition to the recommendation of the pregnant woman's own consultant.
4. The requirement that the woman be a bona fide resident of Georgia.

—*Ms.*, October, 1973

> "The literal alternatives to [abortion] are suicide, motherhood, and, some would add, madness. Consequently, there is some confusion, discomfort, and cynicism greeting efforts to 'find' or 'emphasize' or 'identify' alternatives to abortion."
>
> —Connie J. Downey, director of Women's Action Program, Department of Health, Education, and Welfare, internal working paper, Fall, 1977

Bettye Lane

Right—**Activist Bill Baird displays "alternatives" to safe abortions.** Below—**Pro-choice pickets march on New York City offices of Right-to-Life.**

Laura Landy/LNS

Bettye Lane

Rosie took the piece of paper and a pen. Pauline helped prop her up so that she could write. It took Rosie a while to steady herself, but she was able to scribble some words before the pen fell from her hand. Pauline helped her back into position and straightened out the sheet. The paper was lying on her chest. Pauline lifted it up to the light above the bed. She could not understand the writing. The first word looked like "Please." There was a "me" and another word that started with a "p." "Please . . . me . . . p . . ." Pauline looked carefully at the last word. She got it. P e a c e. Now the whole sentence fell into place. "Please let me die in peace." Pauline turned her head so Rosie would not see her tears.

—Ellen Frankfort, *Rosie: The Investigation of a Wrongful Death* with Afterword by Frances Kissling (Dial), 1979.

Far left—**Rosie Jimenez dies on October 3, 1977, first victim of the restriction of Medicaid funds for abortions.** Below—**Dr. Kenneth Edelin speaks out for the "right to choose."**

Bettye Lane

"Obviously, the decision to perform abortions was not easy for me to make. I don't think it is for any physician, male or female, black or white. But I know what genocide is—and it isn't doing legal abortions. Black women have suffered and died from botched, illegal abortions. *That* is genocide. . . I'm not promoting abortion—I'm for the right to make a choice."

—Dr. Kenneth Edelin (whose conviction for manslaughter in Boston for performing a legal abortion was overturned in 1976) August, 1975

"The Supreme Court decision was too fast and too easy. The grass roots of the country weren't prepared for it. The issue hadn't developed properly at that level."

—Patricia Beyea, director of American Civil Liberties Union Campaign for Choice, June, 1978

. . . A comprehensive pro-life legislative program must . . . include the following elements: a) passage of a constitutional amendment providing protection for the unborn child to the maximum degree possible; b) passage of federal and state laws and adoption of administrative policies that will restrict the practice of abortion as much as possible; c) continual research into and refinement and precise interpretation of *Roe* and *Doe* and subsequent court decisions; d) support for legislation that provides alternatives to abortion.

—"Pastoral Plan for Pro-Life Activities," Catholic bishops of the United States, November, 1975

"Without the institutional backing of the Catholic Church, the pro-life movement would be a much less visible force. There is no other single institution that has gotten involved in such a visible way. The church has provided money, local organization, shock troops, and even mimeo machines."

—Barbara Lindheim, senior research associate, Alan Guttmacher Institute, June, 1978

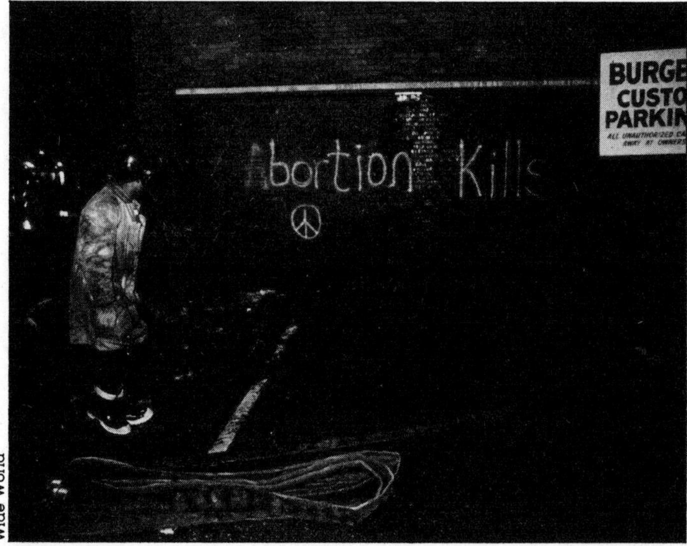

Wide World

"If men could become pregnant, abortion would be a sacrament"

—Flo Kennedy, 1970

Above—**Planned Parenthood Clinic, St. Paul, Minnesota, is firebombed, February, 1977.** Right, opposite page—**Right-to-Life advocates take to the streets.**

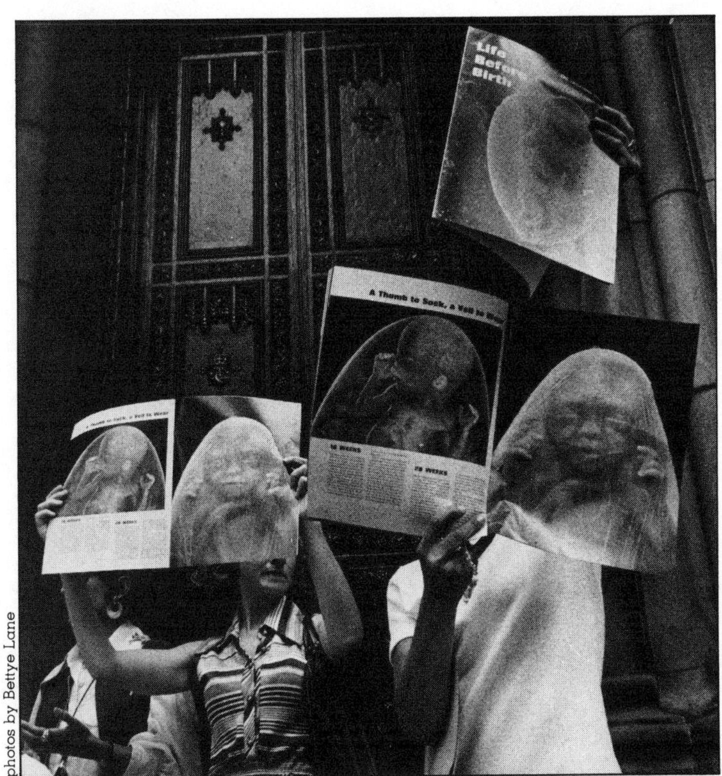

photos by Bettye Lane

70% of Americans agreed that Medicaid should pay for abortions for poor women "under all circumstances" or "under certain circumstances."

—Gallup Poll, June, 1979

1.3 million legal abortions were performed in 1977.

In fiscal 1977, 295,000 abortions were paid for by Medicaid. The projected Medicaid abortion total for fiscal 1978 is 88,000.

—Alan Guttmacher Institute, 1978

76% of Roman Catholics, 82% of Protestants, and 98% of Jews agreed that "if a woman wants to have an abortion, that is a matter for her and her doctor to decide and the government should have nothing to do with it."

—Knight-Ridder Newspapers, 1976 survey in 21 cities

There are between 2 and 3 deaths per 100,000 abortions compared to between 12 and 14 maternal deaths per 100,000 pregnancies carried to term.

91.5 percent of abortions are performed during the first trimester of pregnancy.

Among women who have abortions, 67 percent are white; about one third are aged 19 or younger, one third between 20 and 24, and one third 25 or older.

—Center for Disease Control, 1977 data

Nancy Crampton

" I was given the gifts of the artist, and the trouble that goes with them: So I have that blessing, and there was never a time that I questioned it or doubted it. . . . For forty years, I wanted to jump out of windows. "

—Louise Nevelson, 1975

There *are* no women equivalents for Michelangelo or Rembrandt, Delacroix or Cézanne, Picasso or Matisse, or even, in very recent times, for Wilhem de Kooning or Warhol, any more than there are black American equivalents for the same. . . . The fault lies not in our stars, our hormones, our menstrual cycles, or our empty internal spaces, but in our institutions and our education—education understood to include everything that happens to us from the moment we enter, head first, into this world of meaningful symbols, signs, and signals. The miracle is, in fact, that given the overwhelming odds against women, or blacks, so many of both have managed to achieve so much excellence—if not towering grandeur—in those bailiwicks of white masculine prerogative like science, politics, or the arts.

—Linda Nochlin, "Why There Have Been No Great Women Artists," *Art News*, January, 1971

In 1970, a group of New York women artists stormed the Whitney Museum. They were appalled and desperate over their paltry representation in the museum's prestigious showcase, The Annual. Across the country, another group examined the history of the Los Angeles County Museum of Art and exposed its buying habits—of the thousands and thousands of art works in the permanent collection, a scant 2 percent were done by women.

The "invisible" women artists decided to declare their rage—and their presence. . . . Groups and newsletters emerged in Chicago, Minneapolis, Kansas City, New York, Atlanta, San Francisco, Los Angeles, Seattle, Iowa City. Women artists moved to show their work—mostly by forming co-ops and slide registries, and by mounting exhibitions outside the gallery and museum mainstream; sophisticated publications, educational programs, and workshops sprouted; and historians successfully combed the past for overlooked ancestors.

—Harriet Lyons, "The Arts Explosion Will Change Your Life," *Ms.*, December, 1977

THE ARTS

Erasing the line between "high" art and "craft": (*left*) Miriam Schapiro; (*below left*) modern version of quilting bee; (*right*) Howardina Pindell.

Ellie Thompson

"I question the negative connotations of fabric, of ribbon, of lace. I turn these symbols of our imprisonment around."

—Miriam Schapiro, 1977

Suzanne Opton

Ellie Thompson

The textile and needlework arts of the world, primarily because they have been the work of women have been especially written out of art history. It is a male idea that to be 'high' and 'fine' both women and art should be beautiful, but not useful or functional.

—Patricia Mainardi, "Quilts: The Great American Art," *Feminist Art Journal*, Winter, 1973

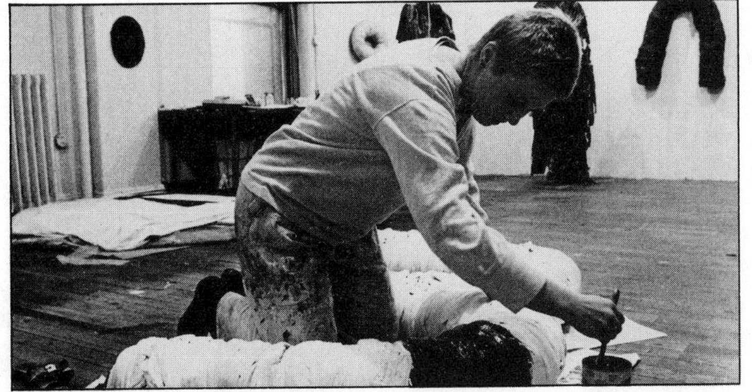

Left—**Harmony Hammond.** Below—**Faith Ringgold.**

> "After I decided to be an artist, the first thing that I had to believe was that I, a black woman, could penetrate the art scene, and that, further, I could do so without sacrificing one iota of my blackness or femaleness or my humanity."
>
> —Faith Ringgold, 1973

"When a woman artist positively identifies herself to us through her work, she commits a courageous and daring act of self exposure, because her contribution has neither spoken to nor been understood by the mainstream of the culture, and the content of her art has been bypassed by interpretations which could not reveal it. Thus a woman's saying, 'I am, I know myself, and I feel a fundamental optimism—a grasp upon my own survival as a model for human survival' is saying something which challenges the prevailing worldview. If consciousness is the content of feminist art, this level of human responsibility and hope is the content of consciousness."

—Arlene Raven, art critic, quoted in *The New Woman's Survival Catalog*, edited by Kirsten Grimstad and Susan Rennie (Coward, McCann & Geoghegan), 1973

photos by Ellie Thompson

Women artists cannot escape exploring their own sexuality, because the connection between sex and inspiration is intimate. They are both forms of intense energy. They connect and correspond. The relationship between the artist and the Muse is a sexual relationship in which it is impossible to tell who is fucking and who is being fucked. If sex and creativity are often seen by dictators as subversive activities, it's because they lead to the knowledge that you own your own body (and with it your own voice), and that's the most revolutionary insight of all.

—Erica Jong, "The Artist as Housewife, The Housewife as Artist," *Ms.*, December, 1972

My goal with *The Dinner Party* was consistent with all my efforts in the previous decade. I had been trying to establish a respect for women and women's art; to forge a new kind of art expressing women's experience; and to find a way to make that art accessible to a large audience. I firmly believe that if art speaks clearly about something relevant to people's lives, it can change the way they perceive reality. In a similar way medieval art had been used to teach the Bible to illiterate people. Since most of the world is illiterate in terms of women's history and contributions to culture, it seemed appropriate to relate our history through art, particularly through techniques traditionally associated with women—china-painting and needlework.

—Judy Chicago, *The Dinner Party: A Symbol of Our Heritage* (Anchor Press/Doubleday), 1979

There is a lot of sexual imagery in women's art—circles, domes, eggs, spheres, boxes, biomorphic shapes, maybe a certain striation or layering. . . . Men's work isn't so much cliché-aggressive, all angles and phallic, as it's closed—the "this is *my* image" number. Women are, for all kinds of reasons, more open, into themselves in a very different way.

—Lucy Lippard, "What Is Female Imagery?" *Ms.*, May, 1975

photos courtesy of The Dinner Party Project

Opposite page top—**Judy Chicago stands before her table set for 39 real and mythological "lost" heroines of history. It takes five years and 400 co-workers to complete "The Dinner Party."** Below—**Ceramic plates for Sojourner Truth, Hatshepsut, Theodora, and needlework details from Hrosvitha runner.**

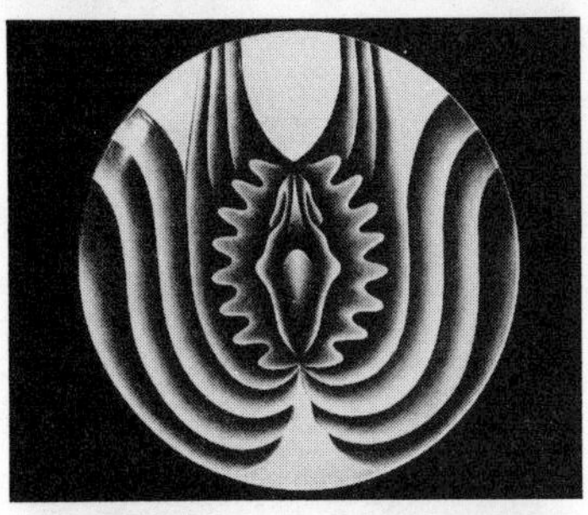

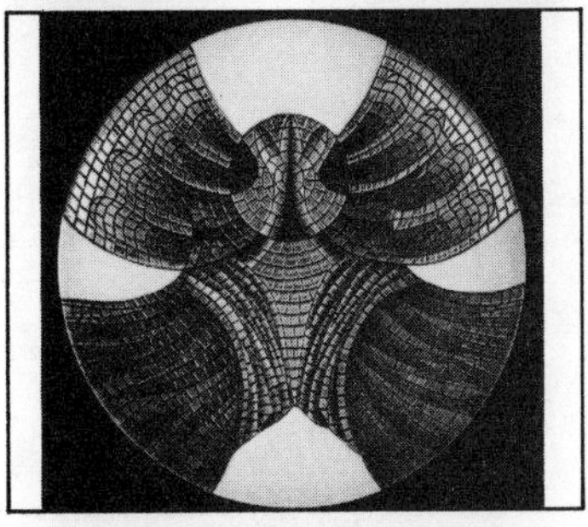

Carole A. Rosen/WCA

A few months after its opening in November, 1973, the Woman's Building [co-founded by Arlene Raven, Sheila de Bretteville, and Judy Chicago] was a Los Angeles landmark. . . . it brought together galleries, workshops, studios, and stores that have produced a staggering number of creations by women. . . .

Here, for the first time, women have had control of all aspects of the art-making process, from education through exhibition. One Woman's Building tenant, the Feminist Studio Workshop, is the first institution in the United States to offer degrees in feminist art education.

—Shirley Koploy, "The Women's Building Alive and Living in L.A.," *Ms.*, October, 1974

Above—**The Women's Caucus for Art presents in January, 1979 its first annual awards for outstanding achievement. The recipients, Alice Neel, Selma Burke, Isabel Bishop (*left to right*), are honored in the White House by President Carter and Joan Mondale. (Not shown are two other winners, Georgia O'Keeffe and Louise Nevelson.)** Left—**Nancy Hanks, now a director of Rockefeller Brothers Fund, serves as Chair of the National Endowment for the Arts, 1969-1977, and secures record-breaking funding from Congress.**

FILM

"Growing Up Female" (1970)

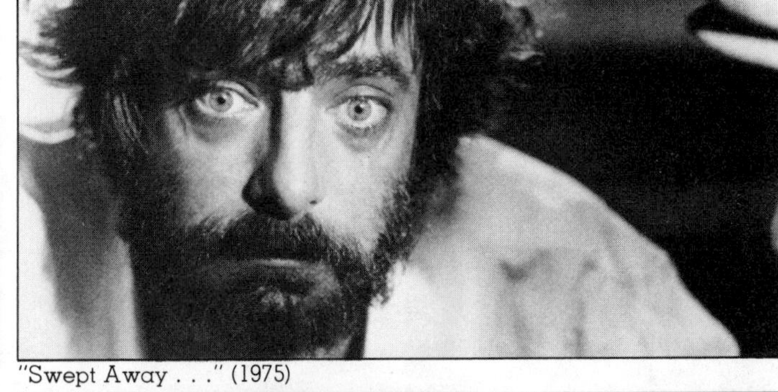
"Swept Away . . ." (1975)

"Alice Doesn't Live Here Anymore" (1974)

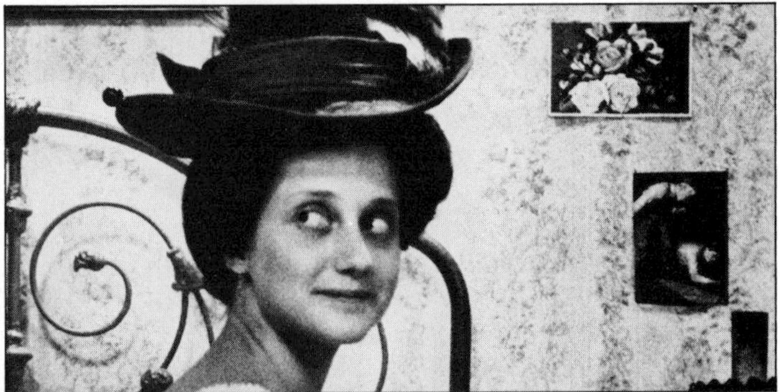
"Hester Street" (1976)

"A Woman Under The Influence" (1974)

"Taxi Driver" (1976)

"The Way We Were" (1974)

"Harlan County, U.S.A." (1976)

"3 Women" (1977)

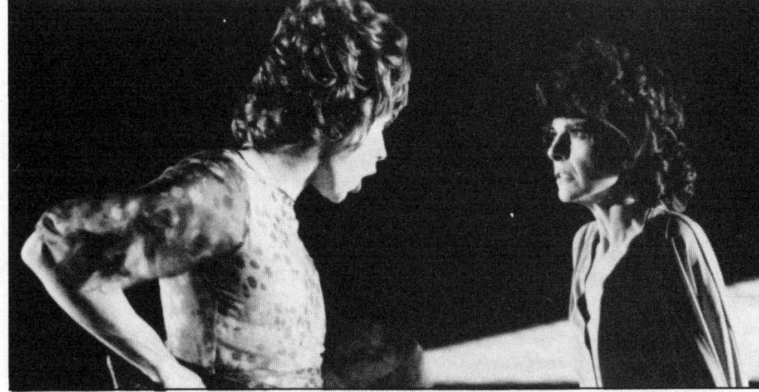
"Turning Point" (1978)

"One Sings, The Other Doesn't"(1977)

"Girlfriends" (1978)

"Looking For Mr. Goodbar" (1977)

"With Babies and Banners: the Women's Emergency Brigade" (1978)

"An Unmarried Woman" (1978)

"Moment By Moment" (1978)

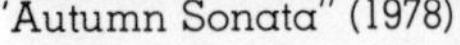
"Autumn Sonata" (1978)

"Klute" (1971)

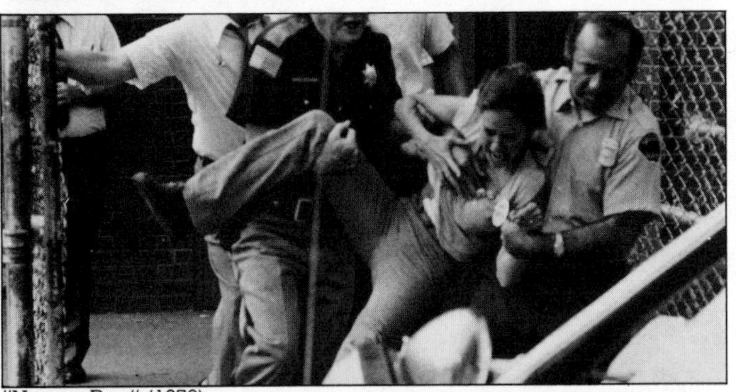
"Norma Rae" (1979)

"Julia" (1977)

"Alien" (1979)

"Coming Home" (1978)

"Kramer vs. Kramer" (1979)

"It's the first time I've been given a role ['Julia'] in which I'm allowed to feel and express friendship for another woman."

—Jane Fonda,
Ms., October, 1977

How will women break through the barriers of a commercial cinema more truly monolithic in its sexism than it ever was in the old days of Hollywood? Where are the women to create new fictions, to go beyond the inner space—as women are doing every day in real life—into the outer world of invention, action, imagination? The women involved in the creative end of commercial films are an illustrious handful. . . .Only outside the industry, in independent filmmaking (or in Europe), is there anything that could call itself a woman's cinema. In documentaries like Nell Cox's *A to B*, Kate Millett's *Three Lives*, Claudia Weill's *Joyce at 34*, Amalie Rothschild's *It Happened to Us*, Julia Reichert and Jim Klein's *Growing Up Female*, and a host of others, women are exploring the "inner space" of their conditioning, discovering long-suppressed anger, contending with the conflicting demands of their lives as mothers and professionals, and finding relief and moral support in a shared experience.

—Molly Haskell,
From Reverence to Rape: The Treatment of Women in the Movies
(Holt, Rinehart and Winston), 1974

The paradoxes in Woody Allen's comedy would seem obvious enough—the simultaneous feeling of horniness and timidity, of sexual obsession and sexual fear, of rapist and virgin—but I think they're more complicated than that. The reason I and so many men I know identify so deeply with his comedy isn't because we secretly regard ourselves as sexual failures. On the contrary, it's because the very man who's built his entire career on his worship of women unconsciously expresses a misogyny we secretly feel but won't admit.

—Ross Wetzsteon,
"Woody Allen: Schlemiel as Sex Maniac,"
Ms., November, 1977

"Annie Hall" (1977)

"Manhattan" (1979)

Through Cicely Tyson's Rebecca [the younger mother in the 1972 "Sounder"], the American audience was introduced to a typical black mother and wife: hardworking, resilient, vigilant, and above all, sensitive. Rebecca functions basically as a follower and sustainer, taking the lead only when conditions (in this case, the imprisonment of her husband) demand that she do so. The role is historically accurate because the black family, no less than the white, is patriarchal, with or without the father present.

—Yvonne,
"The Importance of Cicely Tyson,"
Ms., August, 1974

Bill King

THEATRE

Nancy Crampton

But what of the woman playwright? Virginia Woolf provides the most famous myth. "Let me imagine,' she writes [in a *Room of One's Own*], ". . . what would have happened had Shakespeare had a wonderfully gifted sister, called Judith . . . [who] had the quickest fancy, a gift like her brother's, for the tune of words." This Judith, she continues, "was befriended by Nick Greene, the actor-manager, and found herself with child by that gentleman and so . . . killed herself one winter's night and lies buried at some crossroads where the omnibuses now stop outside the Elephant and Castle."

I had not read *A Room of One's Own* in college but I had internalized the myth of Shakespeare's sister. One aspiring female dramatist was a class-mate. . . . My male cohorts, also in the class, said her writing was "pretty good"—but none of them produced her plays. I never even had a conversation with her. Women should not be playwrights, I theorized from my vantage point in the drama club office where I typed rehearsal schedules. Now I admire her guts.

—Honor Moore,
The New Women's Theatre
(Vantage), 1977

Marianne Barcellona

AP Newsfeatures

Above—**Ellen Stewart, founder of La Mama, one of the few female-owned and directed companies in the country.** Center—**Lynne Meadow, director of the flourishing Manhattan Theatre Club.** Below—**In 1978 American Place Theatre receives first-of-its-kind $80,000 Ford Foundation grant to women playwrights. Julia Miles (*left foreground*), APT's associate producer, heads the Women's Project. Some of the participating playwrights include: (*from left*) Sally Ordway, Patricia Bosworth, France Burke, Sybille Pearson, and Sophy Burnham; (*seated*) Marti Evans Charles, Honor Moore, and Rose Leiman Goldemberg.**

Paul Davis

this ain't yr stuff/put me back
& let me hang out in my own
self
gimme my things
I want my arm wif the hot
iron scar & my leg
the flea bit/i want my
calloused feet & quick
language back/in my mouth
stealing my shit from me/
don't make it yrs
wid alla
my shit/& it was standin there
lookin at myself the whole
time
what ya gotta get from me/i'll
give it to ya/give it to ya/give
it ya/round 5:00 in the winter
when the sky is blue-red
& da city is getting pressed/if
its really my stuff
ya got/ya gotta give it to me/
if ya want it i'm the only one
can handle it

—Ntozake Shange,
"Somebody almost walked off
wid alla my stuff,"
For Colored Girls . . .

If there is one artist whose work best symbolizes the [women's] arts explosion, it is Ntozake Shange. Her choreo-poem, "For Colored Girls . . .," breaks the boundaries between poetry and theater, dance and realism, verbal meters and jazz rhythms, street talk and "high art." Nurtured by both the new voices of black poets and the shared vision of feminist groups, Shange has burst into the nation's consciousness without compromise, and with an art that speaks real life.

—Gloria Steinem,
Ms., December, 1977

MUSIC

" . . . when I wrote ['I Am Woman'] two years ago, I was trying to make a personal statement. I had just passed through a period of time when my ego had been almost totally demolished. I was sitting up in bed one night thinking that if I'd survived that, I could survive anything, and those lines just came into my head: *If I have to, I can do anything. I am strong; I am invincible; I am woman.*

"Also it was very important to me to make a positive statement. I can't bear all those *Take me back, baby/ I'm down on my knees/ If you don't screw me, I'll just die* songs that women are supposed to sing. When I choose songs for my albums, I look for the lyrics first of all to be absolutely truthful in terms of my own experience. "

—Helen Reddy, quoted in "And Now Here's . . . Helen Reddy," by Susan Lydon, *Ms.*, July, 1973

Iris Schneider

Jeff Albertson

Far Left—**Octogenarian blues singer Alberta Hunter makes a successful comeback.** Left—**Composer Pozzi Eschot.** Below—**Bette Midler.**

Bill King

. . .The Divine Miss M.—the woman who's going to do for the seventies what Mick Jagger did for the sixties. . . .

What Bette Midler expresses about our shared-in-common sexuality is dangerous news. She is straining the image of the woman-whore to bursting. The ravening masochism of "I Shall Be Released," for instance, is double-edged-feminine and self-exploiting in the worst way and yet full of hatred for it. Remember me, she growls in the sappy mask of old songs, I am the broken world of love that never worked for anyone.

—Dale McConathy, "Why Bette Midler?," *Ms.*, August, 1973

"I don't know if I could change my face, present a more institutional face to people now that I'm no longer a singer. I'm going to continue about my business as I am, and let the quality of my work be the point. . . .I really do believe I can accomplish a great deal with a big grin. I know some people find that diconcerting, but that doesn't matter."

—Beverly Sills,
general director of
New York City Opera, 1979

Hang in there,
A little bit longer
Though I know it's been
too long
For so many years you
have been fighting,
For so many years you
have been strong.

"Hang in There,"
by Holly Near. ©1973
Hereford Music Company

Twice I was a mother
Once I was a wife
Tore off all the labels
Now all that's left is life
And the changing, oh the
changing
Tomorrow I wonder who I'll be
Got a scrapbook filled with
photographs
And none of them,
Not one of them is me.

—"Changing," music by Nancy Ford, lyrics by Gretchen Cryer.

Inge Morath/Magnum

Left—**Gretchen Cryer (right) and Nancy Ford make women's experience the stuff of hit songs and musicals (*I'm Getting My Act Together . . . and I'm Taking It On the Road*).** Below right—**"Sweet Honey in the Rock," (*left to right*) Evelyn Harris, Yasmeen Williams, Tulani Jordan and Bernice Reagon, express their identities and vision as black women.** Below left—**Beverly Sills enjoys new vantage point.**

Sylvia Plachy

Sharon C. Farmer

Every woman who ever
loved a woman
You oughtta stand up and
call her name:
Mother, sister, daughter,
lover . . . —"Every Woman"

Words and music
by Bernice Johnson Reagon,
©1978, all rights reserved,
used by permission.

The lyrics she [Elizabeth Swados] has chosen for illumination by her music [in "Nightclub Cantata"] have one thing in common; when they are finished with us, we know more about human feeling than before. . . .Swados herself sings a bird lament which is exactly that. A bird, grieving. I wish I could explain to you how like a breaking heart that bird sounded. . . . But until Elizabeth Swados sang it to me, I didn't know birds had the power to express *human* heartbreak.

—Susan Dworkin, "A Sound Track for Emotions," *Ms.*, June, 1977

DANCE

Martha Swope

[Twyla Tharp's] style draws on all kinds of movement—tap, ballet, jazz, and social dancing; the way skaters move or the way Groucho Marx propelled himself bent-kneed across a stage—but it looks only fleetingly like anything else and assumes instead an identity of its own. And it is always, always elegant. Tharp's works [performed, *left*, by herself and Baryshnikov] cajole, nudge, and finally threaten to explode dance forward into new forms. They are also fun to watch.

—Amanda Smith, "Twyla Tharp: Dance Will Never Be Quite the Same," *Ms.*, December 1976

Gwen Phillips

Much of [choreographer Trisha Brown's] work is a witty revelation of the basic awkwardness of physical activity, as well as its risk, even when performed by dancers.

—Jennifer Dunning, "Dance Is Climbing the Walls ...," *Ms.*, December, 1977

Her body arches, as if from sleep.
She begins to dance . . .
She creates her own space, and
fills it, dancing . . .
She is the center of a world.

—Alice Walker, "Judith Jamison Dances 'Cry,' " *Ms.*, May, 1973. ('Cry' is dedicated to 'All black women everywhere—especially our mothers.')

TV

"The Mary Tyler Moore Show" (1973)

Mary [Richards of "The Mary Tyler Moore Show"] is over 30, unmarried and not the least in a panic about it, actually appears to have a sex life, and is neither stupid nor helpless. . . . Still, she has her problems.

Mary is supposedly the associate producer, which would make her second in command on her evening news show. Yet she addresses the producer (the dominant male) as Mr. Grant, and he calls her Mary. . . . Mere writers on the show call him Lou. They, of course, are men, so it's okay.

—Gail Rock,
"Same Time, Same Station Same Sexism,"
Ms., December, 1973

"Mary Hartman, Mary Hartman" (1975)

[Mary Hartman] tries to be a good mother, a loving wife, an interesting sex partner, and a thorough housewife. She waxes her floors relentlessly, sanitizes the toilet every Friday, borrows library books to solve her sexual problems, takes Geritol twice a day, and waits for happiness and fulfillment to find her. . . . The men in the show—particularly her husband Tom—are as trapped on the assembly line as Mary is in the kitchen, bound by rules and regulations that reduce them to the powerlessness of little boys. And they are, if anything, even more out of touch with themselves. Mary, at least, risks asking the questions.

—Stephanie Harrington,
"Mary Hartman, The Unedited, All American Unconscious,"
Ms., May, 1976

Bob Hastings

Donahue with producer McMillen.

"Women have passed by the covered-dishes-and-needlepoint stage. I think they appreciate the issues the show raises and enjoy the challenge of getting emotionally and intellectually involved in what's happening. There are no prizes and nobody screams; we put on an honest sharing of ideas."

— Phil Donahue,
People, April 27, 1979

"An American Family" (1973)

A psychiatrist told a friend of mine recently that in his experience he'd found that there is almost always a third force present when divorce finally happens. The miserable marriage can wobble on for years on end, until something or somebody comes along and pushes one of the people over the brink. . . . It's usually another man . . . or another woman . . . or possibly a supportive psychiatrist; in my case, it was a whole production staff and a camera crew. . . .

—Pat Loud,
Pat Loud: A Woman's Story
(Coward, McCann & Geoghegan), 1974

In a 1977 hour-long segment of "All in the Family," Edith is confronted by a rapist, and rape is dealt with as a violent crime.

Edie Baskin

"Saturday Night Live" (1974)

Gilda Radner, Jane Curtin, and Laraine Newman are, for my money, three of the six most seriously funny women in American television today. The other three are Rosie Shuster, Anne Beatts, and Marilyn Miller, [NBC "Saturday Night]'s female writers. By daring to show women calling each other "bitch" as Emily Litella is likely to do in her cranky encounters with Jane Curtin and doing funny bits about diets and clothes and men, the writers and actresses are saying: "we've transcended all that; we're strong enough and confident enough with who we are now to go back and make irreverent fun of what just yesterday was embarrassing dust to be swept under the political rug."—Sheila Weller, "What Some Women Do For Laughs on Saturday Night,' *Ms.*, October, 1978

"Good Times" (1977)

"When John Amos left 'Good Times' and the show turned into clown routines, I resented it. I wanted a strong, loving father image back. What makes these people not give a black family a father? I'm tired of perpetuating the stereotype of the black single mother. I came from a family of eighteen, and all around me there were black families *with* fathers. When I couldn't convince the producers of 'Good Times,' I quit."

—Esther Rolle, *Ms.*, June, 1978

Janis Klein, Jackie Donnet, Joan Shigekawa, of "Woman Alive" (1973)

"Rhoda" (1975)

"Maude" (1973)

"Roots" (1977)

"Queen of the Stardust Ballroom" (1975)

"One Day at a Time" (1977)

"Carol Burnett Show" (1975)

"Scenes From a Marriage" (1977)

"The Lou Grant Show" (1978)

Dorothy Fuldheim, WEWS anchor

"Upstairs, Downstairs" (1975)

"See How She Runs" (1978)

"The Lily Tomlin Show" (1973)

"Amelia Earhart" (1976)

"Harriet Tubman: A Woman Called Moses" (1978)

"Policewoman" (1974)

"The Bionic Woman" (1976)

"Strangers: The Story of a Mother and Daughter" (1979)

"Margaret Sanger: The Woman Rebel" (1975)

Peggy Charren, president of Action for Children's Television.

Courtesy of Harriett Cody and Harvey Sadis

Joan Cordova

Not wanting to march down any heterosexist aisles, we set about looking for a lesbian ceremony and hit upon the Tryst. A Witch friend explained that it was an ancient ritual of bonding that was not the ownership contract of conventional marriage, but rather a mutual coming together of two equals to bond in love and friendship. She offered to help us do it. "We'll take it!"—*Lesbian Tide*, March/April, 1979

THIS CONTRACT is entered into this 24th day of November, 1972, by and between HARRIETT MARY CODY and HARVEY JOSEPH SADIS, as the parties enter into a marriage relationship authorized by a Marriage License and by an Official of the State of Washington, County of King.

Article I. Names

HARRIETT and HARVEY affirm their individuality and equality in this relationship. The parties reject the concept of ownership implied in the adoption by the woman of the man's name; and they refuse to define themselves as husband and wife because of the possessory nature of these titles.

THEREFORE, THE PARTIES AGREE to retain and use the given family names of each party: HARRIETT MARY CODY and HARVEY JOSEPH SADIS. The parties will employ the titles of address, MS. CODY and MR. SADIS, and will henceforth be known as PARTNERS in this relationship

The word "wedding," in fact, refers to the "wed"—or "bride price." That is, that amount of money, goods, or property paid to the girl's father for her purchase. The level of negotiations would depend on the wealth of the families and the qualities of the girl—her beauty, strength, and abilities. As she was considered more salable if pure, chastity became a big virtue. (In parts of Morocco today, a workingman pays $70 to $100 for a virgin, and only $30 for a widow or divorcée.) Proof of virginity became a necessary part of the wedding ceremonial—inspection of the bridal sheets the morning after or, as in Greece, the bride's stained nightgown left hanging in the window for days.

—Marcia Seligson, "Here Comes the Bride . . .," *Ms.*, February, 1973

Let's get this straight right from the very beginning: I wanted to get married. I wanted a husband—not, of course, any old husband, but the specific potential husband-person I had picked out during my freshman year of college, a man who tells funny stories, likes the same kinds of dogs and pizza that I do, and has never wondered aloud why I can't just behave like other women. I wanted to marry him. What I didn't want was monogrammed cocktail napkins, a new name, an umbrella with streamers on it, life insurance, a Merry Widow undergarment, and engraved stationery from Tiffany's.

—Anna Quindlen, "*Ms.* Goes to a Wedding," *Ms.*, December, 1978

Courtesy of Anna Quindlen and Gerald Krovatin

MARRIAGE

Mary Ellen Mark/Magnum

THE MARRIAGE LICENSE BUREAU OF THE CITY OF NEW YORK

WHEREAS it is common knowledge that women believe the conditions of the marriage contract to be positive and reciprocal feelings between the two parties (known as "love and affection"); and

WHEREAS the marriage contract in fact legalizes and institutionalizes the rape of women and the bondage of women, both their internal (reproductive) and external (domestic labor) functions; and

WHEREAS the marriage contract, known as "license," fails to list the terms of that contract, a failure which would automatically nullify the validity of any other important contract

THEREFORE, WE, THE FEMINISTS, do hereby charge the city of New York and all those offices and agents aiding and abetting the institution of marriage, such as the Marriage License Bureau, of fraud with malicious intent against the women of this city.

September 23, 1969

—Reported in *Sisterhood Is Powerful*, edited by Robin Morgan (Random House), 1970

Above—**Ti-Grace Atkinson (*left*), with members of the Feminists, demonstrates in 1969 at Manhattan's Marriage License Bureau.**

By order of the
Superior Court of the State of Washington
King County, Washington
Teresa M. Shoemaker resumed
the use of her maiden name
Teresa Mary Manning
on December 26, 1973.

This action in no way affects the
validity of the marriage vows
she exchanged with Dean Shoemaker

A week before Janice Champion and David Camesi of Manhattan Beach, California, planned to be married, David decided to change his name to hers.

Why? "I liked her name," says David, an associate professor of music at California State University at Dominguez Hills. "In fact, I loved it."

Janice, an air traffic controller, comments: "My mother thought David must be a very sensitive man to do such a thing. Now Mom, who has been divorced and remarried, is thinking about changing back to Champion, and that wasn't even her family name."

David says that changing his name "made a lot of people realize that many of us are stuck with names we have never liked. I think others will see they can be freer with their names if they desire."

—Joyce McWilliams, *Ms.* "Gazette," June, 1979

. . . The husband's marriage whether he likes it or not (and he does) is awfully good for him. The findings are consistent, unequivocal, and convincing. The superiority of married men over never-married men is impressive on almost every index—demographic, psychological, or social.

After middle age the physical health of married men is better than that of never-married men. But regardless of age, married men enjoy better mental health and fewer serious symptoms of psychological distress. To take an extreme example, in the United States, the suicide rate for single men is almost twice as high as for married men. . . .

It appears conclusive that more wives than husbands report marital frustration and dissatisfaction. More wives than husbands consider their marriages unhappy, have considered separation or divorce, and have regretted their marriages. Fewer married women than married men report positive companionship.

Although the physical health of married women is as good as, or even better than that of married men, the women suffer far greater mental-health hazards.

—Jessie Bernard,
The Future of Marriage
(World), 1972

Not too long ago a male friend of mine appeared on the scene from the Midwest fresh from a recent divorce. He had one child, who is, of course, with his ex-wife. He is obviously looking for another wife. As I thought about him while I was ironing one evening, it suddenly occurred to me that I, too, would like to have a wife. . . . I want a wife to go along when our family takes a vacation so that someone can continue to care for me and my children when I need a rest and a change of scene. . . . If, by chance, I find another person more suitable as a wife than the wife I already have, I want the liberty to replace my present wife with another one. Naturally, I will expect a fresh, new life; my wife will take the children and be solely responsible for them so that I am left free. . . . When I am through with school and have acquired a job, I want my wife to quit working and remain at home so that my wife can more fully and completely take care of a wife's duties. . . .

My God, who *wouldn't* want a wife?

—Judy Syfers,
I Want A Wife
(Know, Inc.) 1971

In New York City recently, a Manhattan jury awarded $56,000 to the husband of Catherine Montalbano for "loss of services." It seems she had been injured in a car crash, and for more than two months her deprived husband had been forced to do all the housework by himself. On an annual basis, the labors of this wife are worth $336,000. *Newsweek* magazine posed the question: Now that Ms. Montalbano is up and around again, can her husband afford her?

—*Ms.* "Gazette," September, 1974

A 1974 protest against *Bride's* magazine.

"Superwoman gets up in the morning and wakes her 2.6 children, feeds them a grade-A nutritional breakfast, and . . . then goes upstairs and gets dressed in her Anne Klein suit, and goes off to her $25,000-a-year job doing work which is creative and socially useful. Then she comes home after work and spends a real meaningful hour with her children, because after all, it's not the quantity of time, it's the quality of time. Following that, she goes into the kitchen and creates a Julia Child 60-minute gourmet recipe, having a wonderful family dinner discussing the checks and balances of the United States government system. The children go upstairs to bed and she and her husband spend another hour in their own meaningful relationship. They go upstairs and she is multiorgasmic until midnight."

—Ellen Goodman,
addressing the Association
of National Advertisers,
November, 1978

Robert: It would seem that after ten or so years of marriage, one wouldn't really have much to talk to the other partner about, but it's not true. There's more joy and excitement now than when we met.
Lois: Yes, I think real discovery comes after you know the superficial things about the other person.

Robert: Lois is sensitive, bright, and creative. Her responses are far more important to me than anyone else's in the world.

—Lois and Robert Gould,
"Taking the Pulse
of A Marriage"
(interview by Angela Wilson),
Ms., February, 1978

Never before has a First Lady shared so fully in her husband's Administration. Rosalynn reads what Jimmy reads, edits his speeches, meets with his aides, sits in on his Cabinet sessions, subs for him on the road, and consults on everything from political strategy to personnel changes. Often compared with Eleanor Roosevelt, Rosalynn functions more like Harry Hopkins, FDR's all-purpose adviser. She is, in short, a one-woman Kitchen Cabinet, Carter's most trusted senior hand.

—*Newsweek*, "Mrs. President," August 6, 1979

White House Photo

Karl H. Schumacher/The White House

Jimmy and Rosalynn Carter at one of their regular working lunches, and (*below*) on return flight from Mideast peace mission in 1978.

. . . She has never officially been appointed to an adviser's capacity, she is not subject to the scrutiny that Cabinet members and aides usually undergo; and, by the very nature of her marital relationship to the President, she cannot be removed or downgraded if her performance as an adviser and policymaker is seen to be lacking. . . .

For Mrs. Carter represents that situation that women have justifiably been appalled at: the woman who derives her influence and power solely from her romantic connection with a man.

—Bob Greene, "Rosalynn: Back to Giving Teas?"
New York *Post*, September 7, 1979

Below—**Joan Kennedy is escorted to the opera in Boston by arts administrator Richard Linzer.** Right—**Margaret Trudeau discos as estranged husband, Pierre Trudeau, is defeated on May 23, 1979.**

UPI

Wide World

"People ask whether the newspaper stories about Ted and girls hurt my feelings. Of course they hurt my feelings. They went to the core of my self-esteem. When one grows up, feeling that maybe one is sort of special and hoping that one's husband thinks so, and then suddenly thinking maybe he doesn't. . . . Well, I didn't lose my self-esteem altogether, but it was difficult to hear all the rumors. And I began thinking, well, maybe I'm just not attractive enough or attractive any more, or whatever, and it was awfully easy to then say, Well, after all, you know, if that's the way it is, I might as well have a drink."

—Joan Kennedy, *McCall's*, August, 1978

From the day I became Mrs. Pierre Elliott Trudeau, a glass panel was gently lowered into place around me, like a patient in a mental hospital who is no longer considered able to make decisions and who cannot be exposed to harsh light. . . .

As Pierre settled down to married life and no longer felt he had to court me, so he returned to spend more and more time at his work, leaving me alone. I waited, and waited, and waited all day for him to come home, devoting the last hours to putting on my makeup and my prettiest clothes so as to look beautiful for him. When he appeared he took *off* his best clothes and climbed into old, baggy slacks. When I told him how bored I was, he looked disgusted: "How *can* you be bored when life is so full, when you have so many options?"

—Margaret Trudeau, *Beyond Reason* (Paddington),1979

Wide World

The Right Marriage Split

Many once-married women were properly envious when Lee Marvin was ordered to pay his former mistress of six years $104,000 for support. That is because Michele Triola Marvin was being treated more fairly by the courts of California than many formally married women have been treated in regular divorce proceedings.

Hearings will soon begin in Washington, for example, to focus attention on a federal law that denies women divorced from Foreign Service officers a share of their former husbands' pensions or survivors' benefits. A recent victim of this policy, Jane Dubs, served beside Adolph Dubs in the Foreign Service for 30 years, until their divorce in 1976. When Mr. Dubs was killed on duty as ambassador to Afghanistan last winter, she was refused any part of his considerable survivor's benefits. The money went instead to the second Mrs. Dubs, his wife of only three years.

Proposed new legislation—part of a broader package of Foreign Service reforms—would give women who were married to officers for at least 10 years the right to a prorated share of the benefits earned during marriage. The proposal is modeled on recent changes in Social Security rules that have enlarged the rights of former mates along similar lines.

—New York *Times*, June 24, 1979

My question to these women was simple: "Can you remain friends with your ex-husband?" Their answers were complex and surprising. Since being divorced, some had dated or slept with their former husbands; others had double-dated with new lovers or even fixed each other up. There were couples who called each other daily, spent holidays or vacations together, lent each other money, entertained together and remained close to each other's families of in-laws. One couple shared a wine cellar they had stocked when they were married; another continued to share a summer beach house. Several couples had nursed each other through illnesses and some continued to celebrate what would have been their wedding anniversaries. I heard about one separated couple who deliberately conceived a sibling for their older child, and another woman whose ex-husband asked her to be the guardian of the children of his new marriage should anything happen to him. Yes, Virginia, there are relationships after divorce and only the exes themselves seem to understand how they work.

—Lindsy Van Gelder,
"Ten Women Talk About Their Ex-Husbands,"
Ms., January, 1979

. . . I wonder if I am afraid I am nothing without the label 'middle-class nice wife.' Am I afraid to admit to having negative feelings—that I want out—I want to reject my husband? What about my mental scenarios about kicking him out? Why am I so sure he's rejecting me? Why am I nervous about what people will think when they look at me at parties, or bump into me at the supermarket? I just don't want them to say, 'She's the one whose husband left her. . . .

—Susan Braudy,
Between Marriage and Divorce: A Woman's Diary
(William Morrow), 1975

- ☐ **In 1976 there were 2,133,000 marriages in the U.S.**
- ☐ **There were 1,077,000 divorces granted in the same period.**
- ☐ **A 1975 national study showed that alimony was awarded in only 14 percent of divorces.**
- ☐ **And of these, less than half were receiving it regularly.**
- ☐ **Only 44 percent of divorced mothers who were granted custody of their children were awarded child support payments.**

For years, Ethelyn Morgan was the financial backbone of the family: she supported both her husband and their young son by working as a secretary, a typist, a data processor, and a baby-sitter. Today, he is a $27,000 per year associate at a prestigious Wall Street law firm; she is a clerical with a salary potential of $10,000. But Ethelyn Morgan wants a medical degree. She also wanted a divorce. A New York judge thinks she deserves both. . . . She said, "I never knew it hadn't been done before. I kept thinking it's only fair. I supported him through school, and it was always understood that once he finished his degree, I would complete mine. We separated after he had accomplished his career goals, but I hadn't come anywhere near mine. I still want to be a doctor."

—Claudia Dreifus, *Ms.* "Gazette," September, 1975

. . . Eventually, I was ready to emerge on the other side of grief. I wanted to taste life again. To live, to work, to love. Suddenly I was frantically impatient with my whole way of life. It didn't last. I wavered back and forth for months. . . .

One of the first things I had to set to rights was money. Money matters. It really does. It is right up there with love and security and identity. I care more about money than I do about sex right now.

There comes a time, as the widow's numbness leaves her, when she discovers that she is ostracized by our couple-oriented society. When she is yearning for comfort, for companionship, to be included in the world of families where she used to belong so naturally, then she finds that she has been excluded from most of the intimacies of her old friends, the social life she used to take for granted.

—Lynn Caine, *Widow* (William Morrow), 1974

Opposite page—**Michelle Triola celebrates winning $104,000 settlement from actor Lee Marvin in 1979 landmark "palimony" suit.** Below—**Widow Lynn Caine with her children.**

Jill Krementz

HOUSTON

Diana Mara Henry

In fact, if anyone was underrepresented [among the 2,000 delegates; 15,000 were in attendance] it was the white upper-middle class. Whites were 64.5 percent of the elected delegates, as opposed to 84.4 percent of the general female population, and women with family incomes of more than $20,000 a year were 14.1 percent of the elected delegates, compared to 25.7 percent nationally. It may be the only conference in which delegates-at-large had to be used to round out the contingent of elected delegates—to achieve racial balance as mandated by the public law creating the conference—by adding white women. It was like a supermarket checkout line from Anywhere, U.S.A., transposed to the political arena: homemakers and nuns, teenagers and senior citizens, secretaries and farmers and lawyers, mahogany skins and white and café au lait. We were an all-woman Carl Sandburg poem come to life.

—Lindsy Van Gelder,
"Four Days That Changed the World," *Ms.*, March, 1978

A lighted torch, passed hand to hand across 2,600 miles from Seneca Falls, New York, arrives in Houston as the First National Women's Conference convenes, November 1977: (*left to right*) Billie Jean King, Susan B. Anthony II, Bella Abzug, Sylvia Ortiz, Peggy Kokernot, Michele Cearcy, Betty Friedan.

THE RESOLUTIONS

ARTS AND HUMANITIES

The President should take steps to require that women: are assured equal opportunities for appointment to managerial and upper level posts in federally funded cultural institutions . . .; are more equitably represented on grant-awarding boards, commissions, and panels; benefit more fairly from government grants. . . .

Judging agencies and review boards should use blind judging for musicians, including singers, in appraising them for employment, awards, and fellowships, as well as for all articles and papers being considered for publication or delivery and for all exhibits and grant applications, wherever possible.

BATTERED WOMEN

The President and Congress should declare the elimination of violence in the home to be a national goal. To help achieve this, Congress should establish a national clearinghouse for information and technical and financial assistance to locally controlled public and private nonprofit organizations providing emergency shelter and other support services for battered women and their children. The clearing-house should also conduct a continuing mass media campaign to educate the public about the problem of violence and the available remedies and resources.

Local and state governments, law enforcement agencies, and social welfare agencies should provide training programs on the problem of wife-battering, crisis-intervention techniques, and the need for prompt and effective enforcement of laws that protect the rights of battered women. ¶ State legislatures should enact laws to expand legal protection and provide funds for shelters for battered women and their children; remove interspousal tort immunity in order to permit assaulted spouses to sue their assailants for civil damages; and provide full legal services for victims of abuse. ¶ Programs for battered women should be sensitive to the bilingual and multicultural needs of ethnic and minority women.

BUSINESS

The President should issue an Executive Order establishing as national policy: the full integration of women entrepreneurs in government-wide business-related and procurement activities . . .

The President should amend Executive Order 11625 of October 13, 1971, to add women to its coverage and to programs administered by the Office of Minority Business Enterprise. ¶ The President should direct the Small Business Administration (SBA) to add women to the definition of socially or economically disadvantaged groups as published in the "Code of Federal Regulations" and take all steps necessary to include women in all the services and activities of the SBA. These steps should include community education projects to encourage women to participate in SBA programs, particularly minority women, including Blacks, Hispanic-Americans, Asian-Americans, and Native-Americans. ¶ The President should direct all contracting agencies to increase the percentage of the annual dollar amount of procurement contracts awarded to women-owned businesses and to maintain records by sex and race or ethnicity for monitoring and evaluation. ¶ The President should direct the General Services Administration to amend, so as to include women, the Federal Procurement Regulations requiring that all firms holding government contracts exceeding $5,000 insure that "minority business enterprises have the maximum practicable opportunity to participate in the performance of government contracts."

CHILD ABUSE

The President and Congress should provide continued funding and support for the prevention and treatment of abused children and their parents under the Child Abuse Prevention and Treatment Act of 1974.

States should set up child-abuse prevention, reporting, counseling, and intervention programs or strengthen such programs as they already have. Child abuse is defined, for this purpose, as pornographic exploitation of children, sexual abuse, battering, and neglect. ¶ Programs should: provide protective services on a 24-hour basis; counsel both victim and abuser; create public awareness in schools and in communities . . .; encourage complete reporting and accurate data collection; and provide for prompt, sensitive attention by

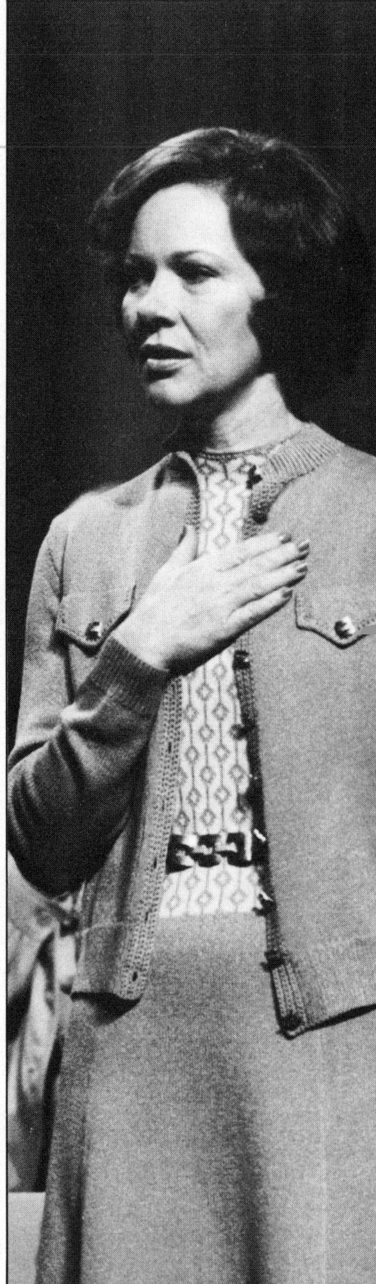
Alex Webb/Magnum

Joan Roth

Diana Mara Henry

Joan Roth

Clockwise—**First Ladies Rosalynn Carter, Betty Ford, Lady Bird Johnson. Margaret Mead. Barbara Jordan. Jean Stapleton.**

Left to right—**High Chief Puhn Peneveta, mayor of Pago Pago, American Samoa. Mary Crisp, vice-chair, Republican Party. Homemaker Alice Bibeau and college student Colleen Wong.**

Diana Mara Henry

Diana Mara Henry

Diana Mara Henry

police, courts, and social services. . . .

CHILD CARE

The federal government should assume a major role in directing and providing comprehensive, voluntary, flexible-hour, bias-free, nonsexist, quality child care and developmental programs, including child-care facilities for federal employees . . . ¶ Federally funded child-care and developmental programs should have low-cost, ability-to-pay fee schedules that make these services accessible to all who need them, regardless of income, and should provide for parent participation in their operation. ¶ Legislation should make special provision for child-care facilities for rural and migrant worker families. ¶ Labor and management should be encouraged to negotiate child-care programs in their collective bargaining agreements. ¶ Education for parenthood programs should be improved and expanded by local and state school boards, with technical assistance and experimental programs provided by the federal government. ¶ City, county, and/or state networks should be established to provide parents with hot-line consumer information on child care, referrals, and follow-up evaluations of all listed care givers. . . .

CREDIT

The Federal Equal Credit Opportunity Act of 1974 should be vigorously, efficiently, and expeditiously enforced by all the federal agencies with enforcement responsibility. . . .

DISABLED WOMEN

The President, Congress, and state and local governments should rigorously enforce all current legislation that affects the lives of disabled women.

The President, Congress, and Administration should expeditiously implement the recommendations of the White House Conference on Handicapped Individuals and develop comprehensive programs for that purpose. . . .

The federal government should enact legislation which will provide higher income levels so that disabled women can afford to live independently and at a decent standard of living. The disabled woman must have the right to determine for herself whether she will live in or out of an institutional setting. . . .

Disabled women should have the right to have and keep their children and have equal rights to adoption and foster care. ¶ The Congress should mandate health training and research programs focused on the health needs of the disabled. . . .

The President and Congress should enact legislation to include disabled women under the 1964 Civil Rights Act and afford them judicial remedy. ¶ The President and Congress and International Women's Year must recognize the additional discrimination disabled women face when they are members of racial, ethnic, and sexual minority groups and appropriate steps must be taken to protect their rights. ¶ In the passage of the National Plan of Action, the word "woman" should be defined as including all women with disabilities. The term "bilingual" should be defined as including sign language and interpreter for the deaf. The terms "barriers" against women and "access" should be defined as including architectural barriers and communication barriers. . . .

EDUCATION

. . . Federal surveys of elementary and secondary schools should gather data needed to indicate compliance with federal anti-discrimination laws, and these data should be collected by sex as well as race or ethnicity. The Civil Rights Commission should conduct a study to evaluate the enforcement of laws prohibiting sex discrimination in physical education and athletics . . .

Leadership programs for working women in postsecondary schools should be upgraded and expanded, and private foundations are urged to give special attention to research on women in unions.

Bilingual vocational training, educational and cultural programs should be extended and significantly expanded . . .

State school systems should move against sex *and race* stereotyping through appropriate action, including:

- Review of books and curriculum.
- The integration into the curriculum of programs of study that restore to women their history and their achievements and give them the knowledge and methods to reinterpret their life experiences. . . .

ELECTIVE AND APPOINTIVE OFFICE

The President, governors, political parties, women's organizations, and foundations should join in

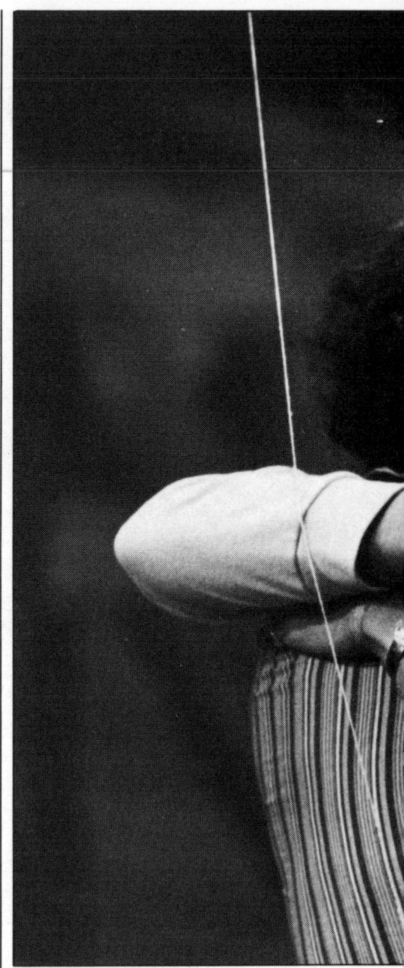

Clockwise from above—**The Sexual Preference vote is celebrated—and jeered. Antiabortion spokeswoman Dr. Mildred Jefferson (*right*): Anti-ERA protesters; Disabled caucus member.**

Christina Thomson

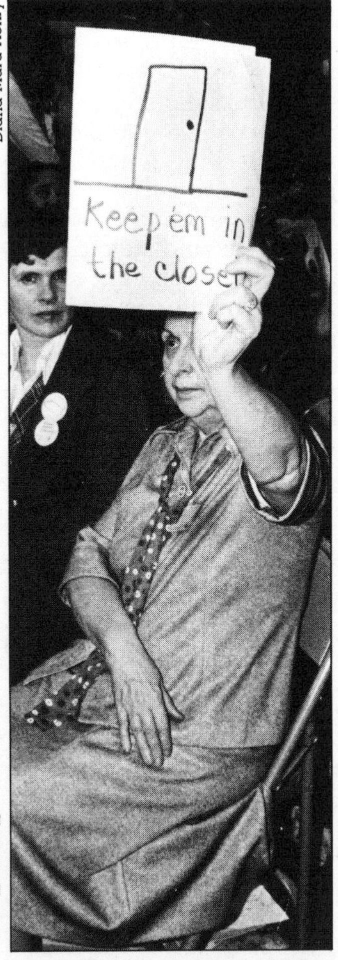

Diana Mara Henry

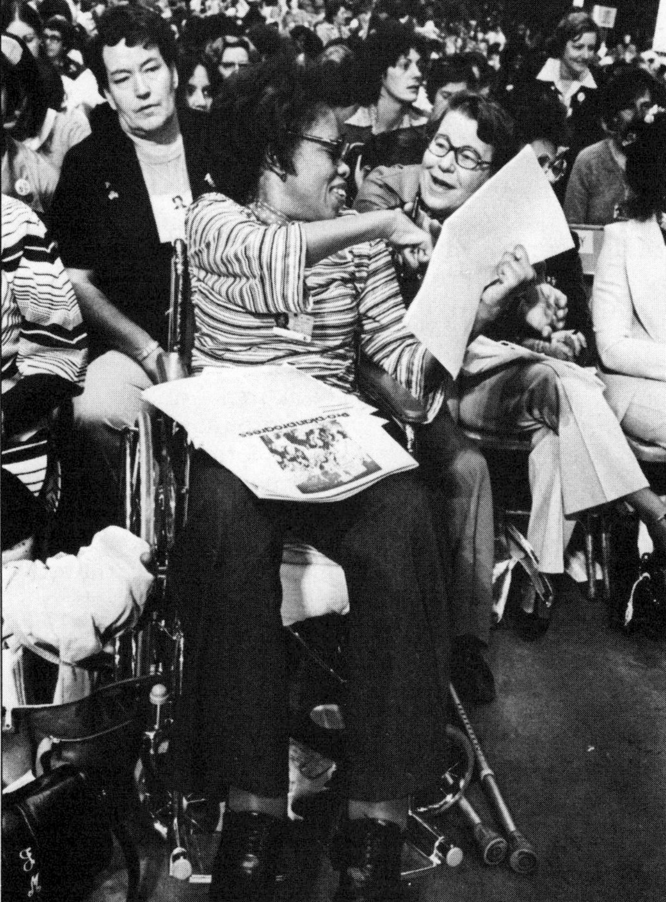

Janie Eisenberg

Christina Thomson

Joan Roth

an effort to increase the number of women in office, including judgeships and policymaking positions, and women should seek elective and appointive office in larger numbers than at present. . . .

EMPLOYMENT

The President and Congress should support a policy of full employment so that all women who are able and willing to work may do so. . . .

The Equal Employment Opportunity Commission should receive the necessary funding and staff to process complaints and to carry out its duties speedily and effectively. ¶ All enforcement agencies should follow the guidelines of the EEOC, which should be expanded to cover discrimination in job evaluation systems. These systems should be examined with the aim of eliminating biases that attach a low wage rate to "traditional" women's jobs. Federal legislation to provide equal pay for work of equal value should be enacted. . . . ¶ As the largest single employer of women in the nation, the President should require all federal agencies to establish goals and timetables which require equitable representation of women at all management levels, and appropriate sanctions should be levied against heads of agencies that fail to demonstrate a "good faith" effort in achieving these goals and timetables. . . .
¶ Agencies and organizations responsible for apprenticeship programs should be required to establish affirmative action goals and timetables for women of all racial and ethnic origins. . . .

Special attention should be given to the employment needs of minority women, especially Blacks, Hispanics, Asian-Americans, and Native-Americans, including their placement in managerial, professional, technical, and white-collar jobs. English-language training and employment programs should be developed to meet the needs of working women whose primary language is not English.

The Congress should amend the Veteran Preference Act of 1944 (58 Stat. 387, Chapter 287, Title V, U.S. Code) so that veterans' preference is used on a one-time-only basis for initial employment and within a three-year period after discharge from military service, except for disabled veterans. . . . ¶Unions and management should review the impact on women of all their practices . . . . ¶ Enforcement of the Fair Labor Standards Act and the Social Security Act as they apply to household workers and enforcement of the minimum wage should be improved. ¶ Federal and state governments should promote Flexitime jobs, and pro-rated benefits should be provided for part-time workers. . . .

EQUAL RIGHTS AMENDMENT

The Equal Rights Amendment should be ratified.

HEALTH

Federal legislation should establish a national health security program. . . .

Health insurance benefits should include preventive health services; comprehensive family planning services; reproductive health care; general medical care; home and health support services; comprehensive mental health services.

States should license and recognize qualified midwives and nurse practitioners as independent health specialists and state and federal laws should require health insurance providers to directly reimburse these health specialists. ¶ States should enact a patient's bill of rights which includes enforceable provisions for informed consent and access to and patient ownership of medical records.

Federal legislation should be enacted to expand the authority of the Food and Drug Administration: to require testing of all drugs, devices, and cosmetics by independent sources. . .; to have immediate recall of hazardous, unsafe, or ineffective drugs, devices, and cosmetics; to require a patient information package insert with every drug and device marketed. . . . ¶ Congress should appropriate funds for increased research on safe, alternative forms of contraception, particularly male contraception. Research to identify the risks of present forms of contraception and estrogen-based drugs should be given higher priority. . . . ¶ The Department of Health, Education, and Welfare should provide additional funds for alcohol and drug-abuse research and treatment centers designed to meet the special needs of women. . . . ¶ Congress should appropriate funds to establish and support a network of community-based health facilities to offer low-cost, reproductive health services. ¶ The President should appoint a special commission to conduct a national investigation of conditions in nursing homes and mental institutions and propose standards of care. ¶ Congress should appropriate funds to encourage more women to enter the health professions and Congress should allocate funds only to those health professions schools whose curricula are clearly nonsexist. ¶ The Secretary of Health, Education, and Welfare should undertake a special investigation of the increase in surgical procedures such as hysterectomy, cesarean section, mastectomy, and forced sterilization.

HOMEMAKERS

The federal government and state legislatures should base their laws relating to marital property, inheritance, and domestic relations on the principle that marriage is a partnership in which the contribution of each spouse is of equal importance and value.

The President and Congress should support a practical plan for covering homemakers in their own right under Social Security and facilitate its enactment.

Alimony, child support, and property arrangements at divorce should be such that minor children's needs are first to be met and spouses share the economic dislocation of divorce. . . . Loss of pension rights because of divorce should be considered in property divisions. More effective methods for collection of support should be adopted. . . .

The federal and state governments should help homemakers displaced by widowhood, divorce, or desertion to become self-sufficient members of society through programs providing counseling, training and placement, and counseling on business opportunities; advice on financial management; and legal advice.

INSURANCE

State legislatures and state insurance commissioners should adopt the Model Regulation to Eliminate Unfair Sex Discrimination of the National Association of Insurance Commissioners. The Regulation should be amended and adopted to include prohibition of the following practices: denial of coverage for pregnancy and pregnancy-related expenses for all comprehensive medical/hospital care . . . denial of coverage to women with children born out of wedlock and denying eligibility of benefits to such children; using sex-based actuarial and mortality tables in rate and benefit computation.

INTERNATIONAL AFFAIRS

Women and Foreign Policy. The President and the Executive Agencies of the government dealing with foreign affairs (Departments of State and Defense, USIA, AID, and others) should see to it that many more women, of all racial and ethnic backgrounds, participate in the formulation and execution of all aspects of United States foreign policy. Efforts should be intensified to appoint more women as Ambassadors and to all U.S. Delegations to international conferences and missions to the United Nations. Women in citizen voluntary organizations concerned with international affairs should be consulted more in the formulation of policy and procedures.

U.N. Commission on the Status of Women. The U.S. Government should work actively for the retention and adequate funding of the U.N. Commission on the Status of Women, and it should recommend that the commission meet annually rather than biennially.

Women in Development. The U.S. Agency for International Development and similar assistance agencies should give high priority to the implementation of existing U.S. legislation and policies designed to promote the integration of women into the development plans for their respective countries.

Human Rights Treaties and International Conventions on Women. In pressing for respect for human rights, the President and the Congress should note the special situation of women victims of oppression, political imprisonment, and torture. They should also intensify efforts for ratification and compliance with international human rights treaties and conventions to which the United States is signatory, specifically including those on women's rights.

Peace and Disarmament. The President and the Congress should intensify efforts to: (a) build, in cooperation with other nations, an international framework within which serious disarmament negotiations can occur; (b) reduce military spending and foreign military sales, convert excessive weapons manufacturing capacity to production for meeting human needs; (c) support peace education in schools and advanced study in the fields of conflict resolution and peacekeeping. . . .

International Women's Decade. The U.S. should give vigorous support to the goals of the U.N. Decade for Women: Equality, Development, and Peace in the General Assembly and other international meetings; should give financial support to Decade activities and should participate fully in the 1980 mid-Decade World Conference . . .

MEDIA

The media should employ women in all job categories and especially in policy-making positions. . . . They should make affirmative efforts to expand the portrayal of women to include a variety of roles and to represent accurately the numbers and lifestyles of women in society. . . .

Appropriate federal and state agencies . . . should vigorously enforce laws which prohibit employment discrimination against women working in the mass media. . . .

Particularly, public broadcasting should assume a special responsibility to integrate women in employment and programming.

Women's groups and advocacy groups . . . should join the campaign to de-emphasize the exploitation of female bodies and the use of violence against women in the mass media.

MINORITY WOMEN

Minority women share with all women the experience of sexism as a barrier to their full rights of citizenship. Every recommendation in this plan of action shall be understood as applying equally and fully to minority women. ¶ But institutionalized bias based on race, language, culture and/or ethnic origin or governance of territories or localities has led to the additional oppression and exclusion of minority women and to the conditions of poverty from which they disproportionately suffer.

Therefore every level of government action should recognize and remedy this double-discrimination and ensure the right of each individual to self-determination. ¶ Legislation, the enforcement of existing laws, and all levels of government action should be directed especially toward such problem areas as involuntary sterilization; monolingual education and services; high infant and maternal mortality rates; bias toward minority women's children; confinement to low-level jobs; confinement to poor, ghettoized housing; culturally biased educational, psychological, and employment testing (for instance, civil service); failure to enforce affirmative action and special admission programs; combined sex and race bias in insurance; and failure to gather statistical data based on both sex and race so that the needs and conditions of minority women may be accurately understood. ¶ Minority women also suffer from government failure to recognize and remedy problems of our racial and cultural groups.

For instance:

American-Indian and Alaskan-Native Women: have a relationship to Earth Mother and the Great Spirit as well as a heritage based on the sovereignty of Indian peoples. The federal government should guarantee tribal rights, tribal sovereignty, honor existing treaties and congressional acts, protect hunting, fishing, and whaling rights, protect trust status, and permanently remove the threat of termination. ¶ Congress should extend the Indian Education Act of 1972, maintain base funding of education instead of replacing it with supplemental funding, provide adequate care through the Indian Health Service, forbid the systematic removal of children from their families and communities, and assure full participation in all federally funded programs.

Asian/Pacific American Women: are wrongly thought to be part of a "model minority" with few problems. This obscures our vulnerability due to language and culture barriers, sweatshop work conditions with high health hazards, the particular problems of wives of U.S. servicemen, lack of access to accreditation and licensing because of immigrant status and to many federally funded services.

Hispanic Women: Deportation of mothers of American-born children must be stopped and legislation enacted for parents to remain with their children; citizenship provisions should be facilitated. ¶ Legislation under the National Labor Relations Act should be enacted to provide migrant farm working women the federal minimum wage rate, collective bargaining rights, adequate housing, and bilingual-bicultural social services delivery. ¶

Classification of existing Hispanic-American media as "foreign press" must be stopped to ensure equal access to major national events. ¶ Additionally, the Federal Communications Commission must provide equal opportunity to Hispanic people for acquisition of media facilities (radio and television), for training and hiring in order to provide Spanish-language programming to this major group.

Puerto Rican Women: emphasize that they are citizens of the United States and wish to be recognized and treated as equals.

Black Women: The President and the Congress should provide for full quality education, including . . . special admission programs and for the full implementation and enforcement at all levels of education. ¶ The President and the Congress should immediately address the crisis of unemployment which impacts the Black community and results in Black teenage women having the highest rate of unemployment. ¶ The Congress should establish a national program for the placement of "children in need of parents," preferably in a family environment, where the status of said children is affected by reason of racial or ethnic origin. ¶ The President and the Congress should assure federally assisted housing to meet the critical need of Black women, especially of low and moderate income, should direct the vigorous enforcement of all fair housing laws, and provide the allocation of resources necessary to accomplish this housing goal. ¶ The President, Congress, and all federal agencies should utilize fully in all deliberations and planning processes, the Black Women's Plan of Action which clearly reflects and delineates other major concerns of Black Women.

OFFENDERS

States should review and reform their sentencing laws and their practices to eliminate discrimination that affects the treatment of women in penal facilities. Particular attention should be paid to the needs of poor and minority women. . . .

Disparities in the treatment of male and female juvenile offenders must be eliminated . . . states are urged to establish more youth bureaus, crisis centers, and diversion agencies to receive female juveniles detained for promiscuous conduct, for running away, or because of family or school problems.

OLDER WOMEN

Federal and state governments, public and private women's organizations, and social welfare groups should support efforts to provide social and health services that will enable *the older woman* to live with dignity and security. These services should include but not be limited to:

•Innovative housing which creates as nearly as possible an environment that affords security and comfort.

•Home health and social services . . . that will offer older women alternatives to institutional care, keeping them in familiar surroundings as long as possible.

•Preventive as well as remedial health-care services.

•Public transportation in both urban and rural areas for otherwise housebound women.

•Continuing education. . . .

•Immediate inclusion of geriatric education in the curriculum and training of all medical personnel. . . .

•Bilingual, bicultural programs—including health services, recreation, and other programs—to support elderly women of limited English-speaking ability.

•Elimination of present inequities in Social Security benefits.

•Recognition of the economic value of homemaking in the Social Security benefits.

•Passage of the Displaced Homemakers bill. . . .

•Older women should be included as active participants on all kinds of policy-making positions at every level of government.

•The image of the older woman is changing and there should be wide publicity focused on this.

•Mandatory retirement should be phased out.

RAPE

Federal, state, and local governments should revise their criminal codes and case law dealing with rape and related offenses to provide for graduated degrees of the crime with graduated penalties depending on the amount of force or coercion occurring with the activity; to apply to assault by or upon both sexes, including spouses as victims; to include all types of sexual assault against adults . . . to specify that the past sexual conduct of the victim *cannot be introduced into evidence;* to require no more corroborative evidence than is required in the prosecution of any other type of violent assault. . . .

Local task forces to review and reform rape law and practices of police, prosecutors, and medical personnel should be established where they do not now exist. . . . Rape-crisis centers should be established (with federal and state funding) for the support of victims and the confidentiality of their records should be assured. Bilingual and bicultural information resources should be made available where necessary.

Federal and state funds should be appropriated for educational programs in the public school system and the community, including rape prevention and self-defense programs. . . .

State legislatures should expand existing victim compensation. . .

REPRODUCTIVE FREEDOM

We support the U.S. Supreme Court decisions which guarantee reproductive freedom to women. ¶ We urge all branches of federal, state, and local governments to give the highest priority to complying with these Supreme Court decisions and to making available all methods of family planning to women unable to take advantage of private facilities. ¶ We oppose the exclusion of abortion or childbirth and pregnancy-related care from federal, state, or local funding of medical services or from privately financed medical services. ¶ We urge organizations concerned with improving the status of women to monitor how government complies with these principles.

We oppose involuntary sterilization and urge strict compliance by all doctors, medical and family planing facilities with the

Department of Health, Education, and Welfare's minimum April, 1974, regulations requiring that consent to sterilization be truly voluntary, informed, and competent. Spousal consent should not be a requirement upon which sterilization procedures are contingent. If the patient does not speak English, appropriate staff must be found to explain the procedures and HEW regulations in the primary language of the patient. ¶ Particular attention should be paid at all levels of government to providing confidential family-planning services for teenagers, education in responsible sexuality, and reform of laws discriminating against unwed parents and their children. ¶ Programs in sex education should be provided in all schools, including elementary schools. . . . ¶ Each school system should assist teenage parents with programs including child-care arrangements that will encourage them to remain in school, provide educational and vocational training leading to economic independence, and teach prenatal health and parenting skills.

RURAL WOMEN

The President and Congress should establish a federal rural education policy designed to meet the special problems of isolation, poverty, and underemployment that characterizes much of rural America. Such a policy must be consciously planned to overcome the inequality of opportunities available to rural women and girls. . . .

A farm wife should have the same ownership rights as her spouse under state inheritance and federal estate laws. Tax law should recognize that the labor of a farm wife gives her an equitable interest in the property. . . .

The President should appoint a joint committee from the Departments of Labor, Agriculture, and Justice to investigate seasonal and migratory workers in all states and territories of the United States.

All programs developed on behalf of rural women should be certain to include Black, migrant, Native-American, Alaskan, Asian, and Hispanic, and all isolated minorities, and that affirmative action programs be extended to include all disenfranchised groups.

SEXUAL PREFERENCE

Congress, state, and local legislatures should enact legislation to eliminate discrimination on the basis of sexual and affectional preference in areas including, but not limited to, employment, housing, public accommodations, credit, public facilities, government funding, and the military.

State legislatures should reform their penal codes or repeal state laws that restrict private sexual behavior between consenting adults.

State legislatures should enact legislation that would prohibit consideration of sexual or affectional orientation as a factor in any judicial determination of child-custody or visitation rights. . . .

STATISTICS

The Office of Management and Budget should require all departments and agencies to collect, tabulate, and analyze data relating to persons on the basis of sex in order to assess the impact of their programs on women.

The U.S. Census Bureau should aggressively pursue its efforts to reduce the undercounts of minority Americans, including Blacks, Hispanic-Americans, Asian-Americans, and American Indians. . . .

WOMEN, WELFARE, AND POVERTY

The federal and state governments should assume a role in focusing on welfare and poverty as major women's issues. All welfare reform proposals should be examined specifically for their impact on women. Inequality of opportunity for women must be recognized as a primary factor contributing to the growth of welfare roles.

Women in poverty, whether young or old, want to be part of the mainstream of American life. . . .

Along with major improvements of the welfare system, elimination of poverty for women must include improvements in Social Security and retirement systems, universal minimum wage, nontraditional job opportunities, quality child care, comprehensive health insurance, and conprehensive legal services. . . .

We support increased federal funding for income-transfer programs (e.g. Social Security, SSI, AFDC). Congress should approve a federal floor under payments to provide an adequate standard of living based on each state's cost of living. And, just as other workers, homemakers receiving payments should be afforded the dignity of having that payment called a wage not welfare.

We oppose the Carter Administration proposal for welfare reform (HR 9030) . . .; and we oppose proposals for "workfare" where welfare mothers would be forced to "work off" their grants, which is work without wage, without fringe benefits or bargaining rights, and without dignity . . . We strongly support a welfare reform program developed from ongoing consultation with persons who will be impacted. This program should (1) be consistent with the National Academy of Science recommendation that no individual or family living standard should be lower than half the median family level for substantial periods (after tax); and this income should not fall below the government defined poverty level of family income even for shorter periods; (2) help sustain the family unit; and (3) that women on welfare and other low-income women who choose to work not be forced into jobs paying less than the prevailing wage. . . .

Quality child care should be a mandated Title XX service, available to all families on an ability to pay basis throughout training, education, job search, and employment.

Congress should encourage education of women by insuring that federal and other education grants do not reduce an individual's or family's eligibility for public assistance in AFDC or any other programs.

IMPLEMENTATION

. . . It is hereby resolved that: a Committee of the Conference be selected by the National Commission . . . after receiving recommendations . . . from the delegates of this body. . . .

Suzanne Opton

AGING

It was not that she had not loved her babies, her children. The love—the passion of tending—had risen with the need like a torrent; and like a torrent, drowned and immolated all else. But when the need was done—o the power that was lost in the painful damming back and drying up of what still surged, but had nowhere to go. Only the thin pulsing left that could not quiet, suffering over lives one felt, but could no longer hold nor help.

—Tillie Olsen, *Tell Me a Riddle* (Lippincott), 1961 reissued 1971.

That a woman of 73 [Anaïs Nin], writing still about herself, could still surprise, shock, anger, and delight me, caused me to ponder, when I learned of her death, her *meaning* for all of us left in life, in the *world*. . . . Throughout her life she believed in her right to record what *she* saw and what *she* felt, and to be serious enough about it to do it *exhaustively*. She made of her own mind and body a perpetually *new* frontier, enlarging our consciousness by exploring and presenting the many and varied exposures of the same Anaïs Nin. Someone said that hers was a professional generosity toward the young.

—Alice Walker, *Ms.*, April, 1977

We have been married 35 years, three children they're all gone so we have the time of our life. We live away in the country, paradice lane I call it. I've never stepped out on my husband or he on me. This is such a nice place. We love going naked all the time . . . We both said we hoped this honeymoon would last forever and it is. We don't care what other people think. It's so much fun to put hay in the barn and lay down on it and fuck. He don't let it come but about twice a week but we fuck all the time. We are always touching. I'm glad I'm not like Mama was—she slept down stairs, Daddy slept up, and they never give each other a good word. My husband loves fuckin good as I do. I know it's nasty to other people but they could enjoy it more if they were out in the country like we are. I cannot express the feelings I have now for this most wonderful place this side of Heaven. This is our summer love story and I hope fall winter spring will be even better.

—a letter quoted in "The Sexual Lives of Women over 60", Carol Tavris, *Ms.*, July, 1977

I had learned from the U.S. government census figures that there were more than 53,000 people 65-and-over living below the national poverty level in Philadelphia alone. Late Start, another federally funded program of this kind, fed about 1,000 of them; the Corporation for Aging was feeding another 1,300 one meal a day, five days a week. That's all most of them ate.

—Loretta Schwartz, "Hungry Women in America," *Ms.*, October, 1977

There are thousands of women staking their territories on city streets. . . . In New York City, there is only one publicly run women's shelter, a converted animal hospital with 47 beds; and there is no program for women—as there is for homeless men—to exchange chits distributed by the city for meals and a place to sleep.

So the women become fixtures in the buried maze of subway haunts, or they spend their days in the emergency waiting rooms at the city hospitals; they stuff papers in the sink and sometimes wash themselves in the ladies' rooms there. They seem to want to be around people, but not be involved. The last thing they want is to be locked away.

—Joan Roth,
"Shopping-Bag Ladies Tell What It's Like To Live on the Streets,"
Ms., March, 1977

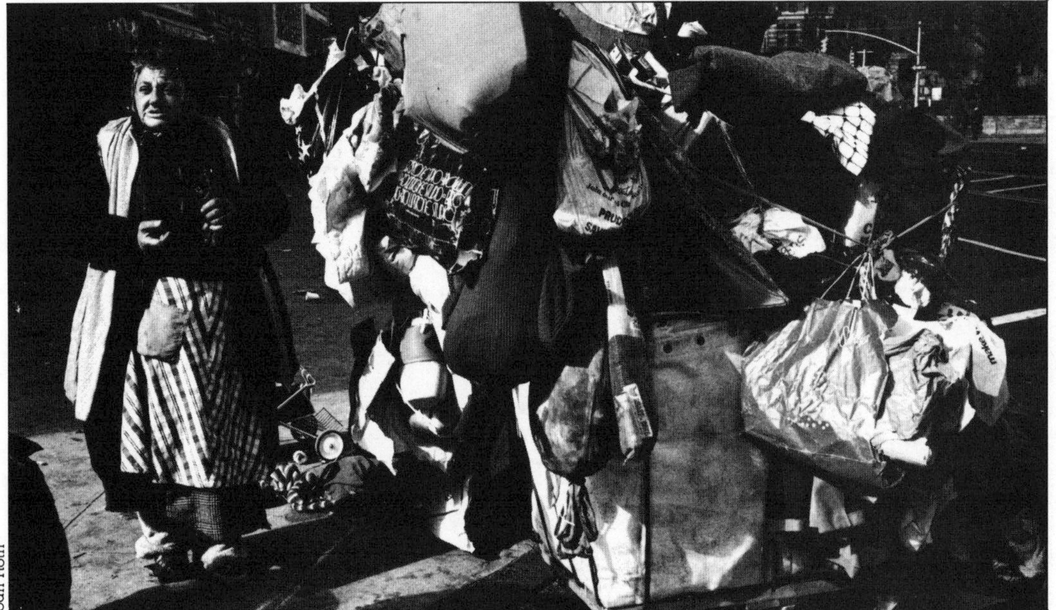

Joan Roth

"Women are considered fit to be used as long as they can give birth. And the excitement of sex is always in relation to what is new. Perhaps they feel that a man's sex, his erection, has no age . . . while a woman . . . it's disgusting that people think that all that is left to an aging woman is plastic surgery."

—"Jeanne Moreau Talks About Seduction, Aging, and Fame,"
by Judith Thurman
Ms., January, 1977

Bettye Lane

Maggie Kuhn (*left*), the 69-year-old activist from Philadelphia who is the chief Gray Panther organizer and publicist, and proselytizer-at-large for rights for our elderly and aging: "We hassled the name for a year and a half. We wanted to show we were taking a stand—rocking the system—not just giving lip service. We decided that if the word 'Panthers' did turn some people off, we were glad. They weren't going to do much radical action anyway. Gray is a symbolic color—everyone gets old, and if you put all the colors of the rainbow together, you get gray."

—*Ms.* "Gazette," June, 1975

> Every time I think that I'm getting old, and gradually going to the grave, something else happens.
>
> —Lillian Carter, *Ms.*, October, 1976

Above—**The indefatigable Lillian Carter.**
Right—**Until her death in 1976 at the age of 92, pioneer photographer Imogen Cunningham spends her time . . . pioneering.**

Judy Dater

Iris Schneider

Edna Robinson, former chess champion, starts after-school program in 1973.

I began once more the well-worn arguments even she could have recited by rote. As I described the imperfect equation of all our lives at the moment, I began to tell her about my life abroad. Leaning against the giant maple tree my father had planted as a sapling almost 50 years ago, I said, "You don't know how hard it is to be so far from your own country. I've lived in places where I can't even wish things could be different; not just for you, for me." As I talked on, hastily and without thought, I was shocked to find that I was crying. My mother reached out and touched my hand. She patted it and said, "There, there, don't cry. We can't always do what we want to do."

That night she said she was ready for the nursing home. She hadn't forgotten that she was a comforter, a mother still. Life reverses itself as we mature and our parents age, and so we forget that we can still receive comfort and solace, just as we comfort them. She'd always been at her best in times of crisis. Now, withered and senile, she decided to do what the family wanted. For us. From that moment on, she never spoke of her home again.

—Bonnie Ghazarbekian, "How My Mother Helped Me Put Her in a Nursing Home," *Ms.*, March, 1979

Lenore Davis

Jill Krementz

Where a tough old matriarch in a traditional society might feel capable of coping with the unexpected, American women have been more likely to hang back. In some cultures old women go up the pecking order to become bossy mothers-in-law and arbiters of morals and social standing. We don't, not often; not since the days of Mrs. Astor and Mrs. Potter Palmer. Older women here are apt to slide down the pecking order toward a lonely old age. . . .

I'm afraid that there are very few older women who are seen as compelling role-models for young women. . . . It may take a long time for true heroines to emerge; but in the meantime, we older women who know we aren't heroines can offer our younger sisters, at the very least, an honest report of what we have learned and how we have grown.

—Elizabeth Janeway, "Breaking the Age Barrier," *Ms.*, April, 1973

GROUPS

And each new feminist undertaking—be it small presses, periodicals, bookstores, galleries, conferences, festivals—has a double function: it makes available new art and new thinking and, by its very existence, it strengthens the network of the community, through which audiences and artists are reached and created. Competition has no meaning here: women's structures can only survive and grow through being nourished by each other. Women's art, though created in solitude, wells up out of community. There is, clearly, both enormous hunger for the new work thus being diffused, and an explosion of creative energy, bursting through the coercive choicelessness of the system on whose boundaries we are working.

—Adrienne Rich,
reviewing Joan Larkin's
Housework, *Ms.*, February, 1977

Judy [Viorst]: I went to a dinner party the other night and started talking about Women's Liberation. And . . . I got attacked as I have never been attacked in my life! One women snapped and said: *"My* trouble is that men don't treat me as enough of a female." One man was talking about "those dykes."

My femininity was so threatened by these attacks that I actually backed down. I felt they would go home saying I was a freak just because I brought up the subject of Women's Liberation.

Betty [Friedan]: That's why you need solidarity, my dear.

—from a symposium in
Pageant magazine,
July, 1970

The National Congress of Neighborhood Women at their first conference in 1974.

"There's a stereotype of the working-class woman as being passive and inarticulate and incapable of thinking about the 'larger' issues outside her home. There's another myth that says the Women's Movement is antifamily, antichurch, antineighborhood. . . . We're not too big on abstract theory. Our main concern is providing direct services—helping women get education, jobs, better child care, health care, and setting up battered women's shelters."

—Christine Noschese,
staff director,
National Congress of
Neighborhood Women,
February, 1979

Janie Eisenberg

Most [C-R] groups find that starting at the beginning works best: childhood and feelings about self and parents raise fewer problems of guilt and defensiveness, since we were less responsible for our lives in those years. Move slowly on from topic to topic, and try to keep a common focus. For instance, a group might explore questions like these:

- What was our earliest childhood awareness of being trained to behave like a girl? How were brothers or boys in the neighborhood raised, treated, or educated differently? What was our feeling about that?
- What was our first experience of sexual fantasies? Sexual realities?
- What was our reaction to bodily changes in adolescence? How were we prepared for those changes? How did we feel?
- What were our earliest fantasies of accomplishment? Of making some difference in the world?
- What was our first work experience? Current work experiences?
- What thoughts are brought to mind by the word, "humiliation"?
- What are our feelings about money? for women? for men?
- What are our feelings about power? when women use it? when men use it?
- Marriage: why did we marry, if we did; why not, if not? Would we make the same choice again?
- How often are we able to be honest about our feelings?
- What situations make us feel guilty?
- How do we feel about our appearance? about wearing makeup, fashionable clothes?
- What are our private terrors?
- How do we feel about childbirth? aging? menopause?
- How do we feel about love? When have our feelings been experienced as love? What are our fears of being unlovable?
- How have our experiences with discrimination against women, whatever their race, compared with experiences of discrimination against black men? Other minorities? What feelings of inferiority have we been taught that are the same? or different?
- What are our hopes for the future? What do we want to do before we die?
- What conditions of our daily lives do we want to change? How are we (or why are we not) changing them?

—from "A Guide to Consciousness-Raising," *Ms.*, July, 1972

. . . Many women have not been able to avoid completely the female experience of disliking, competing with, and feeling betrayed by other women. And the reasons they give are as varied as they are endless: economically and professionally successful women are aggressive elitists; heterosexually committed women are cowards and deserters; happy mothers and Marxist women are fools and fifth columnists; lesbians are sick; white women are racists; black women can't wait to walk behind their men; middle-aged women wear hats and gloves; young women carry spears and throw bombs.

These divisions certainly have valid political and economic bases. However, the psychological basis for such divisions is the female belief that she cannot be enhanced or protected by the success or power of any other women. Also at work here is an absolute terror of differences.

—Phyllis Chesler, *Women and Madness* (Doubleday), 1972

Unstructured groups may be very effective in getting women to talk about their lives; they aren't very good for getting things done. It is when people get tired of "just talking" and want to do something more that the groups flounder, unless they change the nature of their operations.

—Jo Freeman, "The Tyranny of Structurelessness," *Ms.*, July, 1973

Bettye Lane

. . . The small group is especially suited to freeing women to affirm their own view of reality and to think independently of male-supermacist values. It is a space where women can come to understand not only the way this society works to keep women oppressed but ways to overcome that oppression psychologically and socially. It is Free Space. . . . In the beginning of a group experience opening up is a reaching out to find human contact with other women. Later it becomes a way to communicate to others about one's subjective feelings—about the group, about the Women's Movement, about one's life.

—Pamela Allen, "Free Space," *Notes from the Third Year*, 1970

ORGANIZING

"We were not real philosophical in those days [the early 1970s in Pittsburgh]. We became instant experts on everything. On child care. Started our own nursery school. We worked on employment cases. . . . First we started organizing local NOW chapters. Then we organized the state. I went to every village and town, organizing; if you have just one or two people, you can get a chapter going. I organized housewives. Because that's where I was. You have to do what you know. It never occurred to me that we weren't going to get housewives, and we did. We have."

—Eleanor Smeal, president, NOW, February, 1978

Question: What is it that 75 national women's organizations—with more than 30 million members—have created? *Answer:* The U.S. National Women's Agenda—an action program announced this summer.

Coming from the goals of groups with wide-ranging constituencies—such as the Girls Clubs of America, the Association of Junior Leagues, Lesbian Feminist Liberation, and Women's International League for Peace and Freedom—the Agenda specifies 11 women's priorities for action:

I. Fair Representation and Participation in the Political Process.
II. Equal Education and Training.
III. Meaningful Work and Adequate Compensation.
IV. Equal Access to Economic Power.
V. Quality Child Care for All Children.
VI. Quality Health Care Services.
VII. Adequate Housing.
VIII. Fair and Humane Treatment in the Criminal Justice System.
IX. Fair Treatment by and Equal Access to Media and the Arts.
X. Physical Safety.
XI. Respect for the Individual.

—*Ms.* "Gazette," September, 1975

Margaret Sloan, a co-founder of the National Black Feminist Organization.

. . . Black feminists have established the National Black Feminist Organization, in order to address the particular and specific needs of the larger, but almost cast-aside half of the black race in Amerikkka, the black woman.

Black women have suffered cruelly in this society from living the phenomenon of being black and female, in a country that is *both* racist and sexist. There has been very little real examination of the damage it has caused on the lives and on the minds of black women. Because we live in a patriarchy, we have allowed a premium to be put on black male suffering.

—NBFO "Statement of Purpose," *Ms.* "Gazette," May, 1974

Neal Boenzi/NYT Pictures

With Ilene Goldman, and 18 other women, Lola Redford created an organization called CAN—Consumer Action Now. It was an effort to accentuate the positive—to make homemakers think about the environmental impact of their buying habits; to give consumers specific alternatives for environmentally sound lifestyle. . . . They decided to put out a newsletter. That was in 1970. Each issue would cover a single topic of interest to environmentally concerned consumers. It would be "something a woman could read over her coffee," Lola says, "and we wanted it to have pizzazz, flair. Everything else on these subjects was so deadly dull.". . .

Their subscription list grew; people began to give them money; even the government came through with some real funds to launch such projects as a fifth-grade curriculum for environmental studies. They were volunteers edging toward professionalism. And they were changing politically.

For her part, Lola began to understand the importance of getting women into environmental decision-making. "Every conference I went to, it was two other women and seventy men."

In 1974, Lola organized a retreat, during which each CAN woman studied a chapter of Wilson Clark's big book, *Energy for Survival: The Alternative to Extinction* (Anchor). From that time on, CAN stopped being a newsletter with a project here and there and became a solar-advocacy organization.

—Susan Dworkin,
"The Renewable Energy of Lola Redford,"
Ms., July, 1979

Above—**In 1971, Lola Redford and Ilene Goldman (holding poster) lead CAN's first protest—against phosphates in detergents. On May 3, 1978 CAN organizes Sun Day—an event that results in the formation of the Solar Lobby.** Far right—**Members of the Coalition of Labor Union Women at their founding conference, 1974. (*Left to right*) Edie Van Horn of the U.A.W., Josephine Flores of the Farm Workers, Clara Day of the Teamsters, and Olga Madar of the U.A.W.**

The most important characteristic of the groups is their crossing of status lines. When women start rapping about salary, they find the low salary of secretarial jobs is caused by the same sexism as the lower-than-average salary of the professional women's jobs.

—Susan Davis,
"Organizing from Within,"
Ms., August, 1972

"Divide and conquer—that's what they try to do to any group trying to make social change. I call it D&C. Black people are supposed to turn against Puerto Ricans. Women are supposed to turn against their mothers and mothers-in-law. We're all supposed to compete with each other for the favors of the ruling class."

—Flo Kennedy, 1973

WANTED BY THE FBI

INTERSTATE FLIGHT - MURDER, KIDNAPING

ANGELA YVONNE DAVIS

FBI No. 867,615 G

Photograph taken 1969

Photograph taken 1970

Alias: "Tamu"

DESCRIPTION

Age:	26, born January 26, 1944, Birmingham, Alabama		
Height:	5'8"	**Eyes:**	Brown
Weight:	145 pounds	**Complexion:**	Light brown
Build:	Slender	**Race:**	Negro
Hair:	Black	**Nationality:**	American
Occupation:	Teacher		
Scars and Marks:	Small scars on both knees		

Fingerprint Classification: 4 M 5 Ua 6

UPI

Angela Davis is apprehended in 1970—and acquitted in 1972.

"Angela Davis is accused—only *accused*—of buying a gun for somebody, and what happens? She spends months in solitary confinement and hundreds of thousands of dollars on legal defense before she can go free. Lieutenant Calley is convicted of slaughtering kids and women in Vietnam, and what happens? He gets confined to very comfortable quarters, not even sent to jail—and Nixon defends him in public. It makes you wonder: does femocide pay?"

—Flo Kennedy, 1972

Perhaps it is simply the gallantry of Angela Davis, a gallantry so complete that it senses everything, operating by a wisdom all its own to enchant fate, outwit it, and prevail. . . . Here perhaps at last is the Joan one hoped for, come in a day when no one will have a match and the fire will never fly about its target—a woman unwilling to be martyred.

—Kate Millett, "On Angela Davis," *Ms.*, August, 1972

. . . No woman is really an insider in the institutions fathered by masculine consciousness. When we allow ourselves to believe we are, we lose touch with parts of ourselves defined as unacceptable by that consciousness; with the vital toughness and visionary strength of the angry grandmothers, the shamanesses, the fierce market-women of the Ibo, the marriage-resisting women silkworkers of prerevolutionary China, the millions of widows, midwives, and women healers tortured and burned as witches for three centuries in Europe, the Beguines of the 12th century who formed independent women's orders outside the domination of the Church, the women of the Paris Commune who marched on Versailles, the uneducated housewives of the Women's Cooperative Guild in England who memorized poetry over the wash-tub and organized against their oppression as mothers, the women thinkers discredited as "strident," "shrill," "crazy," or "deviant," whose courage to be heretical, to speak their truths, we so badly need to draw upon in our own lives. I believe that every woman's soul is haunted by the spirits of earlier women who took risks and resisted as women today—like Inez Garcia, Yvonne Wanrow, Joan Little, Cassandra Peten—are fighting their rapists and batterers.

—Adrienne Rich,
commencement speech,
Smith College, June, 1979

SYMBOLS

Right—**Sister Maureen Murphy, charged with first-degree manslaughter in the 1976 death of her newborn son, is found not guilty in May, 1977.** Below—**SLA "captive" Patty Hearst is photographed robbing a California bank, 1974.**

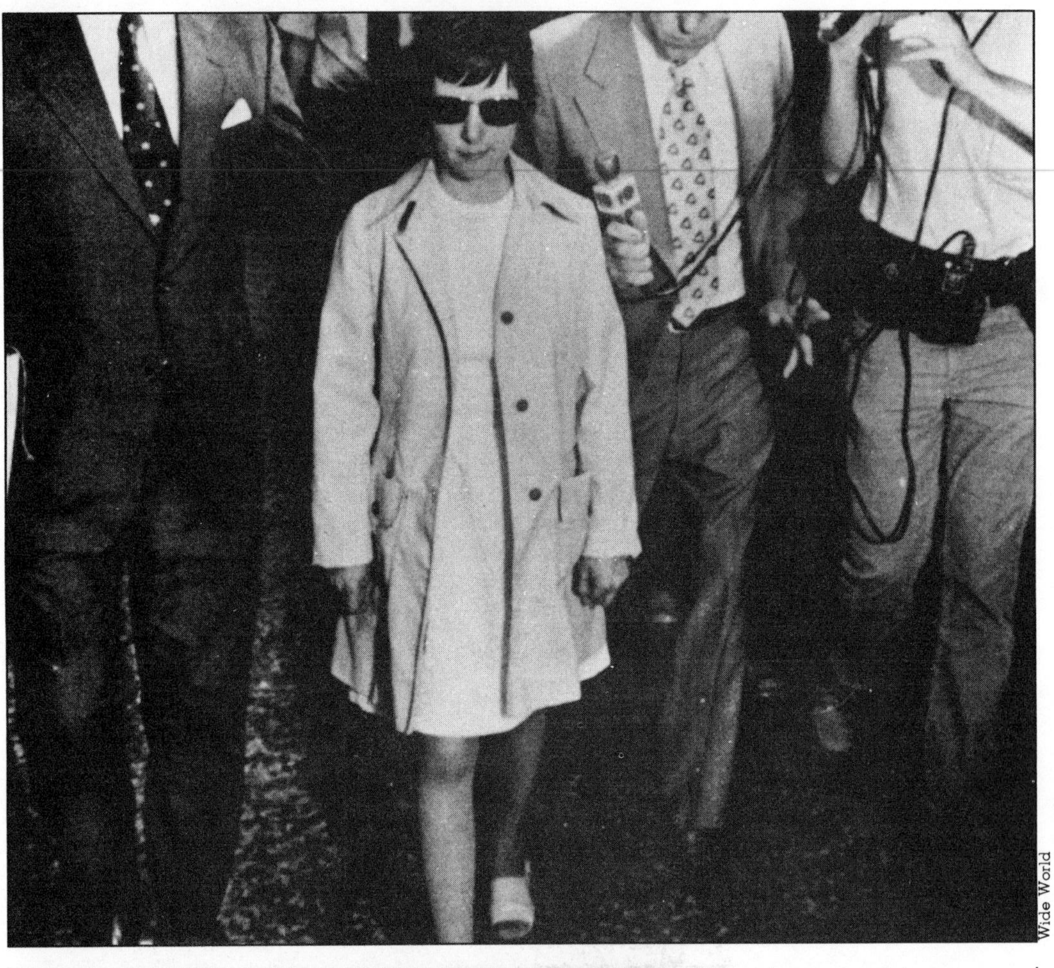

Wide World

In fact, Sister Maureen fell into the chasm presently existing between the old and new Catholic life-styles. In the old days, swaddled in a habit and living behind fortress walls, she would have been treated by a doctor summoned behind the convent walls, a doctor who would probably report his findings directly to her Mother Superior.

A nun who experiences sexual contact—however rarely—is a cruelly likely candidate for pregnancy. Her knowledge of birth control is probably limited, and some of its methods beyond easy reach. Even to *consider* methods of contraception implies a degree of premeditated consent—even welcome—to the act of sex which most nuns are simply unable to make.

—Catherine Breslin,
"Nun On Trial
for Infanticide,"
Ms., March, 1977

Wide World

What happened to me happens to women all the time. I've been kidnapped, held prisoner, threatened, beaten, humiliated, raped, battered. I've been lied to and lied about and disbelieved. The only difference between what happened to me and what happens to other women is that mine was an extreme case.

—Patricia Hearst, 1978

We've discovered more about the ways in which our pain is used, to divide us, when it could unite us—the trick being to support a Patricia *and* mourn for the dead SLA women, to express sympathy for Catherine Hearst *and* for the overlooked Wendy Yoshimura, even to understand the recently sentenced Emily Harris . . .

—Robin Morgan,
"Why Should We Care
About Patty Hearst?"
Ms., March, 1979

I ask Peg [Mullen, whose son Michael's death in Vietnam was the focus of C.D.B. Bryan's *Friendly Fire*] why she was different. With other people, the anger seemed to die out; other women didn't keep protesting. "This is a fallacy," she states firmly. "A lot of women did. I've met them in every state of the Union. Pat Simon of Gold Star Mothers for Peace. The Iowa and Illinois women who went on the peace mission to Paris. I'm not unique, not at all. It was just kept quiet by the press. It *would* have affected the war if some of these women had gotten publicity back in 'sixty-six or 'sixty-seven. Instead, the press treated them as crackpots, out of touch with reality. *Obsessed.*"

—Mary Crawford, "Peg Mullen and the Military: The Bureaucracy of Death," *Ms.*, January, 1977

Bettye Lane

Above—**Iowa farm wife, Peg Mullen (with husband Gene) is radicalized by coverup of son's death in Vietnam, 1970.** Right—**Karen Silkwood (and her supporters) is vindicated in May, 1979 when a federal jury awards her estate $10.5 million to be paid by Kerr-McGee, owner of the plutonium plant where she was contaminated by radiation in 1974.**

One of the last people to see her alive recounts in a sworn affidavit that Karen clenched her hand around a brown manila folder and a large notebook. The affidavit continues: "She then said there was one thing she was glad about, that she had all the proof concerning the health and safety conditions in the [Kerr-McGee] plant, and concerning falsification. As she said this, she clenched her hand more firmly on the folder and the notebook she was holding. She told me she was on her way to meet [union official] Steven Wodka and a New York *Times* reporter to give them this material. . . ."

—B.J. Phillips, "The Case of Karen Silkwood," *Ms.*, April, 1975

Under what conditions is a violent reaction to sexual attack justified? When is it self-defense? Or part of the trauma of rape? We need to understand the current legal possibilities as well as precisely how we wish to change them. We want live activists, after all, not imprisoned martyrs.

Yet, what *do* we do with the rage? It is clearly there—and, if combined with little faith in legal remedies, it seems sure to produce vigilantism. Our question must be: At what cost to women?

—Gloria Steinem, "But What Do We Do With Our Rage," *Ms*, May, 1975

Yvonne Wanrow, who has faced murder charges since 1972 for defending her children against a molester, pleads guilty to manslaughter in April, 1979 and receives five years' probation.

Bettye Lane

Everybody in the house started screaming. The man saw my little two-year-old nephew on the couch, and he went toward him saying, "Oh, what a cute little boy." At that moment my sister stepped between her son and him. When I turned around, he was coming right at me, and that's when I fired. . . .

So I went to prison, and the probation officer recommended prison on these grounds: that I needed to be rehabilitated; that I was inclined to violence, because I purchased a gun in the first place; that he was an expert on Indian culture because he had spent two years on the Colville Indian reservation; that I could pursue my career in art in prison. Because of my intelligence and compassion for other people, he said, "Don't you think you might be of help to other Indian inmates? You know there are other Indian women in prison." I couldn't believe it.

—Yvonne Wanrow,
Ms. "Gazette," July, 1976

Top—**Joan Little is found innocent in 1975 of killing prison guard, who sexually assaulted her while she is jailed on robbery charges.** Bottom—**Inez Garcia serves 15 months of a 1974 second-degree murder conviction for killing a man she said helped rape her, is acquitted in 1977 retrial.**

Bettye Lane

In the case of Inez Garcia, whose alleged rapist was also Latino, not only was he not tried for the alleged crime, but the victim herself was convicted for having spontaneously vented her rage against the alleged rapist's accomplice. . . .

Let us then forge among ourselves and our movements an indivisible strength and with it, let us halt and then crush the conspirary against Joan Little's life.

—Angela Davis, "The Dialectics of Rape," *Ms.*, June, 1975

Cidne Hart/LNS

BEING

How do you accept the risk of falling in love, how do you love with generosity and without meanness—without keeping any loose change in your pocket—and avoid being consumed? How do you integrate romantic love into your life and work without turning it into a vocation?
How is he going to cope with the fact that you're strong?
How is he going to cope with the fact that you're weak?
How are you going to cope with your strengths and weaknesses and allow yourself to be vulnerable again?
Lotsa luck. (And we haven't even mentioned sex. Or jealousy. Or open marriage and all that other stuff.) It's tricky.

—Barbara Grizzuti Harrison, "Is Romance Dead?" *Ms.*, July, 1974

'Falling in love' is no more than the process of alteration of male vision—through idealization, mystification, glorification—that renders void the woman's class inferiority. However, the woman knows that this idealization, which she works so hard to produce, is a lie, and that it is only a matter of time before he 'sees through her.' . . . Thus her whole identity hangs in the balance of her love life. She is allowed to love herself only if a man finds her worthy of love.

—Shulamith Firestone, *The Dialectic of Sex* (Morrow), 1970

It's so much easier to say love is bullshit than to get over a love affair, so much easier to speak of oppression than to confess to private pain, so much easier in the long run to hate men than to love them.

—Ingrid Bengis, *Combat in the Erogenous Zone* (Knopf), 1972

Androgyny is a Greek word meaning, simply, male and female. . . . It makes room for the man in every woman, the woman in every man. Like the word itself, the aspiration toward androgyny is ancient. Again like the word, it may seem initially remote, as estranged from the modern experience and imagination as the Olympians. . . .

Androgyny has been an ongoing human ideal, traceable across civilizations and millenia.

—Harriet Rosenstein, "On Androgyny," *Ms.*, May, 1973

TOGETHER

Eva Rubinstein/Lee Gross Inc.

"In terms of what society says, we shouldn't be together. I mean, I'm [twelve years] older than he is, I'm taller than he is; I'm six feet. How tall are you, Ronnie? Oh, five-seven! Also, we're of different religions. I have a profession, years of schooling, and he's a high school graduate, but it doesn't make any difference. It's so ridiculous—all these things are supposed to be important."

—Emily Martin in "Is It Different With a Younger Man?" *Ms.*, June 1976

Shalmon Bernstein

This new-style man listens so hard to what you say that he can finish your sentences for you. It would be ungrateful of you to suggest that it was not what you intended to say, when he is making such an effort to show you he considers you an equal, and that he recognizes a worthy thought; it was something he might have said himself. It's his way of telling you how smart he thinks you are.

—Donna Allen,
No More Fun & Games, No. 4
February, 1970

The Census Bureau reported today that the number of unmarried couples living together more than doubled in the first eight years of this decade and increased more than eightfold among people under 25 years old.

—New York *Times*,
June 26, 1979

Our friends were furious with us for moving in together. They had trusted in Bill's marriage and my affair with Andrew. Some refused to believe that we were not lovers and intimated that we had merely swapped partners. Others did believe us but felt that in a time when living together and sleeping together had just become acceptable, living together without sleeping together was distinctly perverse.

—Emily Prager,
"Roommates, but Not Lovers,"
Ms., April, 1979

I have growing-up problems—among them, a positive passion for giddiness—but I can respond to beauty and truth when they hit me in the eye. So in deference to Katherine Anne Porter, one cold-sober testimonial story:

A year after I was married, I wanted a divorce. I felt trapped. . . . I had a nice, tall, fond man who made me laugh, but he didn't tango, he didn't bite my ear, and he wasn't sure just exactly what the hell it was I wanted from him.

Luckily for me, he hung in, and he encouraged me to hang in. In the spring of 1975, we were in a car crash. We're still healing, but for the moment, I'm lame and he's halt. His brain is swift, but his feet are slow.

A woman who knew us came to visit and commended me for 'sticking with him.' She talked as though he'd been a bathtub toy, a plastic duck; if it breaks, you throw it away.

I remember the first time I saw him after the accident. I'd been waiting two months for the meeting. Leaning on the shoulders of two smaller men, male nurses, he faltered into my hospital room. His legs were matchsticks, long, pale, brittle under his bathrobe. Nobody had shaved him, his eyes were hollow, he had no power of speech. Yet he looked at me in the high bed, and he knew who I was. He began to make a keening sound. 'Ah, ah, ah, ah,' he sighed, and I knew that the spectacle of me, strung up to tubes and hoses and needles and bottles was hurting him on some level of which he wasn't even conscious.

But the sight of him made me peaceful for the first time since we'd been hurt. I believed if I could touch him, touch his face, touch his once nervous, now quiet, hands, the slab of ice in my chest would melt and I would feel warm again.

Sensuality is complicated. Love is intricate. And the flesh is sweet, but I no longer mistake it for the whole thing.

—Chris Chase,
Ms., November, 1976

Chester Higgins, Jr.

Let's begin with the last line of the story: You may have to leave him.

After all the talk, the lifestyle experiments, the C-R sessions; the battles and the grief—you may end up walking out. Or *he* may call it quits. Because nothing will be the same once you ask the question, "How can I get him to change?"

—Letty Cottin Pogrebin,
"Can I Change Him?"
Ms., January, 1977

. . . She has moved from *loving* (anyone—woman, man, child, the universe) at her own expense, to loving herself at anyone else's expense—only to find that she detests herself for having done so. No grace here, merely hopelessness, although it takes a certain courage to admit it. Is this perhaps the reason some feminists who wrestled with theory (as opposed to sophomoric correct lines) in the '60s went quietly mad with despair in the '70s?

—Robin Morgan,
Going Too Far:
The Personal Chronicle of a
Feminist (Random House), 1977

. . . I know how to make a decision
My opinions are my own
And the one that I love thinks
it's wonderful
That I can get along alone

'Cause he knows I'll never be
a burden
I won't hang on his sleeve
I'm so self-sufficient
I'm so easy to leave . . .
I can handle any crisis
I'm so capable I could scream
I've gotten my whole life together
Reconstructed it bit by bit
But as for finding love, my friend,
This strong woman number . . .
doesn't mean a shit!

—"Strong Woman Number" from *I'm Getting My Act Together . . . and Taking It On the Road* by Gretchen Cryer and Nancy Ford, © 1978, Fiddleback Music Publishing Company, Inc.

It isn't that to have an honorable relationship with you, I have to understand everything, or tell you everything at once, or that I can know, beforehand, everything I need to tell you.

It means that most of the time I am eager, longing for the possibility of telling you. That these possibilities may seem frightening, but not destructive, to me. That I feel strong enough to hear your tentative and groping words. That we both know we are trying, all the time, to extend the possibilities of truth between us.

The possibility of life between us.

—Adrienne Rich, "Women and Honor: Some Notes on Lying," in *On Lies, Secrets, and Silence* (Norton), 1979

Joanne Leonard

**"Me and my friends, Mary, Jess, and Kathy,
get together, sit around and talk to each other about life
have a feelin' what we have in common with each other...
and diggin' that we seem to be three of a kind,
havin' such a good time . . ."**

From "Summer of '71," lyrics by Helen Reddy, music by Jack Conrad.

LNS Women's Graphics

. . . It's perfectly possible to pour the old wine into new bottles. . . . But it does mean partners who are willing to make the effort; it does mean partners who are willing in a very real sense to break with the past, to struggle against the oldest convention of all—sexual oppression. Love is a public as well as a private act, and love between equals has no social history.

—Karen Durbin "What Is The New Intimacy," *Ms.*, December, 1978

Carol Ginandes

. . . She is really a woman. SHE IS REALLY A WOMAN. Her body is soft and her hands and lips are very gentle, and she makes love to me with a caring and concentration and gladness that I've never experienced before.

—Sandy Boucher,
"Mountain Radio,"
Ms., April, 1975

Suzanne Opton

WOMEN'S LIBERATION EQUALS MEN'S LIB
THIS EXPLOITS PEOPLE
You've come a long way, baby.
Virginia Slims.

IMAGE

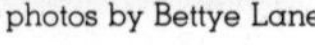

photos by Bettye Lane

"Just pretend that you're a visitor from another planet and all you know about the women of America is what you see on TV. You would see the lady alone in her kitchen polishing her floor, getting the whitest/cleanest/brightest wash in town and dishes you can see your face in. Once in a while she ventures out of the house to get a manicure with Madge or she drops into the supermarket to catch Mr. Whipple squeezing the Charmin. On the way home she pops into Cora's shop to get a little advice on how to make better coffee. Back at home she vacuums her living room until hubby returns from the office to announce that he smells clean. After all this, she goes into a little low-down music and prepares for an Aviance night. . . . No one in our industry has sat around and planned about how we can put women down. And we know that the advertising we see on the screen and in the magazines is the end result of some very careful, sophisticated marketing planning and research on which marketing decision makers build those strategies. . . . [But] if we are really pragmatic about the facts of the marketplace, there is no way we can write ads that show women as competitive housewives working to have the whitest wash or the shiniest floor on the block, or as simple-minded slobs, or as simpering idiots. . . . .

ADVERTISING

". . . The practical reality is that [Alice] doesn't live here any more and what's more, she probably never did. . . . If we really want to keep stereotypes out of our advertising, let's not invent new ones. As we recognize the importance of workingwomen as a market or as we identify the outward-bound housewife who says she 'plans to work,' let's not create new, contemporary stereotypes to replace the traditional ones."

—Rena Bartos, senior vice-president, J. Walter Thompson Company, addressing the Advertising Women of New York, February, 1976

Inglenook
America's Superior Wine

AUNT: ...I'm so happy! (MUSIC UNDER)

FATHER: Well, how does it feel to be a doctor?

DAUGHTER: I wanted to twirl batons... You said be head cheerleader... I just wanted to go to college,

you said be a doctor. Thanks, Pop. (MUSIC UP)

AV/O: Now you should know about Inglenook. America's superior wine.

Very appropriate for those moments in life

that are somehow just a little special.

Remember Inglenook. When the toast is from your heart.

FATHER: To my daughter, the doctor.

PERSONAL STYLE

Below—**Mary Peacock.**
Opposite page top—
Elaine Grove Christensen.
bottom— **Linda Brown.**

"It costs six cents a page to read John Malloy's book *The Woman's Dress-for-Success Book* [Warner Books]. It's worth every penny. I haven't laughed so hard since *Blazing Saddles*. All the years I have been in business I have gone blithely along thinking my clothes were appropriate for the president of an advertising corporation. *Au contraire*! Malloy's research shows my wardrobe to be a total bust. 'My God,' I asked myself when I had completed $9.95 worth of Malloy, 'how on earth did I ever do twelve million a year with *my* wardrobe?' "

—Jane Trahey,
advertising executive, 1978

Now comes *Cheap Chic* to tell me I am right. Or, that given a little direction I could be right. My philosophy is right. In my quest for chic, I am willing to make some terrible mistakes, which is all to the good. I look to the folks who wrote *Cheap Chic* like I look to myself: stylish yet refreshingly idiosyncratic; classic yet breezily irreverent; elegant, witty, original, devil-may-care. Just when you thought I was wearing some weird wrinkled item by accident, I was actually making my own great look.

—Jane Shapiro,
reviewing *Cheap Chic*
by Carol Troy and
Catérine Milinaire
(Harmony Books) *Ms.*, May, 1976

"I hate dresses. Only time I ever put on a dress is to go to church on Sunday. I bought a dress when Jimmy was inaugurated as governor, a special long dress. I have five that I bought while he was in office, and every one of them is out of style."

—Lillian Carter,
Ms., October, 1976

President Nixon chided Helen Thomas, a UPI reporter, about wearing slacks to the White House. After signing a bill in the Oval Room, the President asked, "Helen, are you still wearing slacks? Do you prefer them actually? Every time I see girls in slacks it reminds me of China."

—*Ms.* "Gazette,"
October, 1973

Judith Quist was fired by Jerome Young, owner of the Plaza restaurant in Somers, Connecticut, because she refused to shave her legs. Her boss testified at a State Commission on Human Rights and Opportunities hearing that he fired her because he feared her hairy legs would "hinder" business at his "family-type" restaurant. Quist testified,"I was surprised at what he said. I said, 'Ah, come on, Jerry,I have nice legs, don't I?' " He said a customer had complained. Upon questioning, he replied that he would not fire a black employee if the person's race bothered a customer.

—*Ms.*, "Gazette,"
August, 1975

I buy clothes made for men, every one of whom intends, according to a curiously outdated conviction among clothing manufacturers, to wear his clothes for decades. . . .There is a suitable selection among men's sweaters, pants, jackets, scarves, and, particularly, socks. Hats, too. Sometimes raincoats. . . . Also: I wear clothes that are two sizes "too large," because they are more comfortable than those that "fit." This allows me to stretch my arms as far as they will go without the ominous creaking of seams, to sweat without doing so visibly, to eat a huge meal if I so choose without that fifties' malady, the "shirtwaist's revenge."

—Ingeborg Day,
"One Size Fits All,"
Ms., April, 1979

Recently, we've noticed that while men are usually afforded free alterations on such articles of clothing as suits and slacks, women are given no such courtesy for corresponding articles. This tradition has been with us for years, its origin probably being the archaic notion of sex-role stereotyping. Sewing and alteration of clothing are left for women to do at home, while men, on the other hand, have always had the free services of tailors. This discrimination is even more deplorable in that the industry cannot, in good faith, claim that men's clothing is any more easily altered than women's.

—Barbara L.
—Letters to the editors,
Ms., October, 1973

Fred Seidman

Fred Seidman

Janet Beller

"My hairstyle is a combination of bells, beads, braids, and cornrows. I've been wearing it this way for ten years. It started when I was a student and had to take a swimming class four mornings a week. I had to find a hairstyle that was convenient and easy to groom, and this was it. . . .

"When I started teaching in the New York City Public schools, I got written up for not presenting a positive image of black woman according to the standards of 1971. I was transferred to a less desirable assignment and eventually I left the city school system. . .

"Now people usually like my hair, and when they don't, it's clearly a projection of their own taste and fears. I do my hair myself; it usually takes about six hours, but then once it's finished, I don't have to do much with it except wash it for as long as three months. So in the end, it saves me time."

—Linda Brown,
a teacher/counselor, 1979

"When I became pregnant, I didn't think in terms of maternity clothes because I have always worn oversize things nipped in at the waist—many of them old clothes from thrift shops. I had a whole stock of fat-men's pants that had big, pleated tucks at the waist; as my pregnancy progressed, I let them out."

—Elaine Grove Christensen,
Ms., October, 1979

"Personal style is the essence of fashion. It is the secret of real *chic* and the concept applies equally to feeling attractive in friendly, old, comfortable clothes."

—Mary Peacock,
publisher, *Rags* magazine, 1979

Annie Leibovitz/Contact

"I am 57, but I don't want to wear what some ass-hole who designs clothes for a First Lady says I should wear. I wear what's around—my riding boots, pants—but I refuse to go without nail polish because I dig it. Nail polish or false eyelashes isn't politics. If you have good politics, what you wear is irrelevant. I don't take dictation from the pig-o-cratic style setters who say I should dress like a middle-aged colored lady. My politics don't depend on whether my tits are in or out of a bra."

—Flo Kennedy,
Ms., February, 1974

Bettye Lane

The implication that a woman's underarm and leg hair are superfluous, and therefore unwanted, is but one embodiment of our culture's preoccupation with keeping women in a kind of state of innocence, and denying their visceral selves.

—Harriet Lyons, "Body Hair: The Last Frontier," *Ms.*, July, 1972

Above—**Lily Tomlin as her visceral self, 1978.**

" . . . When I was little, I was small and ugly and I couldn't afford nice things. Now that I can have them, I wear them to please myself. And anyway, lots of women buy just as many wigs and makeup things as I do. . . . They just don't wear them all at the same time."

—Dolly Parton, *Ms.*, June, 1979

Annie Leibovitz/Contact

Annie Leibovitz/Contact

Fred Seidman

"At the time I started, the giant Germans were in demand. Veruschka, who was 6'1", was on top. Jean Shrimpton was 5'9½" and I didn't look like anyone. My features weren't perfect. All my life I'd been told I was ugly. Of the 10 people I saw every day, one might encourage me. The others would look at my book, say thanks and suggest I leave town."

—Lauren Hutton, *Working Woman*, October, 1978

"As far as I'm concerned, being any gender is a drag."

—Patti Smith, *New Times*, December 26, 1975

VIOLENCE

JEB

"Take Back the Night" marches are held in several cities in 1978-79 to demand a woman's right to walk in safety on any street at any hour.

The recent Atlantic Records' release of the Rolling Stones' album "Black and Blue" was advertised by pictures of a brutalized, battered woman. The caption read, "I'm 'Black and Blue' from the Rolling Stones and I love it." A group called the Women Against Violence Against Women is mounting a campaign against this and other distortions in media that show women enjoying abuse. The campaign has supporters such as the J. Walter Thompson Advertising Agency, Proctor and Gamble, and Lily Tomlin. —*Ms.* "Gazette," December, 1976

"A man whose fantasy life is stimulated through adult pornography can find a consenting female, either for money or for companionship. There is no way a man whose fantasy life is stimulated by a five-year-old can find a legitimate and healthy outlet for that stimulation."

—Dr. Judianne Densen-Gerber, founder of Odyssey drug treatment centers, quoted in "America Discovers Child Pornography," by Helen Dudar, *Ms.*, August, 1977

There is a scene in *Deep Throat*, where a man inserts a hollow glass dildo inside Miss Lovelace, fills it with Coca-Cola, and drinks it with a surgical straw—the audience was bursting with nervous laughter, while I sat through it literally faint. All I could think about was what would happen if the glass broke. I always cringe when I read reviews of this sort—crazy feminists carrying on, criticizing nonpolitical films in political terms—but as I sat through the film I was swept away in a bromidic wave of movement rhetoric. "Demeaning to women," I wailed as we walked away from the theatre. "Degrading to women." I began muttering about the clitoris backlash. The men I was with pretended they did not know me, and then, when I persisted in addressing my mutterings to them, they assured me that I was overreacting, that it was just a movie and that they hadn't even been turned on by it. But I refused to calm down. "Look, Nora," said one of them, playing what I suppose he thought was his trump card by appealing to my sense of humor, "there's one thing you have to admit. The scene with the Coca-Cola was hilarious."

—Nora Ephron, *Crazy Salad* (Knopf), 1975

> "The word pornography in its very origins means writing about women captives or slaves. Erotica is something quite different, portraying love as something chosen. Pornography is not sex, and sex need not be violent or aggressive at all. It is violence and domination that are pornographic. . . . It's organic [for feminists to raise the issue now]: having untangled sex and violence on the issue of rape, which came first because it's direct physical violence—as opposed to pornography which is indirect—it's a rational progression toward untangling sex and violence in pornography. *Pornography* is the instruction; rape is the practice, battered women are the practice, battered children are the practice."
>
> —Gloria Steinem, addressing the Women Against Pornography conference, September, 1979

Eric Stein

RAPE

Five women in Dallas, Texas, published the names of some 1,500 men who had been indicted for rape or other sex-related crime in Dallas County from 1960 to 1976. The publication was the result of nine months of combing courthouse records by the *Kitty Genovese Women's Project*, named for the 28-year-old Queens, New York, woman who was stabbed to death in 1964 while many of her neighbors watched.

The members of the project, in their original statement of purpose, said they had reached their decision to publish the names based on information that nearly half of all women who are raped are attacked by men they know.

—*Ms.* "Gazette," March, 1979

[A 1975] *Harper's Weekly* article asks us to imagine a robbery victim undergoing the same sort of cross-examination that a rape victim does:

"Mr. Smith, you were held up at gunpoint on First and Main?"

"Yes."

"Did you struggle with the robber?"

"No."

"Why not?"

"He was armed."

"Then you made a conscious decision to comply with his demands rather than resist?"

"Yes."

"Did you scream? Cry out?"

"No. I was afraid."

"I see. Have you ever been held up before?"

"No."

"Have you ever *given* money away?"

"Yes, of course."

"And you did so willingly?"

"What are you getting at?"

"Well, let's put it like this, Mr. Smith. You've given money away in the past. How can we be sure you weren't *contriving* to have your money taken by force?"

"Listen, if I wanted—"

"Never mind. What time did this holdup take place?"

"About 11 P.M."

"You were out on the street at 11 P.M.? Doing what?"

"Just walking."

"Just walking?

"Weren't you aware that you could have been held up?"

"I hadn't thought about it."

"What were you wearing?"

"Let's see—a suit. Yes, a suit."

"An *expensive* suit?"

"Well—yes."

"In other words, Mr. Smith, you were walking around the streets late at night in a suit that practically advertised the fact that you might be a good target for some easy money, isn't that so? I mean, if we didn't know better, Mr. Smith, we might even think that you were *asking* for this to happen, mightn't we?"

Article 4:

Functions of the [Rape Crisis] Center.

a. Emergency phone service: provides immediate contact and information to women who have been raped or attacked.

b. Discussion groups: groups of 5-10 women will be formed to discuss their reactions to the rape or the attack and how they feel they can resolve these feelings.

c. Escort service to the police or hospital.

d. Emergency housing.

e. Publication and dissemination of information.

—Bylaws of the Rape Crisis Center, Washington, D.C., May, 1972

Bettye Lane

"Confucius once say: 'If rape is inevitable, relax and enjoy it.'"

—former WABC-TV weatherman Tex Antoine's on-camera statement following a news report of the attempted rape of an eight-year-old girl, December, 1976

Man's discovery that his genitalia could serve as a weapon to generate fear must rank as one of the most important discoveries of prehistoric times. From prehistoric times to the present, rape has played a critical function. It is a conscious process of intimidation by which *all men* keep *all women* in a state of fear. —Susan Brownmiller, *Against Our Will*, 1975

- ☐ 60 percent of rapes are planned.
- ☐ 50 percent of rapes are committed in the home.
- ☐ 50 percent of rapes are committed by an assailant known to the victim.
- ☐ Two-thirds of convicted rapists are married and have regular sex.

—Washington, D.C. Rape Crisis Center, 1974

- ☐ An estimated 250,000 rapes are committed every year, but only 56,000 are reported.
- ☐ One reported rape in four results in arrest; one in 60 in conviction.
- ☐ Sixty-eight percent of prosecutors interviewed avoid specializing in rape cases, which are considered to be "too emotional," "frustrating," and "not good for one's career."

—Federal Law Enforcement Assistance Administration, 1978

Bettye Lane

AT HOME

Our examination found the highest rates of marital violence among the following: families living in large urban areas, minority racial groups, individuals with no religious affiliation, people with some high school education, families with low incomes, blue-collar workers, people under 30, and families where the husband was unemployed. . . . Our examination also revealed that families with four to six children had the highest rates of violence. Furthermore, the greater stress a couple experienced, the more violent they were. Last, in homes where husbands and wives shared family decisions, the rate of violence was *lowest*.

Examining the social context and social consequences of marital violence, one finds that irrespective of the kind of hitting that goes on, women are much more likely to get the worst of it. In many cases of marital violence women are physically helpless . . . in many instances the women involved are pregnant and almost completely unable to adequately defend themselves. [I have] found that one in four women who were victims of violence were hit when pregnant.

—Richard Gelles, "The Myth of the Battered Husband," *Ms.*, October, 1979

A massive class action suit filed last December in Manhattan Supreme Court by a coalition of New York-based legal organizations charges that an equally indifferent attitude is shared by New York City police and by the Family Court System. The complaint on behalf of 12 battered wives claims that police "deny the existence, prevalence, and seriousness of violence against married women or treat it as a private privilege of marital discipline." The police refuse to arrest violent husbands, and the Family Court denies women access to orders of protection.

—Marcia Rockwood, *Ms.* "Gazette," April, 1977

One girl out of every four in the United States will be sexually abused in some way before she reaches the age of 18. Although it is widely assumed that her assailant will be a mysterious pervert, according to a 1967 survey conducted in New York City by the American Humane Association, only one quarter of all sexual molestations are committed by strangers. Only 2 percent take place in cars; only 5 percent in abandoned buildings. In a full 75 percent of the cases, the victim knows her assailant. In 34 percent, the molestation takes place in her own home.

—Ellen Weber, "Sexual Abuse Begins at Home," *Ms.*, April, 1977

"There isn't any particular thing that would set me off. Drinking had a lot to do with it. The alcohol justifies any action. After you've slapped a woman around a few times it's no big deal. The woman may be desperate, and the guy doesn't understand that. I'd wonder why a woman would provoke me when she knew what was bound to happen. 'This woman must be crazy,' I'd say. 'She *wants* me to knock her down.' And I know women who are really aggressive, who throw hot water or stab a guy. . . .

"Eventually it dawned on me: 'I'm my pops all over again.' And I went back to the beginning to see what happened. . . .

"What the solution should be to this I don't know, but one obvious way is to talk openly and not sweep such matters under the rug. . . .

"There ought to be a place to go to think things over if either party wants to leave home."

—Bill M., interviewed by Ann Geracimos, *Ms.*, August, 1976

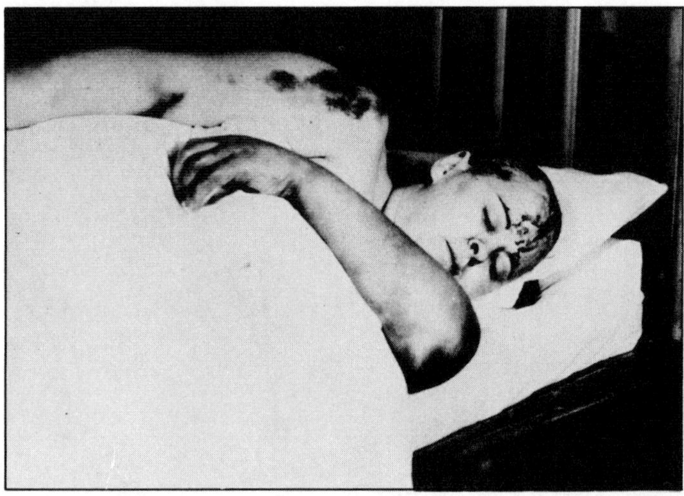

UPI

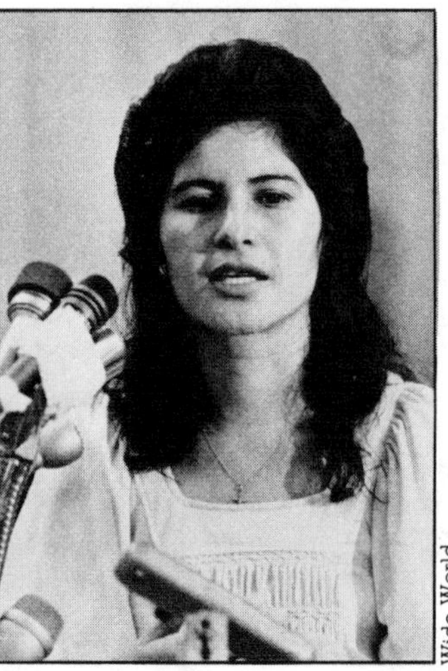

Wide World

Far left—**Wife of a methodist minister is hospitalized after beating by her husband.** Left—**Battered wife Idalia Mejia is acquitted of murdering her husband in 1978.**

The door behind which the battered wife is trapped is the door to the family home. The white-picket-fence stereotype of the American family home still persists from the days of Andy Hardy.

—Del Martin, *Battered Wives* (Glide Publications), 1976

Liaison

Liaison

Bettye Lane

Counterclockwise from bottom right—**In 1978 Sandy Ramos receives major funding for Shelter Our Sisters, her battered wives house in Hackensack, New Jersey. Erin Pizzey in 1971 founds Chiswick Women's Aid, only place in England that would shelter any woman fleeing a violent relationship. Six years later, 70 refuges are operating in Britain. Children who live with their mothers at London's Chiswick shelter.**

HARASSMENT

Woman walks through New York City's Central Park, 1978.

I hate to walk down the street and have men make *psst, psst* noises at me from the sidewalk or from the safety of their cars. I hate riding the subways during the rush hour. Both situations turn me into a man-hater. The *psst, pssts* are bad enough although the assault is exclusively verbal, but the subways represent a worse threat to the command of one's own body.

—Ingrid Bengis, *Combat in the Erogenous Zone* (Knopf), 1972

In a study made by Dr. Stanley L. Brodsky, of the University of Alabama, convicted rapists were shown videotapes of nine different styles of resistance. The women's ploys as reenacted from case histories of actual rapes included pretending they had VD or cancer, were pregnant or virginal, would kill themselves if raped, and various forms of compliance ("You don't need that gun . . . I'll do anything you say.").

The "highly assaultive" rapists said they were sexually excited by resistance, and may have been dissuaded by passivity, crying, and other signs of weakness. But an almost equal number of men said the opposite: that the victims' "body weakness" ploys increased their sexual excitement, but they—mostly men who had approached their victims with relative politeness—would have been stopped by forceful refusal.

—Mary Scott Welch,
Ms. "Gazette,"
March, 1979

It *is* the uprising of women which will presage the end of oppression, but this uprising must be based on more than opposition to oppression and the definition of Woman as Other.

—Jane Alpert,
"Mother Right:
A New Feminist Theory,"
Ms., August, 1973

"It's an open secret," said one young woman aide to a United States Senator from the East Coast, "that some of our Congressmen and Senators just won't hire a woman unless they 'try her out' first. These are the same guys who are supposed to be passing legislation to protect women's rights." Exposés by Elizabeth Ray and Colleen Gardner, both of whom reported sexual favors expected as part of their duties on Congressional payrolls, slowed down some of the sexual pressures for a while. (Though even those exposés sometimes worked against women's employment. Several young women job applicants, in spite of excellent credentials, reported being turned down by cautious Congressmen in their efforts to avoid suspicion.)

—Karen Lindsey,
"Sexual Harassment
on the Job,"
Ms., November, 1977

In February, 1979, the ACLU discovered that they had underestimated the Chicago police when a television reporter broke the story of widespread illegal [strip-searches]. Chuck Collins of WMAQ-TV heard about the searches at a party. Everyone thought it was pretty funny, especially the part about strip-searches allegedly being conducted under the eyes of closed-circuit cameras, with police in other parts of the station following the plundering of women's breasts, vaginas, and rectums on TV monitors.

—Carol Kleiman,
Ms. "Gazette,"
June, 1979

"... knowing karate doesn't mean you'll use it like a gun. It develops a fighter attitude. So if you use an umbrella to beat off an attacker—fine. Maybe it isn't karate. But maybe if you hadn't had that training, you wouldn't have resisted at all."

—Susan Murdock, teacher at Women's Martial Arts Center, New York City, 1975

Bettye Lane

Sexual harassment at the workplace takes many forms. These include verbal harassment, or abuse, subtle pressure for sexual activity, as well as rape and attempted rape. Sexual demands, made by male employers, co-workers, or clients, become coercive when women employees cannot freely choose to say yes or no. In this situation, a woman's economic livelihood is endangered—her ability to keep a job, and to obtain benefits, promotions, or raises.

—Alliance Against
Sexual Coercion,
Cambridge, Mass., flier, 1977

LESBIANISM

JEB

Lesbian and Gay Pride March, New York City, June, 1979.

"I've been known to be violently opposed to the lesbian issue in the women's movement and I have been. I'm someone who grew up in Middle America, and maybe I love men too much. We have all made mistakes and we have all learned. I now see there is nothing in ERA to protect lesbians, and so I urge adoption of this measure."

—Betty Friedan, speaking for the sexual preference resolution, November 21, 1977, The First National Women's Conference, Houston, Texas

JEB

"Women who love women are lesbians. Men, because they can only think of women in sexual terms, define lesbian as sex between women. However, lesbians know that it is far more than that, it is a different way of life. It is a life determined by a woman for her own benefit and the benefit of other women. It is a life that draws its strength, support, and direction from women. . . . You refuse to limit yourself by the male definitions of women. You free yourself from male concepts of 'feminine' behavior."

—Rita Mae Brown, *Ms.*, November, 1976

Catherine Ursillo

In a society in which men do not oppress women, and sexual expression is allowed to follow feelings, the categories of homosexuality and heterosexuality would disappear. . . . But lesbianism is also different from male homosexuality, and serves a different function in the society. "Dyke" is a different kind of put-down from "faggot," although both imply you are not playing your socially assigned sex roles . . . are not therefore a "real woman" or a "real man." The grudging admiration felt for the tomboy, and the queasiness felt around a sissy-boy point to the same thing; the contempt in which women—or those who play a female role—are held. And the investment in keeping women in that contemptuous role is very great. Lesbian is the word, the label, the condition that holds women in line. When a woman hears this word tossed her way, she knows she is stepping out of line.

—"The Woman–Identified Woman" by Radicalesbians, *Notes from the Third Year*, 1970

We are sometimes accused by "straight" feminists of guilt-tripping them about their personal lives; of implying that sexual dependence on men made them somehow less feminist. In fact, we were less concerned about an individual woman's personal choice than about the institution of heterosexuality; less concerned with sex-roles than with sex-power.

—Charlotte Bunch, "Learning from Lesbian Separatism," *Ms.*, November, 1976

Ann Phillips

The anxious fearful confrontation between straight and lesbian feminists should be drawing to a close. Many straight women with strong feminist programs and consciousness are in key positions to mediate between the more radical (withdrawn) elements and the patriarchy, which will weaken and crumble of its own accord as women gradually develop our own strength and identity. As the radical women unfold counter-communities the more conservative women can pacify and deal with the man more directly within his own structure. Both radical and conservative women can reinforce each other and recognize the value of the other in maintaining the revolution along every aspect of its polarities.

—Jill Johnston, "Are Lesbians 'Gay'?", *Ms.*, June, 1975

Eric Stephen Jacobs

In a paradoxical sense, once I accepted my position as one different from the larger society as well as from any single subsociety—or subculture—black or gay, I felt I didn't have to try as hard. To be accepted. To look fem. To be straight. To look straight. To be proper. To look nice. To be hired. To be loved. To be approved. What I didn't realize or couldn't admit then was how much harder I had to try merely to stay alive, or rather to stay human. Yet how much stronger a person I became in that trying.

—Audre Lorde, "I've Been Standing on This Street Corner a Hell of a Long Time," From *Our Right to Love: A Lesbian Resource Book* ed. Ginny Vida (Prentice Hall), 1977

THE BALLOT BOX

Opposite page—
Democrat Ella Grasso of Connecticut in 1974 becomes the first woman governor elected in her own right.

The total number of women in public office has more than doubled since 1975. In October 1975 women held 7,242 offices, about 4.7 percent of the total in the country. By the end of 1978 women held 17,782 offices, about 10.9 percent.

The number of women elected to state legislatures has more than doubled during the decade, from 334 (about 4 percent) in 1970 to 767 (10.3 percent) in 1979. In 1974 Ella Grasso (D-Conn.) was the first woman in her own right elected Governor and Mary Ann Krupsak (D-N.Y.) was the first woman elected Lieutenant Governor. Today there are two women Governors and six women Lt. Governors.

In 1969 there were eleven women in the U.S. Congress—one in the Senate and ten in the House. Today there are 17—one in the Senate and 16 in the House.

The number of women in the state cabinet level and equivalent executive positions has increased from 45 (about 5 percent) in 1974 to 97 (10.7 percent) in 1977. For the first time there are two women members of the President's Cabinet (Secretary of Health, Education and Welfare Patricia Harris and Secretary of Commerce Juanita Kreps). Women hold about 20 percent of the volunteer and paid policy positions in the Carter administration, as compared to 5-10 percent for previous administrations.

In the federal judiciary women held only five of 525 seats in 1975 (less than 1 percent). After the increase of seats on the bench created by the Omnibus Judgeship Act, it is estimated that women will hold about 5 percent of all federal judgeships. In North Carolina in 1974, the first woman became Chief Justice of a state Supreme Court.

The first women national party chairs were chosen during this decade—Jean Westwood was chosen to head the Democratic Party in 1972 and Mary Louise Smith was chosen to head the Republican Party in 1975. In 1968 women composed 13 percent and 17 percent of the delegates to the Democratic and Republican conventions, respectively. By 1976 women were 34 percent of the delegates at the Democratic Convention and 31 percent at the Republican convention. Now the Democratic party rules for 1980 require that states choose an equal number of women and men delegates to its presidential nominating convention. The Republican party rules require that states endeavor to have equal representation.

—National Women's Political Caucus; National Women's Education Fund, September, 1979

First eliminate the 53 percent of the population that is female. Then disqualify the 5.2 percent that is minority male. Now give serious problems to any survivors who are under 30, or don't have four years of college. It is from the remaining pool of only 4.5 percent of the population that our [top] political leadership is selected.

—"An American Success Story," *Ms.*, November, 1977

"I took out the papers, got the signatures, and I was on the ballot [for the Newton, Massachusetts, Board of Aldermen], simple as that. I knocked on something like two thousand doors. . . . Sure there was a difference in the way men and women received me. Many men would ask if I was an attorney, first thing. Many women were willing to hear what I had to say without having to break through something first."

—Susan Schur, quoted in "Grass Roots: Where It All Starts," *Ms.*, April, 1974

Wide World

"The chair recognizes the gentlelady from Texas. . . ."

—Rep. Peter Rodino, House Judiciary Committee, 1974

" 'We, the people'—it is a very eloquent beginning. But when the Constitution of the United States was completed on the 17th of September in 1787, I was not included in that 'We the people.' But through the process of amendment, interpretation, and court decision I have finally been included in 'We, the people . . . "

—Rep. Barbara Jordan, House Judiciary Committee, 1974

Christina Thomson

Bettye Lane

"I ran because I was the most qualified for the job. There was a lot of pressure from some of my supporters in the community not to mention my lesbianism. But I thought it was necessary to state that politically. I mean, we're not purple—right?"

—Massachusetts State Representative Elaine Noble, quoted in *Ms.*, August, 1975

Above left—**In 1976 Congresswoman Barbara Jordan responds to ovation as she is introduced by Democratic National Chair Robert Strauss—the first black and the first woman to keynote a Democratic National Convention.** Right—**Democrat Dixy Lee Ray is elected governor of Washington State, 1976.** Far left—**Democrat Carol Bellamy is elected New York City Council President, 1977.** Left—**Elaine Noble, a self-proclaimed lesbian, is elected in 1974 to the Massachusetts legislature.**

John O'Hara/San Francisco Chronicle

Rachel Cowan

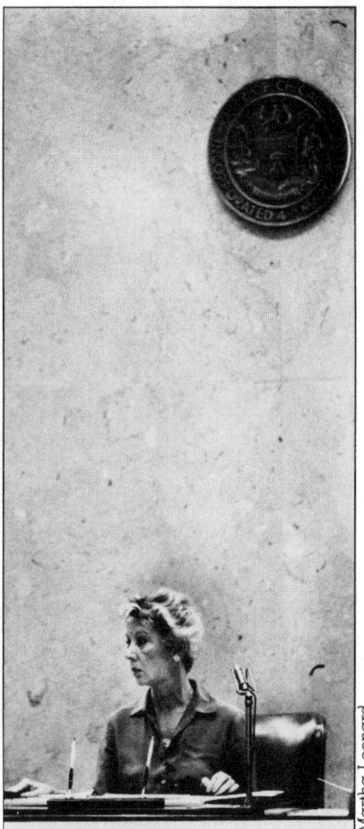

Martha Leonard

Mayors of cities, big and small: Democrat Diane Feinstein (*top left*) is sworn in as Mayor of San Francisco by California Supreme Court Chief Justice Rose Bird, 1978; Unita Blackwell (*left*), Mayor of Mayersville, Mississippi and member of the President's Advisory Committee on Women, visits with a constituent. Democrat Jane Byrne (*above*), elected Mayor of Chicago in 1979.

Cary Herz

"I am a candidate for the Presidency of the United States. I make that statement proudly, in the full knowledge that, as a black person and as a female person, I do not have a chance of actually gaining that office in this election year. I make that statement seriously, knowing that my candidacy itself can change the face and future of American politics—that it will be important to the needs and hopes of every one of you—even though, in the conventional sense, I will not win."

—Shirley Chisholm, June 4, 1972

Below—**Gloria Steinem, Bella Abzug, Shirley Chisholm, and Betty Friedan (*left to right*) announce formation of the National Women's Political Caucus, 1971.** Center—**Koryne Horbal of Minnesota, Democratic feminist organizer and U.S. Representative to the UN Commission on the Status of Women.** Right—**Liz Carpenter, co-chair of ERAmerica.**

Wide World

We must have the imagination to perceive ourselves and other women as autonomous independent creatures—not "co's," not "nice's," not "working for's," not "support staff," but whole human beings. Without this linkage of imagination and mutual support, this bonding that comes first—before we are Democrats or Republicans, and frankly—I will only speak for myself—before I am an American. Without this bonding that connects us to the courageous revolution in the streets of the women of Iran—who suffer problems not so dissimilar from the women of Utah, and different only in degree from the problems all women suffer under patriarchy. Without this bonding that recognizes our ultimate shared interests, and without a sense of where our long-term loyalty lies, we will never become the full human beings we really can be.

—Gloria Steinem,
at the 1979 Convention,
National Women's
Political Caucus

There are feminist publishers, music groups, art galleries, credit unions, health clinics, retreats, work cooperatives. Alternate structures not only serve as rescue stations and laboratories of change, but also as intermediate structures that can evolve and take over gradually as they absorb the change that they themselves have pushed for.

Catherine Ursillo

I think we're realizing more and more that we need to move back and forth; to experiment and make pressure outside, and then to move inside for a while and see just how far we can make the system budge.

But we need to keep a base outside. We need a place to create ourselves.

—Charlotte Bunch,
"Outside the System,"
Ms., July, 1977

A few of us sat down and wrote the principles for the [Minnesota Democratic Farmer Labor Party] Feminist Caucus. We used the word 'feminist' upfront—none of this 'women's' crap. There were fourteen principles—the ERA, the choice of abortion, child care, party reform, supporting feminists for posts in and outside the party—everything. The fourteenth was the most controversial, through, because we pledged to support, as a caucus and as individuals, 'only those candidates who support these principles.' But we kept that fourteenth point. Why mess around supporting candidates who don't support your issues? I'd had enough of that in my life.

—Koryne Horbal,
"Inside the System,"
Ms., July, 1977

"Don't blame me, I voted for Helen Gahagan Douglas."

—button that appeared
in California
during Watergate

Bettye Lane

The ticket that might have been: Congresswoman Shirley Chisholm of New York (*opposite page top*) runs a grass-roots campaign on a shoestring budget for the Democratic Presidential nomination in 1972. Frances (Sissy) Farenthold of Texas (*right*) receives 420 delegate votes for Vice-President at the 1972 Democratic National Convention, second only to Senator Thomas Eagleton. (She later heads the National Women's Political Caucus and becomes President of Wells College in New York State.)

Bettye Lane

"A lady named Farenthold wants to be Vice-President."

—CBS News anchor Walter Cronkite at the Democratic Convention, July 1972

When the nurse, who we later found out is an ardent feminist, came to tell my husband that our baby had been born, she startled him by dryly announcing: "You have a possible future President of the United States—if we ever get the good sense to elect a woman!"

—Shirley E.
—letter to the editors, *Ms.*, August, 1976

Seventy-three percent of the American public told Gallup pollsters that they would vote for a woman for president if she were qualified. Four years ago, 66 percent of the electorate felt this way and back in 1937, a scant 31 percent felt ready and willing. More people now say they would vote for a woman in Congress, as governor of their state, and for mayor or top official of their city or community.

—*Ms.* "Gazette," February, 1976

. . . In 1970 Dr. Edgar Berman, who was an appointee to the Democratic Party's Committee on National Priorities, raised a storm of protest when he attacked Congresswoman Patsy Mink's statement that she "wouldn't see anything wrong with a woman president." Dr. Berman raised the specter of women's alleged instability. "Suppose," he speculated, "that we had a menopausal woman president who had to make the decision on the Bay of Pigs. . . ." Betty Friedan, Shirley Chisholm, and even Dr. Berman's wife rose up in protest. Patsy Mink requested Dr. Berman's ouster from the committee. His response was to attack this as a "typical example of an ordinarily controlled woman under the raging hormonal imbalance of the periodical lunar cycle."

—*The Menopause Book*, edited by Louisa Rose (Hawthorn), 1977

The directors of the Omi Railway Company of Japan are pragmatic students of human behavior and have therefore decided to accept the fact that men have lunar cycles of mood and efficiency. The company operates a private transport system of more than 700 buses and taxis in dense traffic areas of Kyoto and Osaka. . . . The Omi efficiency experts began in 1969 to make studies of each man and his lunar cycles and to adjust routes and schedules to coincide with the appropriate time of the month for each worker. They report a one-third drop in Omi's accident rate in the past two years, despite the fact that during the same period traffic increased. The benefit to the company—and to the men—has been substantial.

—Dr. Estelle Ramey, "Men's Cycles," *Ms.*, Spring, 1972

Pat Field

Mary Anne Fackelman/The White House

Jack Kightlinger/The White House

Jack Kightlinger/The White House

"Carter has appointed a few feminists in visible positions. But we don't have a critical mass yet."

—an HEW staff member, quoted in "All the President's Women," *Ms.*, January, 1978

"You walk into a meeting in one of the departments and now there's another woman there. You see each other, maybe you wink, and you know you're both glad to see each other there."

—Congresswoman Barbara Mikulski, quoted in "All the President's Women," *Ms.*, January, 1978

Sarah Weddington, in addition to being serene, gracious, grave, and dignified, is, depending on whom one consults, either stubborn as hell or possessed of a core of steel.

—Molly Ivins, "What Does Sarah Weddington Have that Midge Costanza Didn't?" *Ms.*, January, 1979

In some very basic ways, American women are in bed with Jimmy Carter—and it's a long time until morning. . . . If 1980 brings enough disillusionment with Carter, however, women are less likely to vote for someone else (or indeed, to have someone much better on women's issues to vote for) than we are to return to our old form of protest: just staying away from the polls.

—Gloria Steinem, "Will Women Make Carter a One-Term President?" *Ms.*, January, 1978

Top to bottom—**The "Ins" and "Outs" of the Carter appointees: Bella Abzug, soon to co-chair the National Advisory Committee for Women, presents President Carter with the report of the National Women's Conference, 1978. Linda Bird Johnson Robb is appointed in 1979 to head the new, more restricted, advisory committee after Bella's ouster. Anne Wexler and Sarah Weddington, Carter's top women aides, join the White House staff in 1978. Midge Costanza leaves after her responsibilities and staff are cut back.**

Christina Thomson

"The only place they can meet without me is in the men's room—and if I thought they were up to anything, I'd kick the door in!"

—Midge Costanza, then Special Assistant to the President, quoted in "One Door from the Oval Office," *Ms.*, January, 1978

Jack Kightlinger/The White House

Column 1—*(top to bottom)* **Lucy Wilson Benson, Under Secretary of State for Security Assistance, Science and Technology, formerly President of the League of Women Voters. Alexis Herman, head of the Labor Department's Women's Bureau. Arvonne Fraser, founder of Women's Equity Action League, is AID Coordinator of the Office of Women and Development.**

Column 2—*(top to bottom)* **Esther Peterson, Consumer Affairs Advisor. Patt Derian, State Department of Human Rights and Humanitarian Affairs. Donna E. Shalala, HUD Assistant Secretary for Policy Development and Research.**

Dana West/The White House

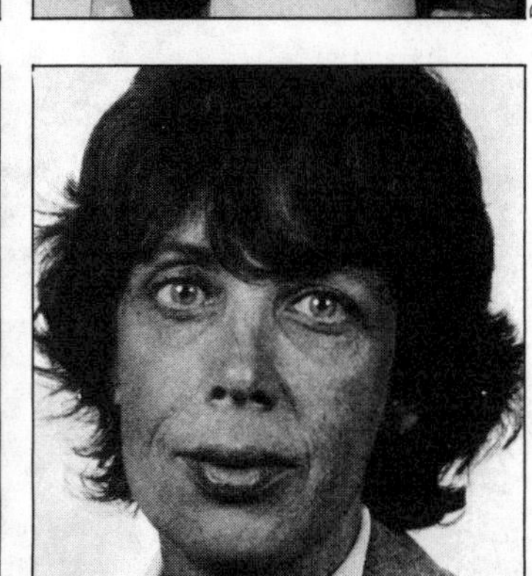

Above—**Patrica Roberts Harris is sworn in as Secretary of Housing and Urban Development in 1977 by Supreme Court Justice Thurgood Marshall as her husband, William Harris looks on. In the 1979 shakeup, she moves to Department of Health, Education, and Welfare.** Below—**Juanita M. Kreps joins Carter Cabinet in 1977 as Secretary of Commerce, after doing important economic research on women and work. She resigns in 1979 "for personal reasons."**

"When men talk about defense, they always claim to be protecting women and children, but they never ask the women and children what they think."

—Pat Schroeder, quoted in *Ms.*, June, 1976

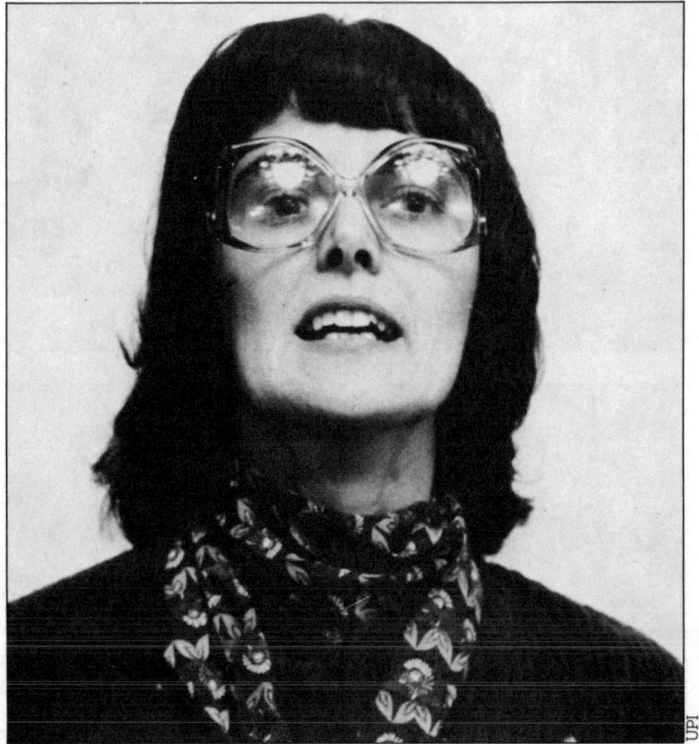

Above—**In 1973, veteran Congresswomen Martha Griffths of Michigan and Shirley Chisholm of New York (*left and second from left*) and Bella Abzug of New York (*far right*) welcome newly elected Elizabeth Holtzman of New York, Barbara Jordan of Texas, and Yvonne Brathwaite Burke of California.**
Left—**Congresswoman Patricia Schroeder, Democrat of Colorado, also comes to the Hill in 1973.**

Newcomers to Congress in 1979 (*left to right*): Congresswomen Olympia Snowe of Maine; Nancy Landon Kassebaum of Kansas, who serves as the only woman Senator; and Congresswoman Geraldine A. Ferraro of New York. With Beverly Byron of Maryland (not pictured), Snowe and Ferraro bring the total number of women in the House to 16.

UPI

Rocco Galatioto

Alan Porter

"America is not a melting pot. It is a sizzling cauldron. . . . Government is polarizing people by the creation of myths. . . . The ethnic worker is fooled into thinking that the blacks are getting everything. Two groups end up fighting each other for the same jobs and schools and recreation centers for their respective communities. What results is an angry confrontation for tokens, when there should be an alliance for a whole new Agenda for America."

—Barbara Mikulski, June, 1970

Above—**Congresswoman Millicent Fenwick of New Jersey, with her Republican colleagues, Senators Charles Mathias of Maryland (*left*) and Roger Jepsen of Iowa, outline their solution to the "tax on marriage" in a 1979 bill.**

UPI

Clockwise from top left—**Congresswomen Cardiss Collins of Illinois. Barbara Mikulski of Maryland. Patsy Mink of Hawaii (pictured with two constituents).**

Like many women who run for office, Bella Abzug comes to elective politics as an issues advocate. A labor lawyer, civil rights, peace, and feminist activist, she seeks and wins a Congressional seat in 1970, campaigning on the slogan, "This Woman Belongs in the House . . . the House of Representatives."

Bettye Lane

At New York's August 26, 1970, Women's Equality march.

Bettye Lane

At a rally in support of Soviet Jewry, 1973.

Bettye Lane

At a UN demonstration against the Franco regime, 1975.

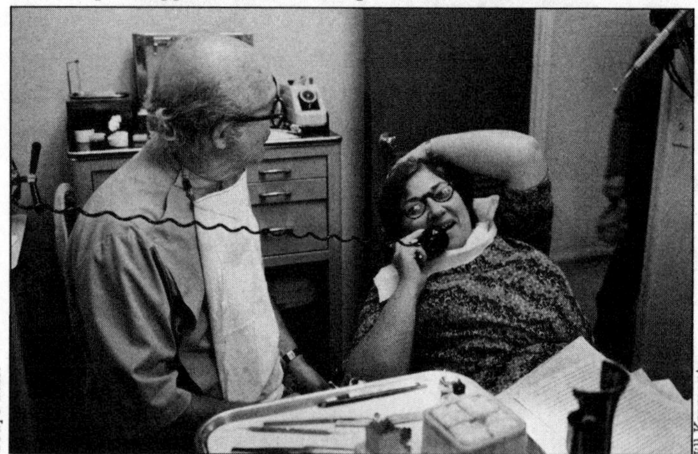
Jill Krementz

Working—even in the dentist's chair, 1975.

Joan Roth

A birthday dance in 1977 with loyal supporter, Shirley MacLaine.

Bettye Lane

Winning friends, but Bella looses the mayor's race, 1977.

I've been described as a tough and noisy woman, a prize fighter, a man-hater, you name it. They call me Battling Bella, Mother Courage, and a Jewish mother with more complaints than Portnoy. There are those who say I'm impatient, impetuous, uppity, rude, profane, brash, and overbearing. Whether I'm any of those things, or all of them, you can decide for yourself. But whatever I am—and this ought to be made very clear—I am a very serious woman.

—*Bella!*, Mel Ziegler, ed., Introduction 1972

Bettye Lane

At meeting to get more women elected, 1974.

Bettye Lane

At a United Farm Workers rally, 1975.

Bettye Lane

With Lily Tomlin in 1976, the year of her unsuccessful Senate race.

Iris Schneider

With husband Martin, Bella throws hat in the ring for 1977 mayoralty.

Ann Chwatsky

At a press conference after the January, 1979, "Friday Night Massacre," when Carter fires Bella as co-chair of the National Advisory Committee for Women. (The committee had challenged his economic priorities.) Behind Bella (*left to right*) are Carolyn Reed of the National Committee on Household Employment and Jean O'Leary of the National Gay Task Force, both of whom, along with co-chair Carmen Delgado Votaw and more than half the committee, resign in protest.

N.Y. Daily News Photo

With Gloria Steinem in August, 1979 to launch an anti-inflation campaign for Americans left "up the creek" by rising prices. The action is sponsored by Women USA, a grass-roots lobby founded by Bella, along with other leaders including Yvonne Burke and Patsy Mink.

"Any woman who chooses to behave like a full human being should be warned that the armies of the status quo will treat her as something of a dirty joke; that's their natural and first weapon."

—Gloria Steinem, "Sisterhood," *Ms.*, Spring, 1972

BACKLASH

Ray Fisher

Learn to capitalize on disappointment and heartbreak . . . stop nagging altogether . . . hold him in reverence, it says in the Bible. . . .It is your nature to give. . . .Tell him you love his body. If you choke on that phrase, practice until it comes out naturally. . . .What if the king makes the wrong decision? . . . The queen is still to follow him forthwith. . . .Are you guilty of that heinous act ingratitude? . . . a wife cannot be grateful if she's grasping for her rights . . .Be prepared mentally and physically for intercourse every night this week. . . .If you're a working wife, he especially needs your reassurance and appreciation, since his masculinity may be threatened by your paycheck.

—Marabel Morgan, *The Total Women* (Pocket Books), 1973

"Why do you think the homosexuals are called fruits? It's because they eat the forbidden fruit of the tree of life . . . male sperm."

—Anita Bryant, 1978

[Anita Bryant and husband Bob Green] . . . stood beneath a portrait of Taurus the Bull in the Zodiac Room of the Holiday Inn, where Green kissed his wife on the mouth and twinkled to the assembled male and female press: "This is what heterosexuals do, fellas."

—Lindsy Van Gelder, "The Lessons of Dade County," *Ms.*, September, 1977

"The pursuit of an orgasm for a woman is an entirely irrelevant undertaking."

—Midge Decter, *The New Chastity and Other Arguments Against Women's Liberation* (Coward, McCann & Goeghegan), 1972

Almost unnoticed, antiabortion forces are seeking a Constitutional Convention as a way of getting an amendment banning all abortions. But is that just the beginning? With such a pretext, a Convention might come together and reconsider all parts of the Constitution. In fact, the whole country might just begin to unravel.

—Lisa Cronin Wohl, "Are We 25 Votes Away from Losing the Bill of Rights . . .?" *Ms.*, February, 1978

The Right offers women a simple, fixed, predetermined social, biological, and sexual order. Form conquers chaos, banishes confusion, makes ignorance look like something instead of nothing. . . .

—Andrea Dworkin, "The Promise of the Ultra-Right," *Ms.*, June, 1979

It is quite incredible that men, whose desire for knowledge is unbounded in every other field . . . are incapable of seeing women as they really are: with nothing else to offer but a vagina, two breasts, and some punch cards programmed with idle, stereotyped chatter; that they are nothing more than conglomerations of matter, lumps of stuffed human skin pretending to be thinking human beings.

—Esther Vilar, *The Manipulated Man* (Farrar Straus & Giroux), 1973

UPI

UPI

"[Theodore Bundy, convicted murderer of two women] supports my career-oriented feminism, and he said he liked the novel [*The Women's Room*] because men and women don't often get a chance to know what it is like to be the opposite sex."

—Carole Boone, quoted in the Boston *Globe*, July 11, 1979

Charles Gatewood/Magnum

GEN

Below—**Four generations of a family gather for a portrait.** Opposite page—**Father and infant son get acquainted.**

Joanne Leonard

ERATIONS

Abigail Heyman/Magnum

But one feature of the old extended family which may be disappearing from the world is a sense of the human life span. Family is a generation-spanning group that transmits history in a uniquely profound way. I have something my daughter doesn't have (and I wish she did): a group of people (some of whom I don't particularly like or wouldn't choose as friends but that's part of what makes it important) whom I've known since I was a baby and whom I've watched progress through the stages of life. There are a number of gray-haired people I remember as radiant infants.

—Dorothy Dinnerstein, *Ms.*, August, 1979

Jill Krementz

Above—**Toni Morrison and son Slade.**
Below—**Letty Cottin Pogrebin with her twins Robin (*left*) and Abigail.**

We all worry about raising our kids to fight what's out there. Feminists with sons have the extra vulnerability of wondering if their sons will be other women's enemies, no matter what Mother tries to do to prevent it.

—Lindsy Van Gelder
and Carrie Carmichael,
"But What About Our Sons?"
Ms., October, 1975

Suppose she had lived long enough for us to be women together? I wonder if I would have gone away to college, then lived alone, traveled, explored sexuality so unguardedly, learned to support myself, taken risks, chosen independence. I think not. I loved her too much to have defined myself without her approval.

Because she was mother and model, I would have assumed her limited aspirations and imitated her passivity. Her gentleness was seductive; strength, anger or rebellion were affronts to her quiet dignity. I saw her role as the supportive, self-effacing wife to be my natural destiny and by the time she died, I had already begun walking in her tracks.

By dying, my mother forced me to live life as an invention of my own. I can only wonder how it would have been between us when I watch other mothers and daughters play out the scenario—not in *what ifs* but in *what is*.

—Letty Cottin Pogrebin,
Ms., June, 1975

Janet Beller

PARENTS & CHILDREN

Probably there is nothing in human nature more resonant with charges than the flow of energy between two biologically alike bodies, one of which has lain in amniotic bliss inside the other, one of which has labored to give birth to the other.

—Adrienne Rich,
Of Woman Born
(W.W. Norton), 1976

Sometimes I try to imagine a little scene that could have helped us both. In her kind, warm, shy, and self-deprecating way, mother calls me into the bedroom where she sleeps alone. She is no more than twenty-five. I am perhaps six. Putting her hands (which her father told her always to keep hidden because they were "large and unattractive") on my shoulders, she looks me right through my steel-rimmed spectacles: "Nancy, you know I'm not really good at this mothering business," she says. "You're a lovely child, the fault is not with you. But motherhood doesn't come easily to me. So when I don't seem like other people's mothers, try to understand that it isn't because I don't love you. I do. But I'm confused myself. There are some things I know about. I'll teach them to you. The other stuff—sex and all that—well, I just can't discuss them with you because I'm not sure where they fit into my own life. We'll try to find other people, other women who can talk to you and fill the gaps. You can't expect me to be all the mother you need. I feel closer to your age in some ways than I do my mother's. I don't feel that serene, divine, earth-mother certainty you're supposed to that she felt. I am unsure how to raise you. But you are intelligent and so am I. Your aunt loves you, your teachers already feel the need in you. With their help, with what I can give, we'll see that you get the whole mother package—all the love in the world. It's just that you can't expect to get it all from me."

A scene that could never have taken place.

—Nancy Friday,
My Mother / Myself
(Delacorte), 1977

Cary Herz

Barbara Love and her mother march for Gay Rights in 1974.

Ethel Diamond/*In sights: Self-Portraits by Women* (Godine)

". . . the only thing that seems eternal and natural in motherhood is ambivalence."

—Jane Lazarre,
The Mother Knot
(McGraw-Hill), 1976

"It took me a long time to get angry with my father, to confront the ultimate. If I weren't a feminist, I probably would not have questioned my right to have a real relationship with my father.

"But I do have a right to be loved, to be respected for my strength, and at the same time to expect to lean on someone else. When I didn't get this feeling in my relationships, I got angry. I feel I've connected with a whole part of me that until now I've completely denied—as if by making friends with my father I've finally been able to make friends with myself. The best part is that I really like what I've found."

—Anne Holton, *Ms.*, June, 1979

Janet Beller

James and Anne Holton.

Mary Helen Washington

Alice Walker and daughter Rebecca.

We are together, my child and I. Mother and child, yes, but *sisters* really, against whatever denies us all that we are.

For a long time I had this sign, which I constructed myself, deliberately, out of false glitter, over my desk:

"Dear Alice,
Virginia Woolf had madness;
George Eliot had ostracism,
somebody else's husband,
and did not dare to use
her own name.
Jane Austen had no privacy
and no love life.
The Brontë sisters never went any-
where
and died young
and dependent on their father.
Zora Hurston (ah!) had no money
and poor health.

You have Rebecca—who is
much more delightful
and less distracting
than any of the calamities
above."

—Alice Walker, "One Child of One's Own," *Ms.*, August, 1979

My fathering had always taken the form of a friendly cloud that floated across the lives of the children, and paused occasionally to cast a shadow. That they would turn out to have their own weather, and that I would profit by the climate, was an immense satisfaction.

—John Leonard,
"The Fathering Instinct,"
Ms., May, 1974

What did you learn from having a child?

I learned vulnerability. So simple, really, the simplicity of it amazed me, tears, my daughter's tears, her pain, her fears, and that I could comfort her, that her body relaxed against mine, that she learned to smile from me, that she was wholly unashamed of her hungers, her tempers, that there was no line of explanation between joy and sorrow but experience itself. The vulnerability and the clear logic of her flesh was a revelation to me. One morning, shortly after her birth, I lay on top of the bed crying because I realized one day I would have to explain death to her. Clearly in all her innocence, she did not deserve death.

—Susan Griffin,
"On Wanting to be the Mother I Wanted,"
Ms., January, 1977

In my puritanical home, there were two large taboos—sex and *money!* I now know why, even though I was a math major at Harvard, I have such difficulty understanding money and financial matters. It was as difficult for me to discuss money with my father as it was to discuss sex.

—letter quoted in
"The First Ms. Survey About Money," by Carol Tavris,
with Susan Sadd,
Ms., May, 1978

Two years ago, when my husband and I were first considering the question of whether or not to have children, I called Planned Parenthood for advice.

"I wonder if you could help us," I ventured. "My husband and I are interested in knowing—"

"You can get contraceptives at any of a number of locations," the clinic supervisor briskly informed me.

"No, no. You see, we have a problem. We—"

"Oh. You mean an abortion. We can refer you to—"

"Wait! We would like some counseling about whether or not to have children."

"Oh. (Pause.) I see. (Longer pause.) That's not our business here. Perhaps you should see a psychiatrist."

—Elizabeth Whelan,
"A Baby? . . . Maybe,"
Ms., April, 1977

Linda Wolfe reports that of the 70 percent who responded to a poll, only 3 babies were born among Bryn Mawr graduates who graduated between 1971 and 1975. Among those who graduated between 1966 and 1970, more than 70 babies had been born to the 70 percent of respondents. In five years the rate of those who had had a child went from over 10 percent to under 1 percent.

—Judith M. Bardwick,
In Transition
(Holt), 1979

Bill King

Margery and Wendy Weil.

My friends have learned to chart the passage of seasons by my mother's annual spring fishing trip to the Beaverkill, a trout stream in Upper New York's Catskill mountains. For 25 years, she has fished there the week before Memorial Day; one of the few women on the stream. My brother and I leave schools and jobs to join her. We come to be with her, to share her excitement and try to catch her style as well as a few fish.

—Wendy Weil,
Ms., June, 1975

Bettye Lane

Counter clockwise from upper left—**Hammers vie with dolls in lives of girls. Eight-year-old Julia looks ahead. Rebels with a cause. The ties between sisters endure—from childhood to old age.**

When we fought, like couples who've lived together for years, we knew the most tender nerve to strike. But when we decided to cooperate, we became a force to reckon with.

—Elizabeth Fishel, *Sisters* (William Morrow), 1979

Ann Chwatsky

Joanne Leonard

LNS

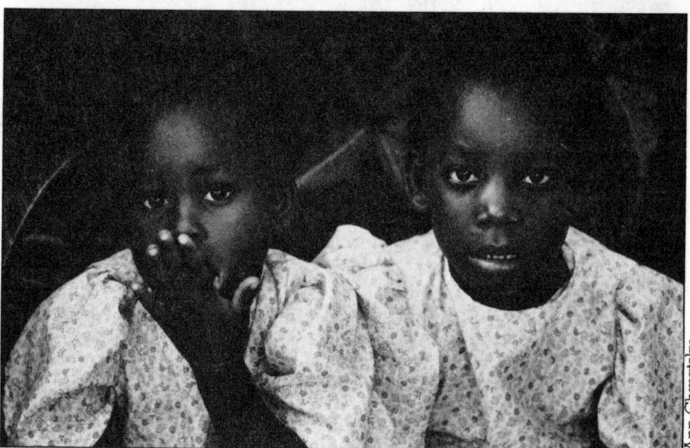

Ann Chwatsky

Opposite page— **Marlo Thomas in the 1974 Emmy award winning ABC special, "Free To Be . . . You and Me," which she originally put together in 1972 as a record album (Bell) "to help girls and boys feel free to be who they are and who they want to be."**
Below—**Another non-sexist classic is Charlotte Zolotow's *William's Doll* (Harper & Row, 1972)—about a boy who wants a doll and a grandmother who understands why.**

GROWING UP

Years ago, a friend of mine used to tell a very funny Embarrassing Moment story. Once, while walking in a department store, she found herself just behind two small boys whose heads came up only a little above her waist. Feeling affectionate and mischievous, she put a fingertip on the top of each boy's head. In an instant, two furious adult faces looked up at her, and in a harsh, high, but adult voice, one of them said, "What the hell do you think you're doing?" They were midgets.

Only quite recently did I realize that behind her act and our laughter at hearing about it was this thought—that if those midgets had really been children, it would have been perfectly all right to walk along with her fingertips on the tops of their heads.

But what makes it such a good idea to touch strange children's heads? What gives us the right to do it? What makes us think that they like us to do it.?

—John Holt,
Escape from Childhood
(E.P. Dutton), 1974

Growing numbers of young people hope to build, through their individual lives, a more just world in which everyone has the chance to realize his aspirations and potential. They are our main hope of salvation, I feel. In trying to undo discrimination against women—and its ill effects on men—some of these young people will lean over backward to avoid imposing on their children traditional stereotypes of boy and girl behavior, man and woman roles. They will, for instance, be as ready to buy dolls for their sons as for their daughters, if asked, and in no hurry to present dolls to their daughters *unless* asked. The same, in reverse, goes for guns.

Rejecting old stereotypes to this extent may seem ridiculous to some people. It is slightly disturbing to a physician trained in older concepts. But such self-conscious deviations from custom may be necessary if new and perhaps more valid and natural definitions of sex roles are to be tested. Letting children discover their own roles, without coaching, does not mean that they will end up sexually confused. And if roles for women and men in the future are not defined nearly as sharply or as oppositely as they are now, individuals with various personalities may be able to find roles that by today's standards are unconventional mixtures but that they can play out more comfortably.

—Dr. Benjamin Spock,
New York Times,
July 13, 1971

The American Family Report: Raising Children in a Changing Society, was based on a probability sampling of 1,230 households with one or more children under 13. It found that 43% of the parents belong to the "New Breed." They stress freedom over authority, self-fulfillment over material success, and duty to self over duty to others—including their own children. The study found that New Breed parents are loving but self-oriented, and they take a laissez-faire attitude to their own child rearing. Says Yankelovich: "It's not the permissiveness of the '50s, which was child-centered and concerned with the fragility of the child. Today, the parent says in effect, 'I want to be free, so why shouldn't my children be free?' "

—Daniel Yankelovich poll,
April, 1977

Others read my strictures on the way in which Americans are brought up—denied all firsthand knowledge of birth and love and death, harried by a society which will not let adolescents grow up at their own pace, imprisoned in the small, fragile, nuclear family from which there is no escape and in which there is little security—and think that I am indeed writing for today's world, so little have we altered the way in which our people are reared.

—Margaret Mead,
preface to the
1973 edition of
Coming of Age in Samoa
(William Morrow),
originally published in 1928

Intensive analyses of toy catalogs, observation in toy stores, interviews with toy executives, and questionnaires probing adult and child attitudes toward certain toys reveal three major findings: (1) "Masculine" toys are more varied and expensive, and are viewed as relatively complex, active, and social. (2) "Neutral" toys are viewed as most creative and educational, with boys receiving the most intricate items. (3) "Feminine" toys are seen as most simple, passive, and solitary.

—Letty Cottin Pogrebin,
"A Report on Children's Toys,"
Ms., December, 1972

In eight [high school civics] texts, there were only 33 index listings for women, compared to 1,104 for men. Ethel Rosenberg, the executed spy, and former Senator Margaret Chase Smith tie for prominence with three listings each.

—Jennifer MacLeod
and Sandy Silver(wo)man,
"Civilizing Civics,"
Ms., December, 1973

During one year a child will see 200 hours of commercials—a total of 22,000 ads for snacks, sweets, drinks, toys, drugs, pills, and household chemicals and detergents.

—Robert B. Choate,
and Nancy M. Debevoise,
"Battling the
Electronic Babysitter,"
Ms., April, 1975

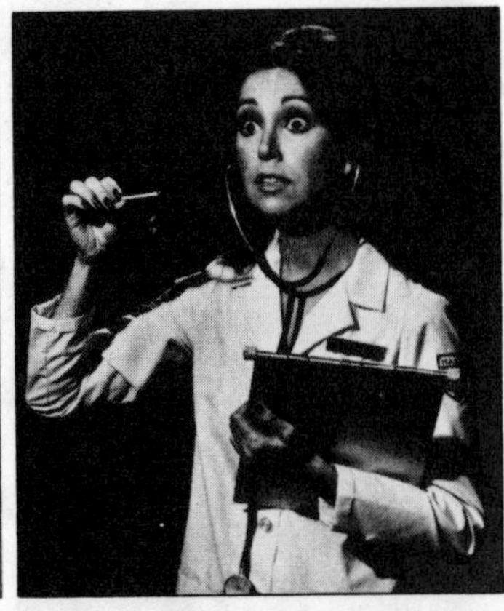

Bettye Lane

FOREMOTHERS

So long has the myth of feminine inferiority prevailed that women themselves find it hard to believe that their own sex was once and for a very long time the superior and dominant sex. In order to restore women to their ancient dignity and pride, they *must* be taught their own history, as the American blacks are being taught theirs.

—Elizabeth Gould Davis, *The First Sex* (G.P. Putnam's), 1971

"To get the word 'male' out of the Constitution cost the women of this country 72 years of campaigning. During that time, they were forced to conduct 66 campaigns of referenda to male voters, 480 campaigns to get legislatures to submit suffrage ammendments to voters, 47 campaigns to get state constitutional conventions to write women's suffrage into state constitutions, 277 campaigns to get state party conventions to include women's suffrage planks, 30 campaigns to get Presidential party conventions to adopt women's suffrage planks and 19 campaigns for the amendment in 19 successive Congresses."

—Carrie Chapman Catt, following ratification of the Women's Suffrage Amendment in 1920

The general pattern was that women would perceive a community need—for a church, an orphanage, an old people's home. They would then organize to meet this need, raise money, buy a building, run the institution. After some years, when the institution would become successful, the community would take it over, it would become incorporated, usually run by male trustees. At that point, it would also enter history, because its records would be preserved. And historians, looking at the records, would find no evidence of women's activities.

—Gerda Lerner, National Women's Agenda Coalition Conference, December, 1978

Below from top—**Sojourner Truth (c. 1797-1883), inspired speaker for the abolitionist and women's rights movement, delivered her famous "And ain't I a woman?" speech in 1851. Amelia Bloomer (1818-1894), temperance reformer, editor, and suffragist, defended women's wearing of "pantellettes" causing a furor and the coining of the name "Bloomer Costume." Emma Goldman (1869-1940), anarchist, free-speech advocate, and feminist. Often called "Red" Emma, she was deported to Russia in 1919.**

Bettmann Archive

N.Y. Public Library

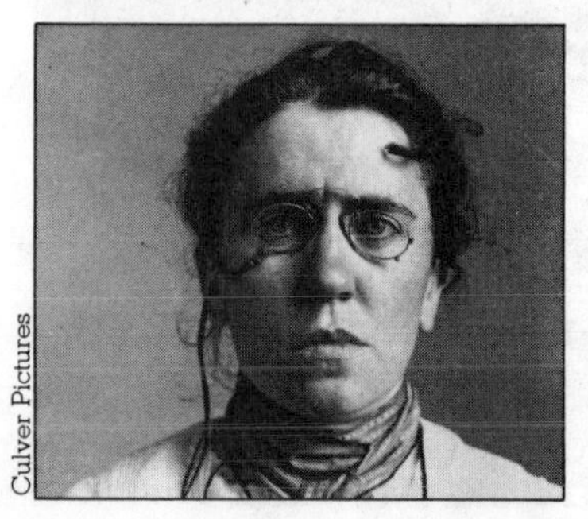

Culver Pictures

Evelyn Hofer

Above—**Alice Paul (1885-1977), militant suffrage leader and author in 1923 of the Equal Rights Amendment, fought for its passage for half a century.** Opposite page—**A suffrage march in New York City shortly before women won the vote nationally made a point of the territories and states where women already had suffrage rights.**

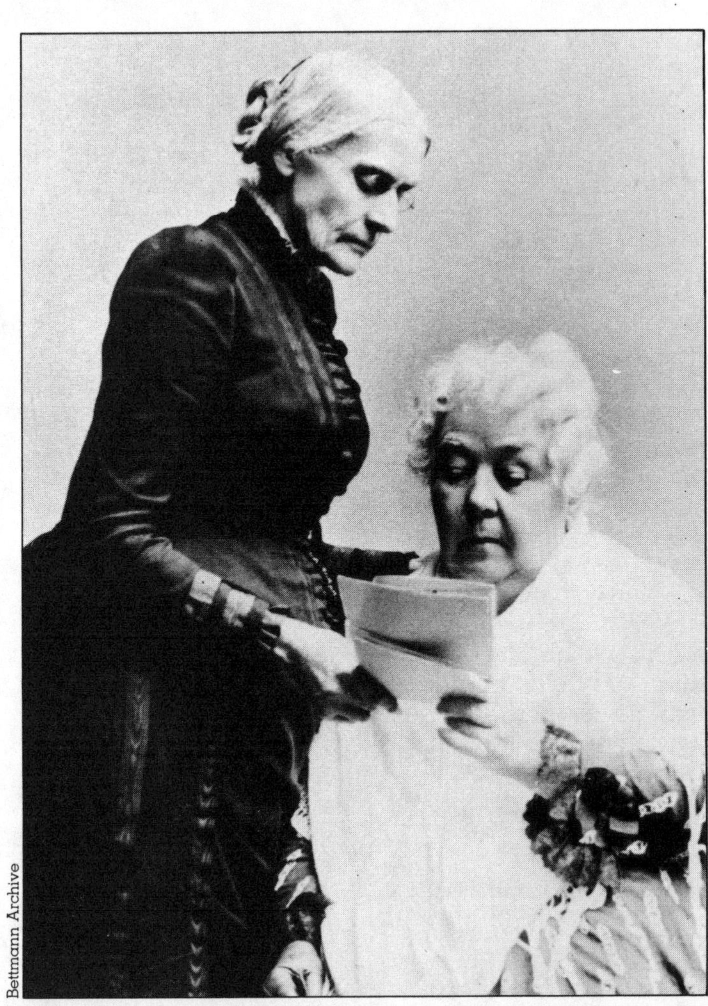

Bettmann Archive

Her crime: that she "did knowingly, wrongfully and unlawfully vote for a Representative in the Congress of the United States."

Mr. Justice Hunt. "The prisoner will stand up. Has the prisoner anything to say why sentence shall not be pronounced?"

Miss Anthony. "Yes, your Honor, I have many things to say; for in your ordered verdict of guilty, you have trampled underfoot every vital principle of our government. My natural rights, my civil rights, my political rights, my judicial rights, are all alike ignored. Robbed of the fundamental privilege of citizenship, I am degraded from the status of a citizen to that of a subject; and not only myself individually, but all of my sex are, by your Honor's verdict, doomed to political subjection under this so-called form of government."

—from the trial of Susan B. Anthony, June, 1873 cited in "The United States of America vs. Susan B. Anthony," by Sophy Burnham and Janet Knight, *Ms.*, November, 1972

Susan B. Anthony (1820-1906, standing) and Elizabeth Cady Stanton (1815-1902) led the 19th century battle for women's rights; close friends, Anthony's organizing abilities complemented Stanton's strengths as a theoretician. "It is a settled maxim with me," wrote Stanton, "that the existing public sentiment on any subject is wrong." Anthony was tried for the "crime" of voting in 1872.

Bettmann Archive

Schlesinger Library/Radcliffe College

Bettmann Archive

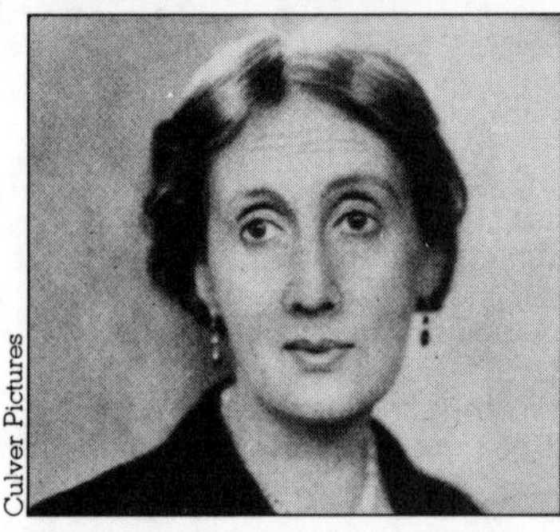
Culver Pictures

Top to bottom—**Crystal Eastman (1881-1928), social investigator, peace worker, feminist, and journalist, wrote in the *Nation* in 1928, "No self respecting feminist would accept alimony. It would be her own confession that she could not take care of herself."**

Elizabeth Blackwell (1821-1910), America's first women doctor, founded the New York Infirmary for Women and Children in 1857 and added a women's medical college in 1868.

Virginia Woolf (1882-1941), author of *Mrs. Dalloway, To the Lighthouse*, and other novels, urged independence for women in her essay, "A Room for One's Own."

It is in vain to look in her work for a modern woman, leading the kind of life that we lead. All we can look for is prophecies of ourselves, and she was our prophetess. There were, in her day, no professional women running homes and jobs with the aid of deep freezers and washing machines; there were no businesswomen; there were no women novelists with many children, rushing from typewriter to school to butcher. There were no middle-class housewives giving dinner parties of extreme sophistication and Elizabeth David cuisine, with no servants in the kitchen and no nanny behind the green baize door, but they were about to be born and she welcomed them.

—Margaret Drabble, "How Not Be Afraid of Virginia Woolf," *Ms.*, November, 1972

We . . . feel a peculiar tenderness for the young women on whose shoulders we are about to leave our burdens. Although we have opened a pathway to the promised land and cleared up much of the underbrush of false sentiment, logic and rhetoric intertwisted with law and custom, which blocked all avenues in starting, yet there are still many obstacles to be encountered before the rough journey is ended. The younger women are starting with great advantages over us. They have the results of our experience; they have superior opportunities for education; they will find a more enlightened public sentiment for discussion; they will have more courage to take the rights which belong to them. Hence we may look to them for speedy conquests. When we think of the vantage-ground woman holds today, in spite of all the artificial obstacles placed in her way, we are filled with wonder as to what the future mothers of the race will be when free to have complete development.

Thus far women have been the mere echoes of men. Our laws and constitutions, our creeds and codes, and the customs of social life are all of masculine origin. The true woman is as yet a dream of the future.

—Elizabeth Cady Stanton, International Council of Women, 1888, *History of Woman Suffrage*, IV, 1902

The knowledge that my grandmother's contemporaries were not just good wives, mothers, housekeepers, and cooks but rather a generation of potentially revolutionary freedom fighters gives a new dimension to their lives and a new strength to mine.

—Midge Mackenzie, *Shoulder to Shoulder*, 1975

Chester Higgins, Jr.

Left—**Fannie Lou Hamer (1917-1977), civil rights and women's leader, electrified the nation at the 1964 Democratic Party Convention with her description of exclusion of blacks from the political process.** Below—**A prospector in 1915, one of the "ordinary women" whose history is being "reclaimed' by women today.**

Adams State College

Bettmann Archive

Bettmann Archive

Above left—**Harriet Tubman *(far left)* (1820?-1913), fugitive slave, with group of ex-slaves she led to freedom on the Underground Railroad.** Above right—**Mary McLeod Bethune (1875-1955), educator and founder of the National Council of Negro Women. Her statue is the only one of a black or of a woman in Washington, D.C.** Right—**Amelia Earhart (1897-1937?) aviator, women's rights advocate, and the first woman to fly the Atlantic alone, disappeared on a round-the-world flight in 1937.**

Schlesinger Library/Radcliffe College

BOOKS 100

It's been said that "literature makes nothing happen," but there were certain books that definitely made this decade of women "happen." Many of them are quoted in the text—along with examples of writings that reacted to (or resisted) the message. The following list is a special sampling based on one of two criteria: that the book was an event in itself (recent, original publications of deBeauvoir, Lessing, Woolf), or that it caused an event or events to happen (Barbara Seaman's *The Doctor's Case Against the Pill*, for instance, was instrumental in bringing about a congressional investigation). Some of these books rescued our buried history, or pioneered new literary genres, or redefined entire subjects—health or rape or battery—as "political." All of them helped break the silence.

What's *not* included here, though (for lack of space), could fill a book. For example, there are no "reissues" (despite such wonderful resurrections as Kate Chopin's fiction or Elizabeth Cady Stanton's political writings); no biographies (there are so many major ones, such as Nancy Milford's *Zelda*, which are revolutionizing the field of biography itself); no books on the male response (pro or con) to feminism, since women writers were our priority. There are also no personal collections of essays; there've been too many important ones, including those by Nora Ephron, Betty Friedan, Kate Millett, Robin Morgan, Adrienne Rich, Diana Trilling. Last, it seemed less imperative to list recent work by such distinguished "mainstream" writers as Joan Didion, Lillian Hellman, Mary McCarthy, Joyce Carol Oates, or Susan Sontag, although their voices—directly or indirectly—certainly influenced the rising consciousness about women.

One more celebratory note: there are now so many thousands of books by and about women that the bibliographies listing them have in turn proliferated into the hundreds. Rather than give a sampling of bibliographies to show the range and focus available (for instance, minority women, child care, women's studies, lesbian sexuality, international feminism), we happily recommend a "bibliography of bibliographies"—Jane Williamson's *New Feminist Scholarship: A Guide to Bibliographies* (The Feminist Press, 1979)—which will send you on to further treasures. Happy reading!

Tillie Olsen

Thomas Victor,

Germaine Greer

Bettye Lane

Maxine Hong Kingston

Kate Millett

Bettye Lane

Toni Cade Bambara

Jill Krementz

Susan Brownmiller

Bettye Lane

Alice Walker

Jill Krementz

Anne Sexton

Nancy Crampton

Margaret Drabble

Jill Krementz

Adrienne Rich

Nancy Crampton

Doris Lessing

Jill Krementz

Jardim/Hennig

Wide World

Gordon/Hardwick

Jill Krementz

Grace Paley

Nancy Crampton

Marilyn French

Alix Kates Shulman

Nancy Crampton

Molly Haskell

Bettye Lane

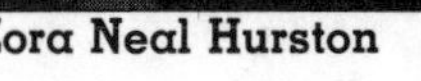

Zora Neal Hurston

Carl Van Vechten

FICTION, POETRY, AND DRAMA

Ai. *Cruelty* (Houghton Mifflin Co., 1974).

Alta. *Burn This and Memorize Yourself: Poems for Women* (Times Change Press, 1971).

Atwood, Margaret. *Surfacing* (Simon & Schuster, Inc., 1973).

Beattie, Ann. *Chilly Scenes of Winter* (Doubleday & Co., Inc., 1976).

Bernikow, Louise, edited and with an introduction by. *The World Split Open: Four Centuries of Women Poets in England and America, 1552–1950* (Random House, Inc., 1974).

Broner, E.M. *A Weave of Women* (Holt, Rinehart & Winston, Inc., 1978)

Broumas, Olga. *Beginning with O* (Yale University Press, 1977).

Brown, Rita Mae. *Rubyfruit Jungle* (Daughters, Inc., 1973; Bantam Books, Inc., 1977).

Brown, Rosellen. *The Autobiography of My Mother* (Doubleday & Co., Inc., 1976).

Chase Riboud, Barbara. *Sally Hemings* (Viking Press, Inc., 1979).

Di Prima, Diane, *Selected Poems: 1956–1976* (Plainfield, Vt.: North Atlantic Books, 1977).

Drabble, Margaret. *The Needle's Eye* (Alfred A. Knopf, Inc., 1972).

French, Marilyn. *The Women's Room* (Summit Books, 1977).

Gordon, Mary. *Final Payments* (Random House, Inc., 1978).

Gould, Lois. *A Sea-Change* (Simon & Schuster, Inc., 1976).

Grahn, Judy. *Work of a Common Woman: The Collected Poems of Judy Grahn, 1964–1977* (Oakland, Ca.: Diana Press, 1978).

Griffin, Susan. *Like the Iris of an Eye* (Harper & Row Pubs., Inc., 1977).

Hardwick, Elizabeth, ed. *Rediscovered Fiction by American Women: A Personal Selection*, 18 vols. (Arno Press, 1977).

Hill, Ruth Beebe. *Hanta Yo* (Doubleday & Co., 1979).

Iverson, Lucille and Kathryn Ruby. *We Become New: Poems by Contemporary Women* (Bantam Books, Inc., 1975).

Jong, Erica. *Half-Lives* (Holt, Rinehart & Winston, Inc., 1973).

Jordan, June. *Things That I Do in the Dark: Selected Poems* (Random House, Inc., 1977).

Katz, Naomi and Nancy Milton. *Fragment From a Lost Diary and Other Stories: Women of Asia, Africa, and Latin America* (Pantheon Books, 1973).

Kaufman, Sue. *The Diary of a Mad Housewife* (Random House, Inc., 1972)

Lamb, Myrna. *Mod Donna and Scyklon Z* (Pathfinder Press, 1971).

Lessing, Doris. *Collected Stories* (Random House, Inc., 1978).

Lorde, Audre. *The Black Unicorn: Poems* (W.W. Norton & Co., Inc., 1978).

Merriam, Eve. *A Husband's Notes About Her* (Macmillan Publishing Co., Inc., 1976).

Moore, Honor, edited and with an introduction by. *The New Women's Theatre: Ten Plays by Contemporary American Women* (Random House, Inc., 1977).

Morgan, Robin. *Monster: Poems* (Random House, Inc., 1972).

Morrison, Toni. *Sula* (Alfred A. Knopf, Inc., 1974).

Paley, Grace. *Enormous Changes at the Last Minute* (Farrar, Straus & Giroux, Inc., 1974).

Piercy, Marge. *Women on the Edge of Time* (Alfred A. Knopf, Inc., 1976).

Rich, Adrienne. *Diving Into the Wreck: Poems 1971–1972* (W.W. Norton & Co., Inc., 1973).

Rukeyser, Muriel. *The Collected Poems of Muriel Rukeyser* (McGraw-Hill Book Co., 1979).

Russ, Joanna. *The Female Man* (Bantam Books, Inc., 1975).

Sexton, Anne. *The Death Notebooks* (Houghton Mifflin Co., 1974).

Shange, Ntozake. *For Colored Girls Who Have Considered Suicide When the Rainbow Is Enuf: A Choreopoem* (Macmillan Publishing Co., Inc., 1977).

Shulman, Alix Kates. *Memoirs of an Ex-Prom Queen* (Alfred A. Knopf, Inc., 1972).

Silko, Leslie. *Ceremony* (Richard Seaver Books, 1977).

Wakoski, Diane. *The Motorcycle Betrayal Poems* (Simon & Schuster, Inc., 1971).

Walker, Alice, ed., with an introduction by Mary Helen Washington. *I Love Myself When I Am Laughing . . . And Then Again When I Am Looking Mean and Impressive: A Zora Neale Hurston Reader* (Feminist Press, 1979).

Walker, Alice, *Meridian* (Harcourt Brace Jovanovich, Inc., 1976).

Washington, Mary Helen, ed. *Black-Eyed Susans: Classic Stories by and About Black Women* (Doubleday & Co., Inc., 1975).

Wittig, Monique. *Les Guerillères* (Avon Books, 1973).

NON-FICTION

Barreño, Maria Isabel, Maria Teresa Horta and Maria Velhoda Costa. *The Three Marias: New Portuguese Letters* (Doubleday & Co., Inc., 1975).

Baxandall, Rosalyn, Linda Gordon and Susan Reverby. *America's Working Women: A Documentary History, 1600 to the Present* (Random House, Inc., 1976).

de Beauvoir, Simone. *The Coming of Age* (G.P. Putnam's Sons, 1972).

Bird, Caroline. *Born Female: The High Cost of Keeping Women Down* (Pocket Books, 1972).

Boston Women's Health Collective. *Our Bodies, Our Selves: A Course by and for Women* (Simon & Schuster, Inc., 1973).

Brownmiller, Susan. *Against Our Will: Men, Women and Rape* (Simon & Schuster, Inc., 1975).

Cade, Toni Bambara. *The Black Woman* (Signet Books, 1970).

Chesler, Phyllis. *Women and Madness* (Doubleday & Co., Inc., 1972).
Corea, Gena. *The Hidden Malpractice: How American Medicine Treats Women* (William Morrow & Co., Inc., 1977).
Daly, Mary. *Beyond God the Father: Toward a Philosophy of Women's Liberation* (Beacon Press, 1973).
Davis, Elizabeth Gould. *The First Sex* (Penguin Books, Inc., 1972)
Dinnerstein, Dorothy. *The Mermaid and the Minotaur* (Harper & Row Pubs., Inc., 1977).
Dworkin, Andrea. *Women Hating* (E.P. Dutton & Co., Inc., 1974).
Ehrenreich, Barbara and Deirdre English. *Witches, Midwives, and Nurses: A History of Women Healers* (Feminist Press, 1972).
Firestone, Shulamith. *The Dialectic of Sex: The Case for Feminist Revolution* (William Morrow & Co., Inc., 1970).
Flexner, Eleanor. *Century of Struggle* (David McKay Co., Inc., 1968).
Friday, Nancy. *My Mother/My Self* (Delacorte Press, 1977).
Greenberg, Selma. *Right From the Start, A Guide to Non-Sexist Childrearing* (Houghton Mifflin Co., 1978).
Greer, Germaine. *The Female Eunuch* (McGraw-Hill, Inc., 1971).
Haskell, Molly. *From Reverence to Rape: The Treatment of Women in the Movies* (Penguin Books, 1974).
Hennig, Margaret and Anne Jardim. *The Managerial Woman* (Doubleday & Co., Inc., 1977).
Hite, Shere. *The Hite Report* (Macmillan Inc., 1976).
Howe, Louise Kapp. *Pink Collar Workers* (G.P. Putnam's Sons, 1977).
James, Edward T., et al, eds., *Notable American Women, 1607–1950: A Biographical Dictionary,* 3 vols. (Harvard University Press, 1971).
Janeway, Elizabeth. *Man's World, Woman's Place: A Study in Social Mythology* (William Morrow & Co., Inc., 1971).
Johnston, Jill. *Lesbian Nation: The Feminist Solution* (Simon & Schuster, Inc., 1973).
Katz, Jane B., ed. *I Am the Fire of Time: The Voices of Native American Women* (E.P. Dutton, 1977).
Kingston, Maxine Hong. *The Woman Warrior: Memoirs of a Girlhood Among Ghosts* (Alfred A. Knopf, Inc., 1976).
Koedt, Ann, Ellen Levine and Anita Rapone, eds. *Radical Feminism* (Quadrangle, 1973).
Lerner, Gerda, ed. *Black Women in White America: A Documentary History* (Pantheon Books, 1972).
Lippard, Lucy. *From the Center: Feminist Essays on Woman's Art* (E.P. Dutton & Co., Inc., 1976).
MacKenzie, Midge. *Shoulder to Shoulder* (Alfred A. Knopf, Inc., 1975).
McPhee, Carol and Ann FitzGerald, compilers. *Feminist Quotations: Voices of Rebels, Reformers, and Visionaries* (Thomas Y. Crowell Co., 1979).
Martin, Del. *Battered Wives* (San Francisco, Ca.: Glide Publications, 1976).
Millett, Kate. *Sexual Politics* (Doubleday & Co., Inc., 1970).
Mitchell, Juliet. *Woman's Estate* (Pantheon Books, 1971).
Moffat, Mary Jane and Charlotte Painter, eds. *Revelations: Diaries of Women* (Random House, Inc., 1974).
Morgan, Elaine. *The Descent of Woman* (Stein and Day, 1972).
Morgan, Robin. ed. *Sisterhood Is Powerful: An Anthology of Writings from the Women's Liberation Movement* (Random House, Inc., 1970).
Nin, Anaïs. Edited by Gunther Stuhlmann. *The Diary of Anaïs Nin,* 6 vols. (Harcourt Brace Jovanovich, Inc., 1976).
Nochlin, Linda and Ann Sutherland Harris. *Woman Artists, 1550–1950* (Alfred A. Knopf, Inc., 1977).
Olsen, Tillie. *Silences* (Dell Publishing Co., Inc., 1977).
Pogrebin, Letty Cottin. *Getting Yours: How to Make the System Work for the Working Woman* (David McKay Co., Inc., 1975).
Porter, Sylvia. *Sylvia Porter's Money Book: How to Earn It, Spend It, Save It, Invest It, Borrow It—And Use It to Better Your Life* (Doubleday & Co., Inc., 1976).
Reed, Evelyn. *Woman's Evolution: From Matriarchal Clan to Patriarchal Family* (Pathfinder Press, 1975).
Rich, Adrienne. *Of Woman Born: Motherhood As Experience and Institution* (W.W. Norton & Co., Inc., 1976).
Russell, Diana E. and Nicole Van de Ven, eds. *Crimes Against Women: The Proceedings of the International Tribunal* (Les Femmes Publishing, 1976).
Seaman, Barbara. *The Doctors' Case Against the Pill* (Wyden Books, 1969; Avon Books, 1979).
Stacey, Judith, Susan Bereaud, Joan Daniels, eds. *And Jill Came Tumbling After: Sexism in American Education* (Dell, 1974).
Sterling, Dorothy. *Black Foremothers* (Feminist Press, 1979).
Twin, Stephanie. *Out of the Bleachers: Writing on Women and Sport* (Feminist Press and McGraw-Hill Book Co., 1979).
Vida, Ginny, ed. *Our Right to Love: A Lesbian Resource Book* (Prentice-Hall, Inc., 1978).
Wallace, Michele. *Black Macho and the Myth of the Superwoman* (Dial Press, 1978).
Women's Action Alliance. *Women's Action Almanac: A Complete Resource Guide* (William Morrow & Co., Inc., 1979).
Woolf, Virginia. *The Diary of Virginia Woolf,* Vols. 1–5, Anne Oliver Bell, ed., (Harcourt Brace Jovanovich, Inc., 1978–9); *The Letters of Virginia Woolf,* Vols. 1–5, Nigel Nicholson and Joanne Trautman, eds. (Harcourt Brace Jovanovich, Inc., 1977–9).

Ms. Books:

Wonder Woman (Holt, Rinehart & Winston, 1972), with Introductions by Gloria Steinem and Dr. Phyllis Chesler.
The First Ms. Reader (Warner Books, 1973), edited by Francine Klagsbrun.
Free To Be . . . You and Me (McGraw Hill Book Co., 1973), Ms. Foundation, Inc.
Women Together: A Documentary History of The Women's Movement (Knopf, 1976), edited by Judith Papachristou.
The Ms. Guide to Women's Health (Doubleday, 1979), by Cynthia Cooke, M.D. and Susan Dworkin. ■

INDEX